Studies in Philosophy
for Children

Harry Stottlemeier's
Discovery

■ ■ ■

Edited by

ANN MARGARET SHARP

and

RONALD F. REED

With Sources and References by Matthew Lipman

Temple University Press

PHILADELPHIA

Temple University Press, Philadelphia 19122
Copyright © 1992 by Temple University. All rights reserved
Published 1992
Printed in the United States of America

Library of Congress Cataloging-in-Publication Data

Studies in philosophy for children : *Harry Stottlemeier's discovery* / edited by Ann Margaret Sharp
    and Ronald F. Reed ; with sources and references by Matthew Lipman.
    p.   cm.
Includes bibliographical references.
ISBN 0-87722-872-8 (alk. paper)—ISBN 0-87722-873-6 (pbk. : alk. paper)
    1. Children and philosophy.   2. Philosophy—Study and teaching (Elementary)—United
    States.   3. Lipman, Matthew. Harry Stottlemeier's discovery.   I. Sharp, Ann Margaret,
    1942–   .   II. Reed, Ronald F.   III. Lipman, Matthew.
    B105.C45S78   1992
    100—dc20   91-3903
                                                                                                            CIP

In memory of

ADAM REED

(1968–1990)

and

PROFESSOR FREDERICK S. OSCANYAN

(1934–1990)

Contents

PART THREE / *Metaphysical and Epistemological Problems*

PART FOUR / *Logical Issues*

PART FIVE / *Pedagogical Dimension*

EPILOGUE

Acknowledgments

We thank Professor Matthew Lipman for the sources and references that he has dictated to Professor Sharp over the past ten years. This bibliography, which correlates line by line to the text of *Harry Stottlemeier's Discovery*, is another manifestation of Professor Lipman's breadth of scholarship, understanding, sensitivity to nuances in several disciplines, and attention to detail. Although compiling it was a tedious and arduous task, Professor Lipman was aware of the importance of providing sources and references to help teachers and scholars understand the relationship of Philosophy for Children to our intellectual tradition.

We also express our gratitude to Professor Frederick S. Oscanyan, who died in the summer of 1990. Professor Oscanyan devoted many years to perfecting the presentation of the logic in the *Harry* manual and to disseminating the *Harry* program to university students, professors, and classroom teachers.

We give grateful acknowledgment to the editors of *Teaching Philosophy* and *Analytic Teaching* for permission to reprint Frederick S. Oscanyan's essay "A Critical Look at *Harry Stottlemeier's Discovery*" and Michael S. Pritchard's "Critical Thinking: Problem Solving or Problem Creating," respectively. We also express our appreciation to the Getty Foundation for permission to use Ronald F. Reed's "On the Art and Craft of Dialogue," which was originally presented at a Getty seminar, Inheriting the Theory: New Voices and Multiple Perspectives on DBAE, in May 1989. We thank the University Press of Kansas for allowing us to publish a slightly revised version of "On Becoming a Moral Agent," a chapter from Michael S. Pritchard's *On Becoming Responsible*, published in 1991.

At Texas Wesleyan University, two administrators have been especially supportive. Mark Wasicsko, provost, and Allen Henderson, dean of the School of Education, have been very helpful in finding creative ways to get the manuscript typed and proofread.

The typists, Pamela Day, Linda Nowell, Cheryl Stone, and Patricia Spears, did a marvelous job. They met the various deadlines with grace and good humor.

Three colleagues, Professors Michael S. Pritchard, Tony Johnson, and Sally Hagaman, gave more intelligent, supportive criticism than they realize.

Finally, thanks to Ann, Jeremy, and Rebecca. Nothing can alleviate the pain of these months. Still, I think Adam would like having a book dedicated to him. I imagine he smiles.

Introduction

PHILOSOPHY FOR CHILDREN is an attempt to reconstruct and present the history of philosophy in such a way that children can appropriate it for themselves so as to reason well in a self-correcting manner. For children to develop the ability to think well for themselves about matters of importance, what is required is an educational enterprise consisting of philosophical dialogue within the context of a classroom community of inquiry. Such a community concerns itself with the development of good critical and creative thinking and the cultivation of good judgment. But it is much more than this: Philosophy for Children is a method of dialogical reflection coupled with twenty-five hundred years of various views and systems of thought regarding the nature of the universe, the characteristics of the good life, and the cultivation of wisdom.

Harry Stottlemeier's Discovery was the first didactic philosophical novel to be written for children. It was created in 1969 by Matthew Lipman, who had been a philosophy professor at Columbia University for fifteen years. Since the publication of Lipman's novel, Philosophy for Children has entered many classrooms. This has been a gradual process involving experimental research, curriculum construction, and teacher education. By 1973, it was apparent that if Philosophy for Children was to be presented to elementary-school children by classroom teachers on a large scale, manuals would have to be constructed that would not only contain a myriad of exercises and discussion plans aimed at fostering dialogue in the classroom and at reinforcing the cognitive skills introduced but would also provide the teacher with an introduction to the content of the philosophical novel and a way of proceeding. The manual accompanying *Harry Stottlemeier's Discovery* is *Philosophical Inquiry*. Together with the novel, it forms the textual core of the initial teacher-education program in Philosophy for Children.

Between 1973 and 1988, six more programs were constructed in Philosophy for Children. *Elfie*, for grades K through 2, concentrates on the making of distinctions, connections, and comparisons within the context of a variety of broad philosophical issues. Two programs were constructed for grades 3 and 4: *Pixie* concentrates on analogical-reasoning skills and philosophy of language, and *Kio and Gus* emphasizes practice in a variety of reasoning skills that prepare students to investigate nature. *Lisa* (for grades 7 and 8) focuses on ethical inquiry, *Suki* (for grades 9 and 10) on aesthetic inquiry, and *Mark* (for grades 11 and 12) on social and political inquiry.

Philosophy for Children is being taught in some five thousand schools in the United States. The program has been translated into eighteen languages, and there are Centers of Philosophy for Children throughout the United States and in Chile, Costa Rica, Brazil, Mexico, Nigeria, Spain (including Catalonia), Portugal, Guatemala, Iceland, Denmark, Canada, Austria, Australia, and Taiwan. Scholars from the Soviet Union, Romania, Hungary, and Czechoslovakia are now establishing such centers.

Experimental research in the United States and in many other nations has demonstrated that children exposed to philosophy by well-prepared teachers gain significantly in reasoning, reading comprehension, and mathematical performance. But what is a well-prepared practitioner of Philosophy for Children? By practitioner we mean a philosopher, educator, parent, or teacher of Philosophy for Children. Is it enough to expose the practitioner to the methodology of the program? Should training in Philosophy for Children revolve around the reasoning skills and some of the philosophical ideas in the program? Should the aim be to enable practitioners to participate in a community of inquiry committed to investigating the ideas and skills in their classroom and to observe them presenting the program? How much formal logic must the practitioner know? How much of the history of philosophy must be mastered? What can one do to make sure that practitioners can facilitate philosophical dialogues in the classroom? These and many other questions have formed the basis of the investigation into the area of the practice of Philosophy for Children.

One could say that over the years experiments have been conducted around the world in an effort to understand how one ought to go about refining the practice of Philosophy for Children. Initially, we thought that didactic presentations had no place in the process, and we advised all professional philosophers never to lecture either on logic or the history of philosophy. Practitioners, we believed, should be prepared in exactly the same way we would want them to present the material to the children so as to mitigate any transfer problems. Training in Philosophy for Children should be rooted in inquiry and dialogue, with the role of the leader being that of the model inquirer, always helping novices become more aware of the process of reasoning they use in discussing philosophical themes. The leader ought never engage in any behavior that could not be transferred to the classroom.

That's what we thought fifteen years ago. And there is a sense in which we still believe in this practice. What we have come to realize, however, is that the refinement of the practice of Philosophy for Children is far more complicated than we had originally thought. Like most theorists, we have learned from teachers and from children. They have taught us a great deal about curriculum construction and how much the existing school curriculum underestimates children's and teachers' abilities. They have also helped us see some of the shortcomings in our approach to training.

This book is an attempt to improve the practice of Philosophy for Children as it applies to the teaching of *Harry Stottlemeier's Discovery* to elementary-school students. Teachers who have been successful with the program have demonstrated that, after gaining some experience in presenting *Harry Stottlemeier's Discovery* in the classroom, they have a strong desire to know the relationship between the ideas set forth by the various characters in the novel and those to be found in the history of philosophy. Teachers are not mere technicians. They want to understand what it is they are doing. Good teachers aim to be good reflective practitioners. They want to present *Harry Stottlemeier's Discovery* well, and they know from experience that much of this expertise rests with asking the appropriate follow-up questions once the dialogue has begun among the children (often with the help of a discussion plan from the manual). This ability in turn necessitates insight into the rich tradition on which the ideas in the novel draw—the conversation of philosophers on such issues as justice, truth, knowledge, beauty, and the good.

Another important event in the history of Philosophy for Children was the creation in 1980 of a master's degree program at Montclair State College in New Jersey for students with an undergraduate degree in philosophy who had a strong interest in working with children and teachers in elementary-school classrooms. In a short time, the graduate program was attracting extraordinary students from many countries interested in bringing Philosophy for Children to their own communities. The degree program aimed to combine theory and practice. It was composed of four semesters; two were residential at a conference center, and two were on campus at Montclair State College during the fall and spring. The residential workshops focused on the creation of a community of inquiry, using the curriculum as the basis of the dialogue. The fall and spring semesters afforded the students an opportunity to study philosophy with elementary- and secondary-school children in a classroom and to participate in seminars on theory.

Upon entering the program, students were given an extensive bibliography for each chapter of the seven novels in the curriculum. As a requirement for the degree, they would select one philosophical source from the bibliography and write a short essay relating a concept from one of the novels to a treatment of the same concept in the body of traditional philosophy. They would do this for each chapter in each of the novels. Thus, in one year, students would write eighty short essays relating various works in the philosophical tradition to the curriculum they hoped to teach in the future.

In a few years we began to realize that as students combined teaching the program to children with writing these papers their practice in the classrooms became more adept. It was as if the simultaneous activity helped them to realize what they were doing and why they were doing it. They began to hear what children were saying in light of the philosophical tradition. They found themselves more capable of helping children formulate their own views more coherently. They began to speak less and listen more, and they heard themselves asking more appropriate follow-up questions. They came to know when to ask for consequences and assumptions and when to ask for alternative positions. They slowly learned how to use the manual that accompanied the philosophical novel. This meant appropriately sequencing the exercises so as to prepare students in essential cognitive skills before commencing dialogue on the complex philosophical issues introduced in each of the chapters. Once discussion about a philosophical issue was under way, they came to know what discussion plans were appropriate to orchestrate the inquiry and, in particular, what specific questions were appropriate at a given time. Exercises and discussion plans in the manual became a vast repertoire for the students to use in building a classroom community of inquiry committed to the investigation of issues introduced in the novel and having wide application in the daily lives of the children. It was as if the more the graduate students immersed themselves in the philosophical conversation of humankind the better they could facilitate philosophical conversations in their classrooms. One activity became a mirror of the other, infinitely reflecting philosophical possibilities. Far from viewing themselves as passive receivers or transmitters of a philosophical tradition not of their own making, the students slowly started to see themselves as active creators and cocreators of philosophical ideas—reflective practitioners using an increasing number of reasoning skills more and more self-consciously in philosophical activity.

This book, then, springs from two sources. The first involves an attempt to answer a question that arises when one tries to move from theory to practice: What must practitioners know in order to translate theoretical claims into action? In the following chapters that question is answered in a variety of ways by philosophers, educators, and practicing teachers. Interestingly, the answers they propose frequently shed as much light on the theory of Philosophy for Children as they do on the practice.

The second source for the book is our experience in the graduate program at Montclair State College. Over the course of the years, it became clear that as students grappled both with the practice of "delivering" philosophy to children and with the tradition of philosophy their understanding of the tradition was enhanced and their "delivery" was facilitated. We hope that this book might contribute, in a small measure, to a similar growth in its readers.

Studies in Philosophy for Children is aimed at what is today a significant audience, the hundreds of philosophers and tens of thousands of teachers who have been trained in Philosophy for Children. In addition, since the book assumes a minimal knowledge about Philosophy for Children, it might introduce this movement to people interested in the wave of educational reform that is sweeping the country as the century draws to a close.

PART ONE

Some Remarks

by Matthew Lipman on

Philosophy for Children

In this first part, Matthew Lipman offers the reader a glimpse at the thought pro-
cesses that resulted in Philosophy for Children and, in so doing, distinguishes
Philosophy for Children from other contemporary modes of educational reform.
The first chapter, "On Writing a Philosophical Novel," will be of most interest to
students of the genesis of Philosophy for Children. In it, Lipman describes the
context that led him to write Harry Stottlemeier's Discovery. *He speaks of his*
discontent, as a student, with the teaching of logic, the relationship of logic to
philosophy in Harry *(the latter was meant to be a "bribe" to facilitate the learning*
of the former), the significance of characters' names, what the characters were
meant to represent, and the influences of such diverse figures and events as John
Dewey, Jean Piaget, Herman Melville, the pre-Socratics, Denis Diderot, and his
own experiences in World War II on the writing of Harry. *Interestingly, Lipman*
admits that the novel was not intended to be a classroom text. He thought of it "as
a book children might find for themselves on browsing through a library."

"How Old Is Harry Stottlemeier?" contains what may be the most explicit
statement Lipman has ever made regarding the relationship of Philosophy for
Children to the discipline of philosophy. "Harry represents for children a device
by means of which the arcane contents of adult scholarship can be decoded and
translated into ordinary language. It makes accessible to them a world of coveted
meanings that tradition has decreed must be restricted to a small number of
adult men."

Lipman goes on, in this deceptively thin and conversational chapter, to sug-
gest that the community of inquiry modeled in Harry *might serve as a goal for*
contemporary educational reform. For Lipman, Harry and his friends are per-
sons who reason well, who are moved by the "vision of a life in which people
reason together, and who feel intensely that they want to live their lives in such a
way that being reasonable will genuinely matter." By including the motivational
and dispositional along with the development of cognitive abilities, Lipman
distinguishes Philosophy for Children from many thinking-skills programs.

Finally, in the more formal chapter "Integrating Cognitive Skills and Con-
ceptual Contents in Teaching the Philosophy for Children Curriculum," he
develops the connection that he sees between logic and philosophy and mentions
two cases—Socrates' question about the notion of the holy in Plato's Euthyphro
and David Hume's attack on the Cosmological Proof of God's existence in Dialogues Concerning Natural Religion—*where the unpacking of philosophical*
significance is, in part, a function of the development of logical skills.

1

On Writing a Philosophical Novel

Matthew Lipman

■ ■ ■

IN 1969, having taught introductory logic to college students for some years, I was beginning to have serious concerns about its value. I had entertained similar doubts while I was a graduate student, for I hadn't found the subject a congenial one. But when one has taught a course for several years, one comes to think of it as useful and meaningful, whatever one's earlier reservations. Yet, I found myself wondering what possible benefit my students were obtaining from studying the rules for determining the validity of syllogisms or from learning how to construct contrapositives. Did they actually reason any better as a result of studying logic? Were not their linguistic and psychological habits already so firmly established that *any* sort of practice or instruction in reasoning would come too late?

At the time, I was a professor of philosophy at Columbia University. No doubt the student riots of 1968 contributed to my uneasiness about what I was doing. As I watched the fumbling efforts of the university to reappraise itself, I couldn't help concluding that the problems of Columbia could not be solved within the framework of that institution. Teachers and students alike, we had all come out of the same matrix of elementary and secondary education. If we had been miseducated in those earlier grades, then very likely we had come to share many misconceptions that would enable us to botch our later schooling in happy collusion with one another.

At about this time, too, I chanced to observe the efforts of a tutor of neurologically impaired children to help his students with their reading. The youngsters seemed able to read the words, but they were unable to extract the meaning of the passage. I suggested giving them exercises in drawing logical inferences, and the tutor reported that such practice was helpful. It confirmed my hunch that children might profit from instruction in reasoning, provided it were given them early in their development.

Was it possible to help children think more skillfully? That children thought as naturally as they talked and breathed I did not doubt. But how to get them to think well?

The idea of a children's story was suggested to me. But what kind of children's story? Surely not the kind in which all-knowing adults benevolently explain to ignorant little folk the differences between thinking well and thinking badly. Nothing so condescending. This would have to be something young people would discover for themselves, with little help from grown-ups. The children in the story would somehow have to constitute a small community of inquiry, in which everyone shared, at least to some extent, in cooperatively searching for and discovering more effective ways of thinking. It was my thought that the little band of children in the story could serve as a model with which the live students in the classroom might identify. Such a portrait, of children living together intelligently and with mutual respect, might give children hope that such an ideal was feasible (as Plato's dialogues had done for adults).

I can recall deliberating over the preliminary task of naming the characters in the story (which I did not anticipate would eventually become a book). The idea of a pun on the name of the founder of logic intrigued me. What about "Ari Startle"? Too awkward and contrived. I settled for Harry Stottlemeier. The other children in the story were given names that suggested different lines of ethnic ancestry, a maneuver I consciously adopted from *Moby Dick*. (In more recent novels, I have tended to omit the surnames altogether.)

The characters were not borrowed from real life, and neither was the plot, such as it was. My own children were eight and nine years of age at the time, but it didn't occur to me to use them as models. What I gained from them primarily was a sense of the possibilities of dialogue with young people.

What would distinguish the children from one another, it seemed to me, would be not so much their characters as their styles of thinking. One could be experimental, another intuitive, a third analytical, a fourth skeptical, and so on, although no one style would be presented as inherently better or worse than any other. Harry himself would be patient and exploratory, given to alternating moods of wonder and self-doubt. I suspected that his frequent blunders and embarrassments might endear him to children more readily than would the virtues of a less fallible protagonist.

As for the plot of the story, I conceived of it as a miniature paradigm of inquiry. The children discover a rule of logic, conversion (finding a converse). They try it out on a number of different sentences, and it works. But someone finds a counterinstance. At first there is consternation and despair. Subsequently, they realize, however, that the principle can be expanded to accommodate the counterinstance. Once again there is testing; as revised, the rule appears to be valid. But will it work in real life? The final episode of the chapter offers the children an opportunity to apply their discovery to an out-of-school situation—it works!

These were some of the immediate circumstances attendant upon the writing of the first chapter of *Harry Stottlemeier's Discovery*. But at that point I concluded that what was needed was not a vignette but a novelette. To be persuasive, the theme of discovery would have to be much enlarged and reinforced. And the principles of reasoning discovered by the children would have to be shown relevant to the more fundamental and problematical aspects of their lives.

Putting it bluntly, it appeared to me that children could be induced to study logic only by bribing them with philosophy. Youngsters and philosophy are natural allies, for both begin in wonder. Indeed, only philosophers and artists systematically and professionally engage in that perpetuation of wonder so characteristic of the everyday experience of the child. Why not borrow the ideas of the philosophical tradition, then, inserting them into the novel so that the children in the story could go beyond wonder and could reflect upon and meaningfully discuss the metaphysical, epistemological, aesthetic, and ethical aspects of their experience?

Eventually I finished the book, despite my virtually total lack of familiarity with the techniques of fictional writing and with the principles of education. Whatever I knew of the latter, I suppose, came from my having carried in my duffel bag, during World War II, a copy of Dewey's *Intelligence in the Modern World*, which contains a number of key passages of his educational theory. Somehow I had chanced upon the book, although I knew nothing of philosophy, and somehow I grasped, through the obscurity of Dewey's prose, a few of his central ideas. I can still recall perusing the book in those occasional relaxed moments an infantryman may have as we were working our way up through the Saar, crossing the Rhine at Mainz, traversing Germany to Bayreuth, and then rolling on into Austria. I would guess that ideas acquired under those circumstances are especially likely to assume a foundational role with regard to one's later thinking.

Yet I cannot omit mention of another contributing factor. Several years after the war, I was fortunate enough to be able to return to France for a period of study. I was impressed that some of the French writers I became interested in, such as Diderot, found it possible to discuss profound philosophical ideas with ease and clarity. As a result, perhaps, ideas were not so much monopolized by an elite minority: Not even poets considered them alien.

In France, too, I thought I perceived a greater intellectual camaraderie between parents and children. They seemed less self-conscious about sharing a common literature, as when a grandfather could be observed discussing *Phèdre* with his grandson and granddaughter. We ourselves, I reflected, lack appropriate models of thoughtful dialogue with which children might identify and from which they could learn. Our dramatizations of children relating with other children, or with adults, are purely social and affective in their emphasis.

But there was an earlier, and probably less imperfect, example of a society at home with philosophical ideas—the Greece of the pre-Socratics. When one thinks of Anaxagoras and Empedocles, Parmenides and Heraclitus, one thinks of philosophers comfortable with aphoristic and poetical modes of expression, as well as with ordinary language. And then the wedding of philosophy and drama in Plato, as already foreshadowed in Sophocles and Euripides! It was clear that the logic of Aristotle, insofar as it was to be presented in the children's book (his logic being that most akin to language), would have to be accompanied by such philosophical ideas as the pre-Socratics discovered, as well as in some similarly appropriate literary vehicle.

A further problem in the organization of the book had to do with the sequence in which the logical themes were to be introduced. Here the organization of college courses in logic provided little guidance. Over thousands of years, the implications of logic had been carried out and integrated into logic texts, with little regard for their relative importance either to logic or to pedagogy. What I tried to do, therefore, was to strip away the inessentials and to take conversion as the basic building block out of which formal logic is constructed and through whose elaborations logic can be understood. At the same time, I found it necessary to introduce some elements of the logic of relations and the logic of propositions. Also, I tried to provide numerous examples of the use of nonformal ("good reasons") logic. But nothing teaches children reasoning better than the close and careful examination of the multiform uses of language itself and their consequent discussion of their own observations and inferences.

Although the philosophical ideas in *Harry Stottlemeier's Discovery* are borrowed freely from the philosophical repertoire, and even Suki's five-word poem is cribbed from Bernard Fontenelle, I tried to avoid reference in the book to the schools and star performers of the tradition; of what value would it be for children to worry over whether Aristotle or Kant should be classified as rationalists or empiricists? I also tried to avoid technical terminology. I suspected that such language too readily lends itself to being a weapon with which to intimidate and crush those who are too unsophisticated to know how to employ it in their own behalf. And I wanted my book to be used, not simply to help children think, but to help them think for themselves.

Having written the book, I began to cast around for a suitable experimental situation. Such an opportunity came about in 1970. Following Piaget's belief that the formal stage of reasoning begins somewhere around the eleventh year, I chose to experiment with fifth-graders. I devised a "true field" experiment, with randomly selected groups from a heterogeneous population. Each group of about fifteen children was taught twice a week for nine weeks, and each was pretested and posttested. At the end of the experimental period, the control group's scores on logical reasoning remained unchanged; those of the experimental group had jumped twenty-seven months! I was encouraged.

It was not until 1975 that I was able to arrange another experiment. This time, two hundred students were taught for four months by their own classroom teachers. This time, the reasoning gains were less impressive, but the improvement in reading (of the experimental group versus the control group) was substantial and in some cases dramatic.

Earlier, I had thought of *Harry Stottlemeier's Discovery* as a book children might find for themselves on browsing through a library or as a book brought home by a parent to be read and discussed, neither too mature for the child nor too childish for the adult. But gradually I had come to conclude that Philosophy for Children was needed in the school as well as in the home. The experimental evidence of academic improvement convinced me that school administrators would eventually accept it as a thinking- and reasoning-skills program, while children in the classroom would welcome it enthusiastically. But could we find teachers competent to teach it?

I think so. The preparation of teachers is moving slowly, but the necessary format is gradually becoming clearer, and progress is being made. We have learned how to produce curriculum materials for the teacher that identify the leading ideas of each chapter and that then put those concepts into operation by providing suitable exercises, activities, and discussion plans for use in the classroom. Eventually there will be philosophy curricula for every grade from kindergarten through secondary school.

If philosophy begins in wonder, it can also be said that it emerges as reflective dialogue whose insights then infuse and enrich living. But the transitions need to be mediated, and perhaps there will someday be a literature that will help children span the chasms between wonder and reflection, between reflection and dialogue, and between dialogue and experience. The impact of such a literature upon today's children might not be immediately noticeable. But the impact upon tomorrow's adults might be so considerable as to make us wonder why we withheld philosophy from children until now.

2

How Old Is Harry Stottlemeier?

Matthew Lipman

■ ■ ■

ASCERTAINING the age of fictional characters can be treacherous. Take Pixie, after whom one of the Philosophy for Children novels is named. Pixie remarks, at the very beginning of the book, "How old am I? The same age you are." If she is addressing us, and we are of all ages, then so is she. But can we be sure that she is speaking to us?

Likewise with Harry Stottlemeier. In 1992, it has been twenty-three years since *Harry Stottlemeier's Discovery* was written. Does that make Harry twenty-three? Or, since one might guess his age in the book to be eleven, does that make him thirty-four? Or must it be said that he was eleven then, he is eleven now, and he will always be eleven?

Another contrast between Pixie and Harry comes to mind. Pixie teases us and tantalizes us with hints about the "mystery story" that she claims to have composed and that she may some day reveal to us. But what she does tell us—and it is the substance of the book that bears her name—is the story of how her mystery story came about. The matter is quite different with Harry. *Harry Stottlemeier's Discovery* is an open book, and hundreds of thousands of children and adults have now perused it. But there is no "story of how the story came about."

One of the first questions reporters ask is "How did you happen to write *Harry?*" and I always answer truthfully, but a bit differently, because each time some other causal sequence comes to mind. I can only entertain them one at a time, and I suspect that even if I could for a moment contemplate them all together they simply would not add up.

I have contributed a minuscule essay of my own to *Studies in Philosophy for Children* in which I argue that, just as one can trace the philosophical concepts in *Harry* back to their antecedents in the academic tradition, so one can trace the major applications of the thinking skills in *Harry* back to noteworthy illustrations in the history of science and the humanities. But, to return to the

8

topic of the etiology of the book, a considerable portion of it is given over to a paragraph-by-paragraph, virtually line-by-line quest for sources and references. I am sure this will be of great value to teachers, graduate students, and instructors who, in the future, will be curious about this bizarre book that still puzzles people because they cannot find a genre to which to assign it. I have cooperated freely in this quest for sources, for I know that such explanations have some value for many people. But in the long run, what counts is not how the book is to be explained, but how its meanings are to be explicated and interpreted. It is this function that links *Harry* to the hermeneutical study of the humanities, to the cultivation of logical reasoning and judgment, and to the strengthening of conceptual and inquiry skills. *Harry* represents for children a device by means of which the arcane contents of adult scholarship can be decoded and translated into ordinary language. It makes accessible to them a world of coveted meanings that tradition had decreed must be restricted to a small number of adult men.

True, many readers turn away from *Harry* unconvinced. "Too much philosophy!" they exclaim. "Too much logic! Can't you just teach children thinking skills without going through all this nonsense?" What they fail to see is that *Harry* is not about a group of weird little eggheads, nor is it primarily about philosophy and logic. It is about a children's community of inquiry whose members find themselves ashamed to think badly and hate being found unreasonable. In other words, they have more than cleverness, more than mere cognitive skillfulness: They have *standards*—standards of reasoning, standards of inquiry, standards of conduct, standards of judgment. It is these standards that liberate children from merely pedestrian thinking, or from unconstructive thinking, or from mechanical thinking. It is these standards and criteria that characterize independent thinkers—the persons who think for themselves. And the great battle in "education for thinking" is over this very point—whether or not we should equip children with the criteria and standards by means of which they can make reliable judgments on their own, instead of always being limited to following the principles or solving the problems that we set for them.

It is because Harry and his friends set high standards for their thinking that they come to feel passionately about their minds and their lives. For having standards and criteria assures not only sound reasoning but strong feelings as well. This, it seems to me, is what we want: children who can reason well, who are deeply moved by the vision of a life in which people reason together, and who feel intensely that they want to live their lives in such a way that being reasonable will genuinely matter. Without these motivational and dispositional considerations, education for critical thinking is bound to be a bloodless and sterile business.

How old is Harry Stottlemeier? There is a sense in which he has hardly been born and another sense in which he is already dead. Ultimately his age is not for me but for you to decide.

3

Integrating Cognitive Skills and Conceptual Contents in Teaching the Philosophy for Children Curriculum

Matthew Lipman

■ ■ ■

THE PROJECT of connecting philosophical concepts in the Philosophy for Children curriculum with the concepts in academic philosophy from which they were derived (or that they resemble) can be of considerable value for teachers and scholars wishing to ascertain the grounds of the curriculum in the philosophical tradition. We should not, however, restrict such an inquiry to philosophical concepts and the history of philosophy. A parallel enterprise might seek to show how the skills of logic have been employed at key points in any history (whether of philosophy, of science, of technology, or of the humanities) so as to provide a pivot that will make possible the deployment of energies in a new direction or the clustering of energies in defense of a new position.

Texts in logic do not characteristically introduce their readers to the ways in which the logical operations under scrutiny have been employed on various historical occasions. Students of the role of thinking skills in education may, however, find such considerations helpful in devising improved approaches to the acquisition of such skills.

As a matter of fact, teachers of philosophy to college students lacking a grounding in logic have often found that such students have not been fully able to appreciate the conceptual content of the philosophical systems to which they were being introduced because they failed to grasp the logical moves being employed by the philosophers they were reading. While it may be true that the logical infrastructure of ancient philosophy is closer to the surface than is the case with modern philosophy, so that the reliance upon logic seems to be much greater, such differences may be more apparent than real. Contemporary philosophical writers probably presuppose in their readers a level of logical acumen that was part of what ancient writers were attempting to teach.

Take the logical move known as conversion. It is introduced into the Philosophy for Children curriculum in the first chapter of *Harry Stottlemeier's Discovery* and constitutes thereafter the elementary logical operation out of which the entire syllogistic is constructed. The teacher learning this material for the first time may well ask, "How important is this move, not in the history of logic, about which I may have only limited interest, but in the history of other disciplines, or even in the history of philosophy?" If time permits, the instructor might at this point introduce the class to Plato's *Euthyphro*, where something like the principle of conversion is employed. Socrates is anxious to help Euthyphro distinguish between two quite distinct notions: If things are loved by the gods, then they are things that are holy, and, second, if they are things that are holy, then they are things loved by the gods. (I have employed the "If . . . then . . ." formulation used in Chapter Sixteen of *Harry* rather than the class-logic formulation employed in Chapter One.) To the novice in philosophy, these two formulations look innocently equivalent; it is only after having worked a bit with the conversion principle that beginners begin to appreciate the enormity of their difference.

It is precisely the enormity of the logical difference that is needed in order to grasp the magnitude of the philosophical distinction that Plato is trying to introduce. The distinction that is the focal point of the discussion in the *Euthyphro* represents one of the great axial turning points in the history of Western civilization, so much hangs on whether we accept the one formulation or the other. Must we obey the gods simply on the basis of their authority, or does our reason have the capacity to examine questions of goodness or rightness independently so that we can come to our own rational conclusions? This is not a question whose scope is limited to the domain of religion; it extends to all matters of authority, and it inquires about the nature of nonrational authority in any domain whatsoever.

Another approach is to attempt to show that philosophical arguments fail because of an improper employment of specific cognitive skills. This would seem to be what is involved in David Hume's attack upon the Cosmological Proof of God's existence in his *Dialogues Concerning Natural Religion*. What Hume is at pains to demonstrate in that work is that such proofs employ analogical reasoning, but they do so incorrectly. Hume's treatise, however, is only one of a vast number of books and articles demonstrating the reliance of those in art, science, and philosophy upon the principle of analogy. An instructor working with graduate students or prospective teachers will find them much appreciative of illustrations that show the enormous importance of this principle in every field of inquiry. (It is equally important to cite occasions in which the inquiry was advanced precisely because the principle of analogy did not seem to work as expected with the materials under examination. Consider, for example, Newton's perplexity as to why the moon did *not* fall to earth like everything else.)

Still another example would be found in the teaching of ethics. One of the problematic areas here is the matter of ethical reciprocity, which appears to beginning students to be deceptively commendable, until they begin to consider such variants of it as vengeance and gift giving. In the Philosophy for Children curriculum (most notably in *Lisa*), the strategy is first to introduce students to the notion of relationships (in *Pixie*), then to the logic of relations (in *Harry*), and then to ethical reciprocity (in *Lisa*), so that they are prepared to deal with the logical aspects of the problem before its ethical complexities are thrust upon them.

To argue that logic is valuable as a preparation for studying ethics is not to argue that it is the only such subdiscipline of philosophy that needs to be introduced antecedently. Epistemology, for example, may be equally valuable (see the articles "Epistemology" and "Ethics" in the *Encyclopedia of Philosophy*). And so might certain aspects of metaphysics and aesthetics. But the cognitive skills alluded to in this chapter are correlated specifically with certain operations in the field of logic.

If we are to explore new directions in curriculum development, it would seem profitable to integrate the building of cognitive skills along with the introduction of conceptual content, so that contents and skills are strengthened and reinforced simultaneously. The failure to do so has been one of the key reasons for the ineffectiveness of much of modern education.

PART TWO

Ethical, Social, and Political Issues

A standard claim in moral philosophy is that the ability to study it is somehow outside the ken of young people. Typically, one argues that because children are inexperienced (that is, have inadequate acquaintance with and understanding of the contexts within which questions of moral character, conduct, and judgment arise) and because children are moved primarily by passions without real regard for rational principles, it is not possible to engage them in serious discussion about ethics. One trains them in correct moral behavior, and then when the time is right, sometime in adulthood, one begins to discuss the reasons for that behavior.

In "Moral Education: From Aristotle to Harry Stottlemeier," *Michael S. Pritchard, using the work of Lipman, Ann Margaret Sharp, and Gareth Matthews, in addition to his own experience with children, argues that philosophers and psychologists from Aristotle to John Locke through R. M. Hare and Lawrence Kohlberg have seriously underestimated children's moral capabilities. While recognizing that there are significant differences between adults and children, Pritchard holds that not only is it possible to engage children in discussion of moral questions but that childhood reflection on ethical issues may also be essential to moral development.*

Ronald F. Reed, in "Discussion and the Varieties of Authority," looks at the discussion that takes place in Chapter Nine of Harry Stottlemeier's Discovery. *There, Mr. Partridge, the principal of Harry's school, engages the children in what he (Mr. Partridge) calls a "free and open" discussion of a serious ethical question: Does Dale have an obligation to stand for the salute to the flag? Reed argues that not only is the discussion not free and open but it is a grab bag of logical fallacies. Reed then goes on to suggest that there is reason to believe that the principal takes advantage of the appearance of dialogue as a not-so-covert way of forcing the children to think and to act as he would have them do. Rather than examining a moral issue, he is using the dialogue as an instrument for indoctrination. The discussion in Chapter Nine then becomes a sort of antimodel, a compendium of ways in which adults ought not to talk with children.*

In the last chapter in this part, Ann Margaret Sharp, starting from her own experience as a girl attending parochial schools in the 1950s and 1960s and as a young woman drawn to philosophy in the 1960s university, recalls how she and her female classmates were excluded from serious participation in philosophical discussions. Echoing such feminist thinkers as Simone de Beauvoir and Jean Grimshaw, Sharp points out that the exclusion of women, children, and various minorities from philosophical discussion not only deprives them of their right to discover their own humanity within the context of the conversation but also severely limits the ability of the conversation to produce objectivity and meaning.

4

Moral Education: From Aristotle to Harry Stottlemeier

Michael S. Pritchard

■ ■ ■

PHILOSOPHY, says Aristotle, begins in wonder. So does childhood. *Harry Stottlemeier's Discovery* and the other Institute for the Advancement of Philosophy for Children (IAPC) materials join philosophical wonder with childhood. Ironically, I doubt that Aristotle would be pleased, at least not in regard to IAPC's approach to moral education. Shakespeare's *Troilus and Cressida* reminds us that Aristotle insists that moral philosophy is not for the young. It mentions

young men, whom Aristotle thought
Unfit to hear moral philosophy.[1]

Aristotle's doubts focus on two apparent limitations of the young—inexperience and lack of rational principles.

If Aristotle is right, then we should not expect to find much that is philosophical in the moral thinking of children, who can be seen, basically, as lacking what (at least some) adults have. The relative neglect of the philosophical thinking of children in the writings of philosophers suggests that Aristotle's position is widely shared. Until I confronted *Harry Stottlemeier's Discovery*, I was not inclined to challenge the prevailing view. But I have discovered that Harry and his friends can hold their own against Aristotle.

THE PROBLEM OF INEXPERIENCE

If moral understanding requires a basic comprehension of the social and political world of adults, then we can all agree that even older children are relatively inexperienced (as are many adults). But, as *Harry* amply illustrates, the world of children is filled with analogues to the complex social and political institutions characteristic of our adult world. For example, Harry and his classmates critically discuss institutional aims, authority, and rules within the context of formal education. Although the issues of fairness and rights may not have the complexity of problems addressed by the American Civil Liberties Union or by our criminal-justice system, rudiments of the moral concepts and principles relevant to addressing those more complex issues are evident in the children's discussions.

If the eighteenth-century Scottish philosopher Thomas Reid is basically right about morality, we should not be surprised at the richness of children's moral thinking. Reid insists that morality is everyone's business, "and therefore the knowledge of it ought to be within the reach of all."[2] He also denies that "in order to understand his duty a man must needs be a philosopher and a metaphysician" (*AP*, p. 643). This does not mean that philosophical thinking is not necessary—only that this need not be one's preoccupation. That is, one need not be a Plato, Aristotle, Descartes, Locke, or Hume. Reid acknowledges that *moral systems* "swell to great magnitude." But this is not because there is a large number of general moral principles. He says that, actually, they are "few and simple." Moral systems are complex because applications of moral principles "extend to every part of human conduct, in every condition, every relation, and every transaction of life" (*AP*, p. 642). Given the wide reach of such principles, it is clear that the limited experience of children restricts their ability to apply them. The same, to a lesser degree, is true of adults as well, since their range of experience, though more extensive, is also limited. Nevertheless, as *Harry* illustrates, there is no shortage of opportunities for children to test out moral concepts and principles within their familiar range of experience.

LACK OF RATIONAL PRINCIPLES

Still, it might be objected, this has little bearing on the moral development of children. Consider what Aristotle says about our beginnings:

> For while one must begin from what is familiar, this may be taken in two ways: some things are familiar to us, others familiar without qualification. Presumably, then, what *we* should begin from is things familiar to *us*. This is the reason why one should have been well brought up in good habits if one is going to listen adequately to lectures about things noble and just, and in general about political (social) affairs. For the beginning (starting point) is "the *that*," and if this is sufficiently apparent to a person, he will not in addition have a need for "the *because*."[3]

Since Aristotle's lectures on moral philosophy concern "the *because*" and not just "the *that*," presumably the young are not ready for them. First there must be good habits of feeling concerning "the *that*." Only those with good habits will hear what reason has to say.

As for people who lack these habits, Aristotle says that arguments are of no use, "for these do not by nature obey the sense of shame, but only fear, and do not abstain from bad acts because of their baseness but through fear of punishment."[4] Children, therefore, are not suited for moral philosophy:

> For he who lives as passion directs will not hear argument that dissuades him, nor understand it if he does; and how can we persuade one in such a state to change his ways? And in general passion seems to yield not to argument but to force. The character, then, must somehow be there already with a kinship to virtue, loving what is noble and hating what is base.[5]

Thus, we find in Aristotle a theme familiar to twentieth-century psychology—namely, that early "morality" is shaped by fear and punishment. For Freudians, the internalization of these external threats is nearly all there is to morality; adult morality is hardly more than variation on this early theme. For cognitive-developmental theorists like Jean Piaget and Lawrence Kohlberg, there is much more to the story.[6] But, even for them, it begins with fear and punishment imposed on the self-centered child. Only later does the story take a rather remarkable shift in the direction of reasonable concern for others.

For Piaget and Kohlberg, early moral development is highly egocentric. Before the age of seven or eight years, children see things only from their own point of view, and they are motivated primarily by fear of punishment and not being loved. Kohlberg, for example, characterizes "justice" for very young children as the threat of punishment for violating a rule emanating from authority or power. The second stage of moral development emphasizes the idea of reciprocal exchange ("You scratch my back and I'll scratch yours"); but this is still basically self-interested motivation. Only at a third stage does "empathy" enter in, enabling children to get beyond egocentricity to some extent. At this point, limited golden-rule reasoning is possible because children are finally able to imagine what it would be like to be in another person's situation.

Whether we are talking about Aristotle, Freud, Piaget, or Kohlberg, the idea that moral reasoning might play a significant role in moral education before age seven or eight is simply rejected. Of the four thinkers, Piaget and Kohlberg take the most optimistic view that reasoning might contribute to the moral development of young children. But even they offer little hope that sophisticated reflection can occur before age ten or eleven. This is when they believe that children are first able to "think about thinking" to any significant degree. If they are right about children's capabilities, then we should see Harry and his friends as just *beginning* to reflect on various aspects of their moral lives; and we are probably well advised not to expect too much too soon.

If they are wrong, however, important opportunities may be missed, and both children and adults will be the losers. IAPC programs are designed not to miss the earliest possible opportunities to engage children in moral reflection.

Harry does not present its fifth-graders as neophytes when it comes to moral reasoning. IAPC programs designed for earlier grades assume that younger children are capable of reflecting on a variety of moral concepts (for example, fair/unfair, right/wrong, good/bad, cruel/kind). Is this a misguided effort on the part of IAPC, or is there evidence that even very young children have such capacities?

Richard Shweder, Elliot Turiel, and Nancy Much present evidence that children as young as four have an intuitive grasp of differences among prudential, conventional, and moral rules.[7] Characterizing young children as "intuitive moralists," they say, "Although four- to six-year-olds have little reflective understanding of their moral knowledge, they nevertheless have an intuitive moral competence that displays itself in the way they answer questions about moral rules and in the way they excuse their transgressions and react to the transgressions of others."[8] They continue:

> In fact, at this relatively early age, four to six, children not only seem to distinguish and identify moral versus conventional versus prudential rules using the same formal principles (e.g., obligatoriness, importance, generalizability) employed by adults, they also seem to agree with the adults of their society about the moral versus conventional versus prudential status of particular substantive events (e.g., throwing paint in another child's face versus wearing the same clothes to school every day).[9]

There is also a growing body of evidence that even much younger children are capable of empathizing with others,[10] and there is substantial evidence that children have the cognitive ability to reason nonegocentrically much earlier than Piaget's studies suggest.[11] All of this suggests that the IAPC programs portray ordinary rather than philosophically precocious children.

ILLUSTRATIONS

Young children have a very keen sense of fairness within their spheres of experience. Favoritism, taking more than one's fair share, not taking turns, and so on, are staples in the lives of children—in school, on the playground, and within their family structures. That they (like the rest of us) may more readily recognize unfairness in others than in themselves does not mean that they do not understand what fairness is. That they will later extend their conceptions of it to situations they cannot now understand (e.g., taxation)—and that they will discover conflicts with other fundamental moral values—does not imply that they do not now have access to morality at its most basic level.

It might be argued that children begin with particular examples and only through unreflective habituation develop a sense of fairness. But even if this were so, some of the foundation seems well in place rather early on, thus allowing room for reflection much earlier than Aristotle seems to acknowledge. Of course, children do learn from examples. But examples provide only a starting point from which they may go on to deal competently with novel instances. Ronald Dworkin makes an important point in this regard:

> Suppose I tell my children simply that I expect them not to treat others unfairly. I no doubt have in mind examples of the conduct I mean to discourage, but I would not accept that my "meaning" was limited to these examples, for two reasons. First, I would expect my children to apply my instructions to situations I had not and could not have thought about. Second, I stand ready to admit that some particular act I had thought was fair when I spoke was in fact unfair, or vice-versa, if one of my children is able to convince me of that later; in that case I should want to say that my instructions covered the case he cited, not that I had changed my instructions. I might say that I meant the family to be guided by the *concept* of fairness, not by any specific *conception* of fairness I might have had in mind.[12]

If we think of particular moral conceptions as workable, but somewhat inadequate, renderings of basic moral concepts, then we can understand how we might learn from children as they wrestle with these concepts.

This way of looking at moral development differs in an important respect from the cognitive–developmental approach of Piaget and Kohlberg. Characteristically, it claims that children's moral development goes through sequential stages, with each subsequent stage replacing inadequate concepts in preceding stages. Concepts in different stages differ in kind, not simply in degree. Although the concepts in later stages build on earlier ones, the process is more a matter of *reconstructing* than *enlarging* them. Children at the earlier stages are viewed as lacking the ability to understand and assimilate the reasoning of the higher stages. Although emphasizing that greater understanding comes with maturation, stage theories imply that children live in a quite different moral world from adults. Thus, they encourage a condescending attitude toward children's moral thinking and discourage genuine moral dialogue between children and adults. That there are striking moral differences between children and adults cannot sensibly be denied. But there are ways of characterizing those differences that at the same time indicate even more striking similarities.

Gareth Matthews suggests a promising alternative to stage theories. He emphasizes the importance of paradigms:

> A young child is able to latch onto the moral kind, bravery, or lying, by grasping central paradigms of that kind, paradigms that even the most mature and sophisticated moral agents still count as paradigmatic. Moral development is then something much more complicated than simple concept displacement. It is: enlarging the stock of paradigms for each moral kind; developing better and better definitions of whatever it is these paradigms exemplify; appreciating better the relation between straightforward instances of the kind and close relatives; and

learning to adjudicate competing claims from different moral kinds (classically the sometimes competing claims of justice and compassion, but many other conflicts are possible).[13]

In a view such as this, children as well as adults can be acknowledged to share some ground-level understanding of moral concepts and principles. Although adults may typically have the upper hand in regard to breadth of experience and understanding, there is no warrant for entirely excluding children from the adult world of morality.

If the idea that young children are capable of imaginative and provocative moral thought seems farfetched, consider one of Matthews's examples:

> IAN (six years) found to his chagrin that the three children of his parents' friends monopolized the television; they kept him from watching his favorite program. "Mother," he asked in frustration, "why is it better for three people to be selfish than for one?"[14]

This question reflects much more than mere habituation of thought or feeling. Matthews suggests it may be an incipient challenge to utilitarian thought. At the very least, Ian seems to have a rudimentary grasp of two fundamental moral concepts: fairness and selfishness.

Matthews used Ian's remark to construct a story for a group of eight- to eleven-year-olds. In Matthews's story, Freddie is watching his favorite program, "The Abbott and Costello Show," when three younger children invade his home and take over the television set. Here is how the story ends:

> Douglas, who acted as the leader of the group, walked calmly to the TV, reached for the knob, and switched the program to the Moomins.
> Freddie got up sadly and went out to the kitchen.
> "Why the sad face?" said Freddie's mother, as she filled the kettle. "I know they're younger than you, but they're nice kids, really. And their mum and dad are very old friends of your mum and dad. Please be nice to them."
> "But they want to watch the Moomins!" said Freddie in disbelief.
> "I'm sorry," said Freddie's mother, "I know you can't stand that program. But think of it this way. Three people are being made happy instead of just one."
> Freddie reflected a moment. "Mother," he said, slowly and deliberately, "why is it better for three people to be selfish than for one?"[15]

Matthews wrote the story in such a way that the challenge to utilitarian thinking is made explicit. In addition, of course, the utilitarian voice is that of parental authority. Still, none of the children who heard the story picked up on utilitarian themes.

David-Paul commented on the meanness of the three children; after all, they could have played together. He added: "They have to respect other people's rights as well. The Moomins are on almost every day." Martin commented that he would hate to have something like that happen to him. He concluded, "I mean, they could easily have watched what Freddie was watching." The children discussed whether either program could be watched on some other occasion. They recalled related examples from their own lives, and they constructed analogous imaginary examples. Still, says Matthews, "they found utilitarianism unattractive, and they were not inclined to search for any similarly high-level principle or theory to replace utilitarianism."[16]

Finally, Matthews pressed the utilitarian case. "What about this argument," he asked, "that if we let the three visitors have their way, three people will be made happy instead of just one?" Martin replied, "It's not really fair if three people get what they want and leave one person out. That one person will feel very hurt." The discussion then turned to specific considerations—the types of programs involved, relationships among the children (relative ages, siblings or strangers), and whether one really wants others to share the television screen.

Despite further efforts, Matthews was unable to elicit utilitarian responses. He observes:

> Everyday ethics, like the common law, arbitrates disputes and conflicts of interest by appeal to cases, as interpreted, perhaps, by low-level "maxims," or "rules of law." This arbitration may succeed without anyone's having to show that the reasoning fits into some coherent system that will resolve all conceivable disputes. Of course, someone might insist that disputes resolved in this fashion are not resolved correctly unless the resolution can be shown to fall appropriately under some absolutely general principle or to fit properly into some universal system.[17]

Matthews adds, however, despite the children's strong feelings about the case and their efforts to bring analogous situations to bear on this one, "I was interested that none of my kids seemed attracted by the pull to general theory."

A Kohlbergian might reply that what happened here is just what a stage theory would predict. Utilitarian reasoning occurs only at the most advanced level of moral development (postconventional, or critical, morality), and even relatively few adults attain that level. However, this is implausible, as a variation on Matthews's example will show. Suppose he told the children a story about a hermit writing into his will what to do with his modest life savings. He has no friends, but he wants to make sure that his money is put to good use after he dies. Then Matthews asks the children, "Should he give his money to a few rich people so that they'll be a little bit richer, or should he give it to a needy children's hospital?" Surely even very young children can entertain the thought that it would do more good, and for that reason be preferable, to give the money to the hospital rather than to a few wealthy people.

It is no objection that the children's thoughts might be mistaken, since the hospital might misuse the money or the wealthy might themselves put the money to more constructive use for others. The only issue here is whether young children can see that there are circumstances in which it is better to "make three people happy rather than one." It might be suggested that, in Freddie's case, the children simply do not see that more good is served by giving in to the three children. But this does not seem to be their concern. More prominent in their thinking is the issue of fairness, as well as the issue of rights. (Note, also, Martin's incipient Kantian remark that he would not want such a thing to happen to him.) That is, they may resist the appeal to utility because they reject the idea that the "greater good" is the point at issue in *this* case.

THOMAS REID AGAIN

I have suggested that cognitive–developmental theories like Piaget's and Kohlberg's invite condescension toward children's moral thought (as well as that of most adults). This is because built into these accounts of moral development is a moral philosophy that has just the features Thomas Reid challenges. Both utilitarian and Kantian views of morality try to show that there is one supreme moral principle that provides the grounding for all more particular moral ideas (e.g., that we should keep our promises, not lie, not hurt others). This is what Reid calls a *geometrical* model of moral thought, to which he contrasts his own *botanical,* or *mineralogical,* model.

> A system of morals is not like a system of geometry, where the subsequent parts derive their evidence from the preceding, and one chain of reasoning is carried on from the beginning; so that, if the arrangement is changed, the chain is broken, and the evidence is lost. It resembles more a system of botany, or mineralogy, where the subsequent parts depend not for their evidence upon the preceding, and the arrangement is made to facilitate apprehension and memory, and not to give evidence. (*AP*, p. 642)

The philosophical issue of whether morality is best understood on a botanical or a geometrical model cannot be adequately addressed here. On this matter I am inclined toward the botanical model. The geometrical model is, at best, a philosophical aspiration. None of the leading candidates (e.g., Kantianism, utilitarianism, egoism) is free from serious philosophical criticism. Lack of consensus among philosophers does not imply that pursuit of a unified, hierarchical moral theory is misguided. But it does suggest that it is unwise to select, as Kohlberg does, a favored geometrical model as the basis for assessing the moral development of children and adults. At the same time, opting for the botanical model does not imply moral relativism. Reid is no relativist. His concern is mainly that we not lose sight of the fact that morality is practical, not merely theoretical. Again, morality is the business of *all* of us and, therefore, it should be accessible to everyone.

As for the proper role of theory, Reid says: "There is in Ethicks as in most Sciences a Speculative and a practical Part, the first is subservient to the last."[18] Although Reid insists that "the practical Part of Ethicks is for the most part easy and level to all capacities," he does not underestimate the obstacles to clearheaded thinking in our practical circumstances:

> There is . . . no branch of Science wherein Men would be more harmonious in their opinions than in Morals were they free from all biass and Prejudice. But this is hardly the case with any Man. Mens private Interests, their Passions, and vicious inclinations & habits, do often blind their understandings, and biass their Judgments. And as Men are much disposed to take the Rules of Conduct from Fashion rather than from the Dictates of reason, so with Regard to Vices which are authorized by Fashion, the Judgments of Men are apt to be blinded by the Authority of the Multitude especially when Interest or Appetite leads the same Way. It is therefore of great consequence to those who would judge right in matters relating to their own conduct or that of others to have the Rules of Morals fixed & settled in their Minds, before they have occasion to apply them to cases wherein they may be interested. It must also be observed that although the Rules of Morals are in most cases very plain, yet there are intricate and perplexed cases even in Morals wherein it is no easy matter to form a determinate Judgment.[19]

For Reid, experience and reflection can correct, modify, or enlarge the moral understanding that begins in childhood, but they cannot totally *displace* it—a point that "Speculative Ethicks" should constantly bear in mind. Even so, as the passage just cited makes clear, there is plenty of work to do in getting clear about moral matters—more than enough for a lifetime. So, Reid might say, it is better to get started sooner rather than later.

His account of moral agency begins with a contrast between humans and "brute animals." They have no power of self-government—nor would we if we "had no power to restrain appetite but by a stronger contrary appetite or passion" (*AP*, p. 534). Some might object to the severity of this contrast, but even if Reid somewhat underestimates brute animals, this would simply bring them closer to moral agency than he suggests. His fundamental claim concerns the close relationship between the capacity for self-government and moral agency.[20]

Reid points out that humans share with nonhuman animals the tendency to react to harm and threats of harm with "sudden resentment"—a defense mechanism that can strike fear in the aggressor. But humans are also capable of "deliberate resentment," which requires "opinion of injury" (*AP*, p. 567). Such an opinion supposes that the cause of harm is a responsible agent, rather than an inanimate object or animals that have no conception of right or wrong. Thus, the natural sentiment of "sudden resentment" can gradually become transformed, through the influence of reason, into "deliberate," or moral, resentment. But our "opinion of injury" can involve bias, distortion, and other excesses. So we must take care that "deliberate resentment" itself be amenable to reasonable constraints.

How is this to be done? *Harry* models this through self-examination (e.g., when Harry realizes that he should not resent Lisa's helping him to see *his* mistake) and discussion (e.g., when he and Bill Beck open themselves up to developing a friendship). In both kinds of cases a broader and deeper understanding can result and thereby alter one's moral attitudes and judgments. Such self-examination and discussion at an early age is not only possible, it is desirable. It can be a useful supplement to adult modeling. Furthermore, if it does have a constructive influence on controlling excessive and unreasonable resentment, it can provide an alternative to the more usual, punitive methods of controlling unwanted behavior—methods that are often themselves met with resentment.

Reid acknowledges that our moral conceptions develop gradually, just as our rational capacities do. Like the power of reasoning, the "seeds of moral discernment" do not appear in infancy, and they require careful cultivation: "They grow up in their proper season, and are at first tender and delicate and easily warped. Their progress depends very much upon their being duly cultivated and properly exercised" (*AP*, p. 595). Reid points out, however, that "as soon as men have any rational conception of a favour and of an injury, they must have the conception of justice, and perceive its obligation" (*AP*, p. 654).

It is clear that he is not restricting his discussion to adults, as the "notions of a *favour* and of *injury* appear as early in the mind of man as any rational notion whatever" (*AP*, p. 654). Further:

> One boy has a top, another a scourge; says the first to the other, If you will lend me your scourge as long as I can keep up my top with it, you shall next have the top as long as you can keep it up. This is a contract perfectly understood by both parties, though they never heard of the definition given by Ulpian or by Titius. And each of them knows that he is injured if the other breaks the bargain, and that he does wrong if he breaks it himself. (*AP*, p. 663)

If we add to this children's natural sociability and their early, rudimentary grasp of the central idea that "we ought not to do to another what we should think wrong to be done to us in like circumstances" (*AP*, p. 590), there seems little reason to deny that children are quite capable of undertaking, and benefiting from, just the sorts of reflective moral inquiry illustrated in *Harry* and the other IAPC programs.

Reid offers no timetable for when fruitful discussion might begin, but it is clear he does not believe that reflective discussion of morality is only for older children or adults. He observes: "Our first moral conceptions are probably got by attending cooly to the conduct of others and observing what moves our approbation, what our indignation. These sentiments spring from our moral faculty as naturally as the sensations of sweet and bitter from the faculty of taste" (*AP*, p. 641). Reid also reminds us of our tendency to view human actions from partial and biased perspectives: "Prejudice against or in favour of the person, is apt to warp our opinion. It requires candour to distinguish the good from the ill, and, without favour or prejudice, to form a clear and impartial judgment. In this way we may be greatly aided by instruction" (*AP*, p. 641). Again, this is modeled in *Harry* when the children catch each other (and their teachers) jumping to conclusions, stereotyping, and failing to see things from other points of view. However, the "instruction" is accomplished through *discussion* rather than Aristotle's *lectures* on moral philosophy. In this way, the children's moral capacities are respected at the very time they are enlarging.

MORE ILLUSTRATIONS

I have said that the children in *Harry Stottlemeier's Discovery* are not neophytes when it comes to moral reasoning. Neither are the fifth-grade readers of *Harry*. Consider this passage:

> The bell was about to ring, and the two monitors were still standing at the door. Both boys were large and rather heavy, and they decided to tease Fran by not giving her much room to pass. Maybe she thought they did it because she was a girl, and most likely she thought they did it because she was a girl and black, too, but she didn't care for that kind of teasing, and she pushed them out of her way. Mrs. Halsey turned around just in time to see what Fran had done, and she spoke to Fran very sharply about it.[21]

The word "fair" does not appear in this passage—nor do "unfair," "just," "unjust," or any other terms normally associated with issues of fairness (e.g., "discrimination"). Yet, when I asked a group of fifth-graders with whom I met every week, "What do you think fairness is?" Larry immediately reminded us of this passage—something we had read a few weeks earlier, but that we had not discussed in any detail.[22]

I asked my question after we had been discussing other philosophical matters for half an hour. It seemed time to move on to another topic. So I thought the group might enjoy talking about fairness for the remaining fifteen minutes of our session. What followed Larry's reminder of Fran's situation was a barrage of examples. Fairness, the students said, requires getting all the facts straight and hearing all sides of any issue. (Fran, they said, was not even given a chance to explain to Mrs. Halsey why she pushed the boys.) They objected to the deliberate distortion of facts. This led to a discussion of lying. Later, while acknowledging he should not lie, Rick said it is unfair to assume that, just because he used to lie a lot, he still does: "My Mom said that, you know, I used to be the kid who lied because I was afraid when I was young that I'd get a spanking. But now I've stopped lying for about two years now, and my Mom still doesn't believe me." Mike replied, "Rick, but you've earned that responsibility. You lied when you were young. If you never started lying, your mother would have believed you all the time." Is it unreasonable (and unfair) to doubt the word of those who have consistently lied in the past? Regardless of the answer, once doubt sets in, it is very difficult to reestablish trust. (This is a major theme in Sissela Bok's widely read book, *Lying*.) [23] Here is ten-year-old Mike making the same point to his classmates that Bok makes to her very large adult audience.

Mike's comment opened up questions of responsibility and desert. So, I decided to read a short story about treating people equally.[24] Before she can distribute candy to the students in her class, the teacher is called out of the classroom. While she is gone, the students fight over the candy she left on her desk. The biggest, strongest children each have a handful of candy, while the smallest children have only one piece each. When the teacher sees what has happened, she announces that she will treat everyone equally and take back one piece of candy from each student. As might be expected, my students strongly protested the teacher's action. However, what was most interesting about the ensuing discussion is that the students' attention very quickly shifted to a variety of other examples in order to explain their ideas of fairness. They discussed the fairness of group punishments and rewards. They discussed problems of rewarding people according to merit, effort, or ability. And they explored the idea of giving special opportunities to those with special shortcomings or disabilities.

The students did not attempt to subsume their examples under a comprehensive theory. Perhaps with more time they would have tried to do so; and no doubt, like adults, they would have faltered along the way. Questions of punitive and distributive justice are among the most difficult ones we face—whether they concern criminal law, the allocation of scarce resources, or taxation. Given more time, however, the children might simply have continued as they were, sorting out nuances that need attention, modifying their judgments as the examples change, and taking delight, as Rick did, in each new shade of meaning. After all, it was Rick who said, after suggesting that fairness is having the person who cuts a candy bar get the last piece, "It's not only just that. But there's really a lot of meanings." It was also Rick who asked, "Mr. Pritchard, who thinks of these questions? They've always got a two-way answer to them."

Although the IAPC programs encourage the kind of moral reflection that supports Rick's observation, this is accomplished by very different means from Lawrence Kohlberg's use of moral dilemmas.[25] Kohlberg's cognitive–developmental theory claims that moral reasoning is advanced by being thrown into "disequilibrium." Children find that their customary modes of reasoning are not adequate for handling certain moral problems. Successful resolution of such problems requires advancing to the next stage of moral reasoning. Stages form a hierarchy involving progressively greater cognitive complexity and advancement toward a universal moral perspective in which rights and duties stand in a fully reciprocal relation to one another. Since moral development depends on conflict, Kohlberg recommends the use of hypothetical moral *dilemmas* at strategic times as a teaching device in moral education.

In contrast, IAPC programs place no special emphasis on such dilemmas. They do provide children with opportunities to sort out subtle and complex features of situations calling for moral reflection, but only a relatively small proportion of such situations involve dilemmas. A steady diet of dilemmas risks creating the impression that moral problems typically resist confident resolution. However, underlying our recognition that a situation poses a moral dilemma is the belief that there are competing moral values that in more ordinary circumstances, are decisive. (For example, Kohlberg's famous Heinz dilemma—Should Heinz steal a cancer-curing drug to save his wife if this is the only way he can obtain it for her?—presupposes that property is an important value, that stealing is generally wrong, and that saving a life, especially a loved one's, is very important. It is precisely because these are *all* morally important considerations that Heinz is faced with a moral *dilemma*.)

However, it is not just moral dilemmas that give rise to moral puzzlement and call for careful thinking. For example, there is a passage in *Lisa* in which Harry, Lisa, and Timmy wonder when it is right to "return in kind" and when it is not—and, equally important, *why* it is or is not. The passage involves Timmy retaliating after being tripped, Harry and Timmy discussing trading stamps and lending money, and Lisa finally remarking: "It looks like there are times when it is right to give back what we got and other times when it is wrong. But how do we tell which is which?"

How does discussing a passage like this differ from discussing a moral dilemma? When we face a moral dilemma, we are pulled in conflicting directions. We think we have reasons for going either way—or for avoiding both ways. None of the choices seems to be without moral cost, and we are very likely perplexed about what the right choice is (or even whether there is a right choice). Timmy, Harry, and Lisa *might* have viewed the situations they discussed as posing dilemmas of this sort. But, in fact, they do not. Timmy, at least initially, has no doubt that retaliation is called for. Even if Harry succeeds in raising doubt in Timmy's mind, it is not clear that this creates a *dilemma* for him. He might wonder if he really did *have* to get even. Or he might wonder, as the group of fifth-graders with whom I discussed this passage did, what it *means* to "get even," whether it is possible to get even, and whether it is *desirable* to try.

Harry, on the other hand, has little doubt that Timmy's act of retaliation was inappropriate. He also has no doubt that trading stamps is appropriate and that one ought to repay borrowed money. What puzzles him is how to *explain* the differences among these instances of returning in kind. Lisa, too, is puzzled about this. Making progress in resolving such puzzlements is a fundamental part of moral development. But it is not clear that the discussion of moral dilemmas has any distinctive contribution to make here. On the other hand, it would seem useful to compare and contrast what Gareth Matthews calls paradigms—both with one another and with less familiar cases.

When my group of fifth-graders discussed this episode from *Lisa*, they addressed a variety of topics other than dilemmas. Here are some of the things the group discussed:

1. The likely *consequences* of retaliating. They worried that retaliation sets off a chain of events that no one wants—other than, perhaps, the initiator, who wants attention and an excuse to be even more aggressive.
2. Does retaliation really "get things even"? Does this notion even make sense? First Larry, and then Carlen, suggested that it does not.
3. Is it important to distinguish between *wanting* to do something and *having* to do it?
4. Is it right to respond to an acknowledged wrong by returning it in kind? (Do two wrongs make a right?)
5. What *alternatives* are available, and what are the likely consequences of each? (For example, will hitting back make things worse? Will doing nothing in return discourage the initiator, or will it simply encourage more of the same and perhaps contribute to the aggressor growing up to be an undesirable kind of person? Is self-defense needed—as a first response, or as a backup to it?)
6. What should the person who is hit or tripped be trying to *accomplish* in responding one way rather than another? Avoiding making things worse? (For whom?) Getting even? Teaching a lesson? (Are these last two different? If so, how?)
7. *How* is hitting back different from making an exchange of goods, paying back a debt, returning a favor, or responding to someone who does not return a favor or who refuses to extend a favor?
8. Keeping all of these examples in mind, what does the Golden Rule *mean*? Is it a good rule?

The children discussed questions like these in great detail, and with great understanding, for more than half an hour.

Without reaching consensus about how each of the situations should be handled, the students recognized that reciprocal relations in human affairs tend to generate chains of "returning in kind": Attacks encourage counterattacks, counterattacks encourage counter-counterattacks; favors encourage favors in return, extending trust encourages trust in return. But, as children are well aware, reciprocity does not always occur. Counterattacks do sometimes work. Favors are sometimes not returned. Trust sometimes simply renders one vulnerable. How to stop an undesired chain (e.g., hitting) from getting started, or how to stop it once it starts, is a challenge at any age. So, as the children again realized, ideals have to be related to realities. Chip suggested a two-stage strategy: Ignore the instigator at first, but defend yourself if that doesn't work. In response to those who expressed reluctance to extend favors without evidence that they would be reciprocated, Rick replied that it was worth the risk: If everyone would give, everyone would benefit—from someone, even if not from those for whom one does favors. These were thoughtful responses, made in full awareness of the uncertainties present in the situations under discussion.

For me, an occasional prodder but largely a witness to their conversation, the most fascinating aspect of the discussion was its thoroughness. What, I have since wondered, would adults want to add that was not considered in some way? Adults might wish to make comparisons with other kinds of situations that ten-year-olds will understand but have to wrestle with only later. This does not, however, detract from their understanding of the moral nuances of situations *within* their range of experience. I take this as further confirmation of Thomas Reid's view that morality is the business of all of us—and that it is accessible to all of us as well.

COMMUNITY OF INQUIRY

All the IAPC programs emphasize the importance of the classroom becoming a "community of inquiry." In such a classroom, students are encouraged to explore ideas together. Teachers often ask how discussions of moral concerns differ from "values clarification," which they see as designed to encourage students to clarify their moral values. Although such programs do help students become clearer about their own values, children are discouraged from making evaluative or critical remarks about one another's values. Thus, respect is shown for each student's point of view, and charges of indoctrination in the classroom are avoided. However, the underlying message is that moral values are relative to those who happen to embrace them. Morality is quietly endorsed as being "subjective," with each person's ideas being as "valid" as anyone else's.

For some teachers this implicit relativism is anathema, and they want nothing to do with IAPC programs if this is what they amount to. Others welcome this supposed feature of the IAPC approach but fail to see how Philosophy for Children is different from what they are already doing in "values clarification." But it is important to realize that IAPC programs do *not* discourage students from evaluating one another's views. Reason giving is a central activity, not only in clarifying one's views but also in dialogue in which students try to evaluate one another's thinking. Although teachers should refrain from simply imposing their values on students (indoctrination), it is also not their role to reinforce the notion that all views are equally well thought out, plausible, defensible, valid, or the like (relativism).

Although critical dialogue can degenerate into shouting matches and "put downs," it will not if the teacher establishes the appropriate environment for thoughtful discussion. In such an environment, reflective exchanges promote a number of important values. First, they help the participants become more aware of what they believe, why they believe what they do, and what the limitations of their beliefs are. Second, participants become clearer about the beliefs of *others*, thus enabling them to see that there may be more to another person's perspective than "meets the eye" when answers are not accompanied with supporting reasons. This encourages a kind of mutual respect and care that is based on better understanding of the perspectives of others—something without which golden-rule reasoning flounders. Third, participants may learn, as Harry and his friends do, that sometimes "a graceful error corrects the cave." Learning that one's thinking is inadequate, or even mistaken, is not "the end of the world"—it may be, as in Harry's case, the beginning of a new and exciting one. Finally, participants are encouraged to acquire the virtue of reasonableness—an openness to reasoning *with* others.

Taking all of this into consideration, we can see that a community of inquiry is actually a *moral* community, thus itself contributing to one's moral education—not through the indoctrination of some particular set of beliefs, but through a certain kind of practice.

NOTES

Acknowledgment. Portions of this chapter are revisions from chapter 2, "On Becoming a Moral Agent," of Michael S. Pritchard, *On Becoming Responsible* (Lawrence: University Press of Kansas, 1991).

1. William Shakespeare, *Troilus and Cressida* (II, ii, 166 f.). This is cited by David Ross in commenting on Aristotle's *Nicomachean Ethics* (Oxford: Oxford University Press, 1980), p. 3.

2. Thomas Reid, *Philosophical Works*, with notes by Sir William Hamilton, vol. 2, *On the Active Powers of the Mind* (Hildesheim: Olms Verlagsbuchandlung, 1985), p. 594. All further references to this work, abbreviated *AP*, will be included parenthetically in the text. Reid's *Philosophical Works* was first published in 1788.

3. Cited in M. F. Burnyeat, "Aristotle on Learning to Be Good," in *Essays on Aristotle's Ethics*, ed. Amelie Rorty (Berkeley: University of California Press, 1980), p. 71.

4. Ibid., p. 75.

5. Ibid.

6. See Jean Piaget, *The Moral Judgment of the Child* (London, 1932; reprint, New York: Free Press, 1965), and Lawrence Kohlberg, *The Philosophy of Moral Development: Essays on Moral Development*, vol. 1 (San Francisco: Harper and Row, 1981).

7. Richard A. Shweder, Elliot Turiel, and Nancy Much, "The Moral Intuitions of the Child," in *Social Cognitive Development: Frontiers and Possible Futures*, ed. by John H. Flavell and Lee Ross (Cambridge: Cambridge University Press, 1981), pp. 288–305.

8. Ibid., p. 288.

9. Ibid.

10. See, for example, M. L. Hoffman, "Empathy, Role-Taking, Guilt, and the Development of Altruistic Motives," in *Moral Development and Behavior*, ed. Thomas Lickona (New York: Rinehart and Winston, 1976), pp. 124–43; William Damon, *The Moral Child* (New York: Free Press, 1988); and Morton Hunt, *The Compassionate Beast* (New York: William Morrow, 1990).

11. See Damon, *Moral Child*, and Margaret Donaldson, *Children's Minds* (New York: Norton, 1979).

12. Ronald Dworkin, *Taking Rights Seriously* (Oxford: Oxford University Press, 1977), p. 133.

13. Gareth Matthews, "Concept Formation and Moral Development," in *Philosophical Perspectives in Developmental Psychology*, ed. James Russell (Oxford: Basil Blackwell, 1987), p. 185.

14. Gareth Matthews, *Philosophy and the Young Child* (Cambridge, Mass.: Harvard University Press, 1981), p. 28.

15. Gareth Matthews, *Dialogues with Children* (Cambridge, Mass.: Harvard University Press, 1984), p. 92–93.

16. Ibid., p. 94.

17. Ibid., p. 95.

18. Thomas Reid, *Practical Ethics*, ed., with commentary, by Knud Haakonssen (Princeton, N.J.: Princeton University Press, 1990), p. 110.

19. Ibid., pp. 110–11.

20. Reid carefully avoids an excessively individualistic conception of self-government and moral agency. We are naturally sociable, and, Reid says: "Without society, and the intercourse of kind affection, man is a gloomy, melancholy, and joyless being" (*AP*, p. 566).

21. Matthew Lipman, *Harry Stottlemeier's Discovery* (Upper Montclair, N.J.: Institute for the Advancement of Philosophy for Children, 1974), p. 11.

22. This session is discussed in greater detail in chapter 5, "Fairness," in Michael S. Pritchard, *Philosophical Adventures with Children* (Lanham, Md.: University Press of America, 1985). Portions of transcripts that are included here are taken from that chapter.

23. This story is taken from *Philosophical Inquiry*, the workbook for *Harry*, p. 63.

24. Sissela Bok, *Lying: Moral Choice in Public and Private Life* (New York: Pantheon, 1970).

25. The rest of this section is based on my "Reciprocity Revisited," in *Analytic Teaching* 9, no. 2 (May 1989): 54–62. A much more detailed critique of Kohlberg is contained in that article. See also, chapters 7 and 8 of my *On Becoming Responsible*. The full transcript of the children's discussion is in my *Philosophical Adventures with Children*, chapter 9, "Reciprocity."

5

Discussion and the Varieties of Authority

Ronald F. Reed

■ ■ ■

CHAPTER NINE OF *Harry Stottlemeier's Discovery* is interesting for several reasons. First, by the ninth chapter the children have had a good deal of time to talk and to reflect on the nature of their talk. They are beginning to realize that the discussion patterns that they fall into when they talk about the subjects that occupy their attention in Chapters One through Eight may be qualitatively distinct from other sorts of discussion patterns.[1] That realization, of course, is inchoate, but, as evidence to support the claim that such a realization is beginning, one need only point to the last few lines of Chapter Nine. There, Mr. Partridge asks Harry if the discussion held throughout the chapter is an example of what he (Mr. Partridge) calls a "free and open" one.[2] Harry responds that it is a start (*HSD*, p. 47). That, alas, leads to the second reason that the ninth chapter is so interesting.

Stated baldly, the discussion held in this chapter is a grab bag of fallacies, failed and successful attempts at intimidation, and insensitivity to the feelings of others that, if not cruel in intent, is unkind in outcome. In Chapter Fourteen, Suki is upset when her friend, Anne, wants to take her home to meet Anne's parents because, according to Anne, they would find her "interesting"—interesting like an exotic butterfly (*HSD*, p. 71). Suki feels, with good reason, that she is being treated like an object. Even more so, Dale, in Chapter Nine with far better reason, feels that his personhood is being ignored. Thus, the question arises as to what the reader is to make of Harry's belief that the discussion in the chapter is a move in the right direction.

Finally, Chapter Nine is interesting because it involves the first prolonged conversation between an adult and a group of children in a classroom. Previously, there had been relatively brief exchanges that included adults. The reader had witnessed children talking with Mr. Bradley, Mr. Spence, Mr. and Mrs. Portos, Mr. Mellilo, Mrs. Stottlemeier, and Mrs. Olsen. Some of those

32

exchanges took place inside the classroom, some outside, but none of them had anything approaching the emotional intensity of the one in this chapter. And in none of them did the "schoolmaster" play such a central role.

Here, after underscoring some of the more pernicious elements of the discussion in Chapter Nine, I will attempt, using arguments from John Dewey's "My Pedagogic Creed," *Democracy and Education, Art as Experience,* and *A Common Faith,* to explore the general significance of that chapter and, in particular, Harry's claim at the end of it that the discussion held there is a start in the right direction.

Chapter Nine begins with Dale Thompson, previously a minor character, sitting at his desk, weeping. Dale has run afoul of the substitute teacher, who sends him to see the principal, Mr. Partridge. After forcing Dale to wait in his outer office for nearly half an hour, Mr. Partridge finally deigns to meet Dale. With a "hearty" voice and a "friendly" tone, Mr. Partridge asks Dale what his problem is (*HSD*, p. 43). Dale's answer is a complex one. He explains his refusal to stand for the salute to the flag by reference to at least four distinct reasons (*HSD*, p. 43). Dale says he was obeying his parents' command, it was against the commands of *their* religion, it was against the commands of "*our*" religion, and it was against the commands of the Bible, specifically a biblical injunction against idolatry (*HSD*, p. 43).

Mr. Partridge ignores the complexity of Dale's answer and, instead, chooses to focus on the single issue of idolatry. He questions Dale on the meaning of the word. Dale responds with his father's definition—"bowing down to images"—coupled with the biblical commandment "Thou shalt have no other gods before me." Mr. Partridge's rejoinder borders on the ludicrous. He points out that the flag is not an image, but an emblem or a symbol, and that there is a difference between standing up and bowing down (*HSD*, pp. 43–44).

Dale does not laugh. Instead, he continues to treat Mr. Partridge in a serious and respectful manner. Dale admits that standing for the salute to the flag might not involve worshiping the flag, but it could involve worshiping what the flag stands for, and "that's what my father and mother object to, because they say we're supposed to worship God and nothing else" (*HSD*, p. 44). It is here that Mr. Partridge exercises his authority in a particularly disturbing manner. After Dale has made his telling point, Mr. Partridge decides simply to end the conversation. He leaves Dale with the knowledge that his personal problem will be discussed later that day with his classmates (*HSD*, p. 44).

One thinks of the boy's feelings during the long interlude between his exchange with Mr. Partridge and the principal's appearance later that afternoon in Dale's classroom. It takes only a modicum of sympathy to see Dale as one of Anne's butterflies, waiting patiently for the pins that will hold him to the page.

When Mr. Partridge does arrive, he explains Dale's problem (one thinks here of a therapist entering a faculty lounge and explaining Professor X's rash

behavior by a reference to X's recent marital woes), ignores Dale's claim regarding worship of the country, and tells the class that respect for flags has
nothing to do with religion (*HSD*, p. 44).

Mark Jahorski's response is classic in its simplicity. "Mr. Partridge, you say
it has nothing to do with religion. But when we pledge allegiance to the flag,
we're supposed to mention God, and that seems to me to have something to do
with religion" (*HSD*, p. 44). In a pattern that is disturbingly familiar, Mr. Partridge changes the subject. He says, ignoring Mark's claim that God may very
well have something to do with religion, that the words of the pledge are "standard" (*HSD*, p. 44). Mark really does not know how to respond to that, and so
he allows his sister Maria to go off on a different tack. The children talk about
majority rule, obedience to the law (national and divine), obedience to parents,
and the biblical claim that children ought to honor their parents. Dale ends that
part of the discussion with a question: "Would I be honoring them if I disagreed
with them about what the Bible tells me to do?" (*HSD*, p. 45).

Mr. Partridge reenters the discussion. He suggests to Dale that biblical
claims need interpretation and that the interpretation that Dale's parents give
such claims could be wrong (*HSD*, p. 45). Dale agrees to both assertions, but
he points out that just because his parents' interpretation might be a minority
one it does not follow that they are wrong (*HSD*, p. 45).

Once again, Mr. Partridge ignores Dale's answer. Once again, he changes
the subject. This time he does it in a particularly nasty and particularly effective way. He introduces what could qualify as a textbook example of the fallacy
that goes under the rubric "false analogy" or "misleading analogy." He suggests to Dale that his parents, by refusing to allow him to stand for the salute
to the flag, might be significantly like those parents who, on the basis of an
interpretation of the Bible, refuse to allow their sick children to receive needed
blood transfusions (*HSD*, p. 45). In effect, Mr. Partridge comes very close to
suggesting to Dale that his parents might be the sort of persons who would let
him die, and, hence, Dale may not have an obligation to obey them.

For the first time in the course of the discussion, the principal puts Dale in
a position in which he can utter no reasonable response. Dale squirms uncomfortably and finally accedes to his request to have Dale's parents come to see
him. Mr. Partridge takes this episode revolving around the blood-transfusion
analogy as indicative of "progress." One wonders in what the progress consists. Is it that Dale has been scared into silence? Is it that a seed of mistrust
has been planted? Is it that Mr. Partridge has finally compelled Dale to act in a
certain way?

The children, at any rate, are not ready to let the matter drop. They talk
about what counts as honoring or dishonoring one's parents and whether it is
possible to honor yet disagree. Mr. Partridge rejoins the discussion. That re-
entry is breathtaking in the quality of either the principal's own stupidity or of

his conscious attempt to manipulate Dale. He says: "Dale, I'd never counsel you to do something that went against your religious principles. Nor would I tell you that you ought to disagree with your parents. But when you talk with them tonight, couldn't you try to make them see that you wouldn't be dishonoring them if you came to your own conclusions?" (*HSD*, p. 46). The reader, weary at this point, might respond that Mr. Partridge has, indeed, been counseling Dale to do something that went against his religious principles and has, indeed, been suggesting to Dale that he ought to disagree with his parents. Once again, Dale is silenced by Mr. Partridge's maneuverings.

Fortunately, Mickey Minkowski has something to say. He points out to Mr. Partridge that if it is right that one could honor by disagreeing, then Mr. Partridge himself might feel honored by Dale's disagreeing with him (*HSD*, p. 46). Mr. Partridge puts an end to that discussion:

> "Mickey, . . . there are some things that people expect of you, and we in the schools wouldn't be doing our duty if we didn't try to show you what's expected of you. We try to make good citizens of you because society expects you to be good citizens when you finish school. I know that it isn't easy to accept that fact, just as it isn't easy to swallow some bad-tasting medicine. But just as you'll be a healthier person for swallowing the medicine, so you'll be a better person for accepting what I've told you." (*HSD*, pp. 46–47)

Ultimately, what Mr. Partridge is saying is that if he cannot convince the students of the truth of his position by reasoned argument they should still accept that position as true. In effect, the principal is trying to get the children to play a game in which it is impossible for him to lose. It is this "fixed" game that Harry takes to be a start. And that, the mere fact that a curious, intelligent boy like Harry could be put in a position where he took this pernicious exchange to be a first example of the sort of discussion he had in mind, is what makes Chapter Nine so interesting. Simply, one wonders how could Harry be so badly mistaken? To answer that question, it will prove helpful to look at Dewey's critique of "suggestive questioning."

While criticizing the educational theories of Friedrich Froebel, G.W.F. Hegel, and the rest of the group who, according to Dewey, view education as a sort of "unfolding," Dewey has this to say about principles of education. When the teacher has some idea in mind,

> by "suggestive questioning" or some other pedagogical device, the teacher proceeds to "draw out" from the pupil what is desired. If what is desired is obtained, that is evidence that the child is unfolding properly. But as the pupil generally has no initiative of his own in this direction, the result is a random groping after what is wanted, and the formation of habits of dependence upon the cues furnished by others. Just because such methods simulate a true principle and claim to have its sanction they may do more harm than would outright "telling," where, at least, it remains with the child how much will stick.[3]

The difficulty with the discussion in Chapter Nine is that it does, in fact, *simulate* the sorts of *discussions* the children and the adults have been having. Mr. Partridge does not come in and dictate to the class. He does not, as it were, stand at the podium and present a lecture about proper behavior. Instead, *almost* as a good Deweyian, he begins with the psychological side of education (the interest of the child—here, Dale's interest in the question of whether he should stand for the salute to the flag) and connects that with the sociological side (the interest of the community—here, its putative need for uniformity of response to a symbol of the society). The "connecting" takes place within the course of a discussion in which children are given the opportunity to speak their minds, offer reasons for their conclusions, and differ with one another. If one does not know the salient characteristics of the sort of conversations that the children are developing, if one does not have a checklist for gauging the worth of that discussion, if that checklist can only be developed in use, then it is understandable that the novice user would be misled.

With a little experience, however, Harry, in later chapters, will begin to see the problems with the discussion in Chapter Nine. The reader, fortunately, does not have to wait that long. He or she can begin to use the conversation as a sort of antimodel—a compendium, in effect, of things not to do. Using the discussion that way, the reader can begin to build a checklist.

The first thing that becomes apparent is that the sorts of discussions that the children have in mind (let us call them Philosophy for Children ones) make a distinction between interests of the children that are suitable starting points for the discussion and those that are not. A child does not give up his or her right to privacy when he or she enters the discussion. Just because Mr. Partridge is interested in Dale's "problem," and just because the children are interested in talking about the implications of Dale's action (or lack of action), it does not follow that Dale's problem is suitable for discussion. Interest, then, is a necessary but not sufficient point of departure for a Philosophy for Children discussion. Acting on that interest, having a Philosophy for Children discussion about that interest, may be precluded by the child's right to privacy.

The second point is that suggestive questioning, as defined by Dewey, has no place in a Philosophy for Children discussion. It encourages "random groping" after answers, contributes to a dependence of the students on the teacher–questioner, and, with the case of Harry, runs the risk of confusing the real thing with its counterfeit. If questioning is to occur in a Philosophy for Children discussion, it ought to involve the asking of questions where the answers are not already known to the person asking the question.[4]

The third point is that Philosophy for Children discussions are both non-authoritarian and anti-indoctrinal. Here are Matthew Lipman, Ann Margaret Sharp, and Frederick S. Oscanyan talking about Philosophy for Children novels:

One of the merits of the novels of the philosophy for children program is that they offer models of dialogue, both of children with one another and of children with adults. They are models that are non-authoritarian and anti-indoctrinal, that respect the values of inquiry and reasoning, encourage the development of alternative modes of thought and imagination, and sketch out what it might be like to live and participate in a small community where children have their own interests yet respect each other as people and are capable at times of engaging in cooperative inquiry for no other reason than that it is satisfying to do so.[5]

Clearly, Mr. Partridge's behavior in the discussion does present an antimodel. He is involved in the exchange for reasons other than the mere fact that it gives him satisfaction. And his behavior at the end of the discussion, where he suggests agreement even if there is no reasoned support for it, does not show much respect for the values of inquiry and reasoning.

So far, I have attempted to deal with the model of discussion that is suggested by Chapter Nine. It may prove helpful now to shift the focus a bit and to look more at the place of the discussion. Better yet, it may prove helpful to look at other discussions of other places.

In *Art as Experience*, Dewey criticizes museums in the industrial, capitalistic West. He suggests that museums tend to segregate art (more properly art objects) from its connection with ordinary experience. This segregation leads to the mistaken belief that the aesthetic sense (which enables one to discover order in one's environment and to interact harmoniously with it) is best satisfied, or perhaps only satisfied, by infrequent trips to museums. Such visits trivialize the art object, turning it into something fine but useless, and deprive ordinary experience of one of the primary tools, the aesthetic sense, that is essential to the process of reconstructing experience.[6]

Dewey, of course, does not suggest the destruction of museums. But what he does propose may have similar repercussions for aesthetic theory. Dewey says that an adequate aesthetic theory is still waiting to be developed, that it will not grow out of an analysis of the stuff of museums (what goes, typically, under the rubric "fine art"), but that it will be discovered by attending to the various qualities of ordinary experience.

> The comprehension which theory essays will be arrived at by a detour; by going back to experience of the common or mill run of things to discover the aesthetic quality ordinary experience possesses. Theory can start with and from acknowledged works only when the aesthetic is already compartmentalized, or only when works of art are set in a niche apart instead of being celebrations, recognized as such, of the things of ordinary experience. Even a crude experience, if authentically an experience, is more fit to give a clue to the intrinsic nature of aesthetic experience than is an object already set apart from any other mode of experience. Following this clue, we can discover how the work of art develops and accentuates

what is characteristically valuable in things of everyday enjoyment. The art product will then be seen to issue from the latter, when the full meaning of ordinary experience is expressed, as dyes come out of coal tar products when they receive special treatment.[7]

Not only, then, is the aesthetic a function of some relationship to ordinary experience: So, too, is knowledge about the aesthetic, and, by extension, knowledge of aesthetic theory, a function of knowledge about ordinary experience. If the museum is to be important to aesthetics, it must grow from ordinary experience and accentuate that which is "characteristically valuable in things of everyday enjoyment." To the extent that the museum is viewed as divorced from the concerns of everyday experience, it will be viewed as a place that has little or no use in the education of the person, in that continual process of reconstruction of experience. Therefore, the wise museum director will take steps to ensure that the museum does exist on a continuum with the museumgoer's ordinary experience and does select the "characteristically valuable."

Look, now, at another place—the church. Dewey, it is true, did not write much about religion. Over the course of a career that spanned nearly eighty years, he produced the famous religious language of article five of "My Pedagogic Creed" ("the teacher always is the prophet of the true God and the usherer in of the true kingdom of God"),[8] the pamphletlike *A Common Faith*, and not much else. His criticism, sparse as it was, had a trenchancy about it, however, and was clearly an extension of his experiential theory.

Dewey's criticism of the church is analogous to his criticism of the museum. First, he posits an industrial change. At one point in human history, the affairs of the church dominated the life of the individual. One lived and breathed one's religion. It permeated the society, and, hence, there was no distinction between the secular and the religious. If there was an *X*, then *X* was religious. Then a change took place (Dewey is not clear about when). The church became a separate institution and the distinction between secular and religious affairs became significant. As a separate institution, the church adopted a hierarchy and suggested a special path to knowledge and salvation—a path that led through itself. Unfortunately for the church, along with secularization and the rise of modern society comes a change in what Dewey refers to as the social center of gravity.[9] "The shift in what I have called the social center of gravity accompanies the enormous expansion of associations formed for educational, political, economic, philanthropic and scientific purposes, which has occurred independently of any religion. These social modes have grown so much that they exercise the greater hold upon the thought and interest of most persons, even of those holding membership in churches."[10] Thus, not only has a new element been introduced into society—the distinction between the secular and the religious—but religion is no longer, according to Dewey, the prime element in decision making. In fact, Dewey views the historical process as an ongoing trivialization of the role of the church.

His criticism does not stop there. Dewey goes on to say that the church, by virtue of beliefs in the supernatural and by the development of church-related paths to salvation, works against the like-mindedness and fellowship that are essential to democracy. "Lip service—often more than lip service—has been given to the idea of the common brotherhood of all men. But those outside the fold of the church and those who do not rely upon belief in the supernatural have been regarded as only potential brothers, still requiring adoption into the family." [11]

Dewey's solution to what he has identified as the problem of the church is markedly similar to his solution to the problem of the museum. The religious function, defined naturalistically as a sort of interconnectedness with one's fellows,[12] is essential to the educative process of reconstruction of experience. It could and should be the business of the church to safeguard and nurture that function. To paraphrase Dewey's remarks on the museum, the church must grow from ordinary experience; it must exist on a continuum with ordinary experience, and it must accentuate that which is "characteristically valuable" in the things of everyday life.

Returning now to Mr. Partridge, it is clear that he contributes to a segregation of the classroom that is similar to the segregation that Dewey warns against when he speaks about museums and churches. Mr. Partridge does this in two ways. First, by his actions in the course of the conversation in the classroom, he suggests that the ordinary rules of discussion do not apply *in the context of the classroom*. For example (and, since the first part of this chapter was devoted to an analysis of the discussion, this example will have to suffice), in an ordinary discussion the discussants have an obligation to try to respond. This means that if Sue is a discussant with Ron, then when Sue says X, Ron has an obligation to give some indication that he has heard her say X; he also has an obligation to attempt to tailor his remark Y so that it has some relation to X. What distinguishes a discussion from a series of monologues is this process of give-and-take. When Mr. Partridge "discusses" with the children, his remarks are unpredictable.[13] One cannot look at preceding remarks by Dale and predict that, since he has said X, therefore Mr. Partridge will say something that has some relationship to it. The chances are great that the principal will lapse into silence or say some Y that is clearly unrelated to X. His behavior suggests a breakdown in the continuum that could exist between ordinary discussion and one in a classroom.

Second, by his concluding remarks, Mr. Partridge suggests that exchanges in a classroom involve an area of expertise that is beyond the ken of most of the discussants, that there are privileged members in such a conversation (the "priest–teacher"), and that the appropriate behavior toward those members is belief, obedience, or both.

So, Mr. Partridge drives a wedge between the classroom and the other "rooms" of the children's lives. And since those other rooms have a built-in vitality, when the child experiences the classroom as "other" he or she also experiences it as less vital. If Dewey is right, and if we could extend the principal's classroom discussion into a fictional future, we could expect to find a place of tedium. Again, if Dewey is right, a wiser Mr. Partridge would model classroom discussion after the discussions the child has in the home and the neighborhood, accentuating that which is "characteristically valuable."

The obvious question now will be this: What is characteristically valuable about ordinary discussion? Stated another way, How does one go about separating the discussional wheat from the chaff, and delivering the wheat to the classroom? Dewey does not answer those questions. They may, however, set the agenda for further discussion about Philosophy for Children. Looking at Mr. Partridge's behavior in Chapter Nine gives the reader a fairly clear idea as to some of the patterns that he or she might want to avoid. It also points to some of the patterns the reader might want to embrace. Ultimately, what the reader should be most grateful to Mr. Partridge for, however, is that he so disturbs one's "dogmatic slumber" as to force one to realize that the question of what makes something a Philosophy for Children discussion is still open.

NOTES

1. For other analyses of these patterns, see Matthew Lipman, Ann Margaret Sharp, and Frederick S. Oscanyan, *Philosophy in the Classroom*, 2d ed. (Philadelphia: Temple University Press, 1980), pp. 102–28; Ronald F. Reed, "Discussing Philosophy with Children: Aims and Methods," *Teaching Philosophy* 8, no. 3 (1980): 229–34; Judy Kyle, "Managing Philosophical Discussions," *Analytic Teaching* 3, no. 2 (May 1983): 13–16; and Michael Whalley, "Some Factors Influencing the Success of Philosophy Discussions in the Classroom," *Thinking* 4, no. 3–4 (May 1989): 102–5.

2. Matthew Lipman, *Harry Stottlemeier's Discovery* (Upper Montclair, N.J.: First Mountain Foundation, 1982), p. 47. All further references to this work, abbreviated *HSD*, will be included parenthetically in the text.

3. John Dewey, *Democracy and Education* (New York: Free Press, 1966), p. 57.

4. Reed, "Discussing Philosophy with Children," 229–34.

5. Lipman, Sharp, and Oscanyan, *Philosophy in the Classroom*, p. 105.

6. John Dewey, *Art as Experience*, (New York, 1934; reprint, New York: Capricorn Books, 1958), pp. 3–19.

7. Ibid., pp. 10–11.

8. John Dewey, "My Pedagogic Creed," in *The Philosophy of John Dewey*, ed. John J. McDermott (Chicago: University of Chicago Press, 1981), p. 454.

9. John Dewey, *A Common Faith* (New York, 1934; reprint, New Haven, Conn.: Yale University Press, 1960), pp. 59–87.

10. Ibid., p. 60.

11. Ibid., p. 84.

12. Ibid., p. 87.

13. For further examination of the relationship of predictability to philosophy discussions, see Lipman, Sharp, and Oscanyan, *Philosophy in the Classroom*, pp. 102–5.

6

Women, Children, and the Evolution of Philosophy for Children

Ann Margaret Sharp

■ ■ ■

THERE IS SOMETHING wonderful, yet shocking, about waking up one morning and finding yourself in the midst of feminism in philosophy and Philosophy for Children. It seems like such a short time ago that both concepts were not only unheard of in professional philosophical circles but not even considered as possibilities in education. I remember myself in my freshman year at a Catholic girls' high school. It was spring, and the nuns had told us that we would have a five-day retreat. Speakers (priests) would come to lecture us in the mornings, while the afternoons would be reserved for reflection and reading. Of course, it was to be a silent retreat. No talking for five days.

Many of my classmates were not very happy about the prospect of spending five days listening to some priests, reading, and keeping silence. But I remember being thrilled. I had never had such an experience.

"Each girl is to bring in a book that you will read and think about in the afternoons," Sister said. "Not all books will be approved. It must be a book of some substance."

And she looked at us with that stare of hers as if to say, "You know what I mean!"

I remember going to the school library, a very small room, and asking the nun in charge for a "book of substance." She pointed to the theology section and said, "Anything from those shelves will do."

My eyes scanned the titles and caught sight of a red, leather-bound book with gold letters, *The Confessions*, by Saint Augustine. I had been going to confession since I was seven years old. Sin was something I thought about a lot.

"It would be interesting to hear about other people's sins," I thought. "I wonder how others feel about going to confession." With that, I checked out the book.

Sister Mary Jeremiah, who was not only my homeroom teacher but also my algebra teacher (and, I might add, my hero at the time), looked at me very intently when I submitted my book for approval on a Friday morning.

"Heavy reading," she commented. "Go to it, Ann."

I do not remember understanding anything of what I read for the next five afternoons. But I do remember reading greedily. I knew nothing about Saint Augustine.

"Here was a man who lived," I thought to myself. As I look back today, I realize that I had no idea of the purpose of the book. Actually, Saint Augustine is very clear very early on in the work about why he wrote *The Confessions*: "That I myself and whoever else reads them may realize from what depths we must cry unto God." Somehow the young adolescent missed the point.

There was a time set aside between two and two thirty in the afternoon to talk to one's spiritual adviser during the retreat. Sister Mary Jeremiah was my adviser. A big, fair-skinned woman, she spoke with a strong Brooklyn accent and had a habit of grinding her teeth when she became annoyed. This happened quite often. One day she kicked her chair right across our classroom in a frenzy. She was my hero. We used to clean chapel together in the late afternoons, just she and I, and we would talk.

"Sister, who is this Saint Augustine?"

"A philosopher," she said. "A great thinker. A Father of the Church." And she told me the story of Saint Monica, Augustine's early life and his decision to become a priest, and later his appointment as bishop of Hippo.

"I'd like to be one of those," I said.

"It's not for girls, Ann. Only boys become philosophers. Only boys become priests."

"You're a woman and you teach math," I said. (I had also thought I might want to become a math professor.)

"I *teach* math. That's not the same thing as *being* a mathematician. And you might be able to *teach* philosophy, but women don't *become* philosophers."

Later, at a Catholic liberal-arts college run by Ursuline nuns at which everyone took twenty-four credits in philosophy whether they liked it or not, I met my first female philosophy teacher. A short, dark, dynamic nun with green eyes, she taught Introduction to Philosophy in the first semester and Aristotelian Logic in the second semester of freshman year. Now *she* became my hero. Her courses were my favorite, and I remember coming home on weekends and telling my brother everything I could remember that she had told us. Sophomore, junior, and senior years were also filled with philosophy. But these courses were always taught by men. I understood little of the Thomistic babble, but I caught the spirit of the quest. I remember one teacher in particular, who appeared to be talking to himself rather than to the class as he would pace up and down and look out the window, often using terms that no one understood. For some odd reason, however, I loved going to philosophy classes.

I was an exception, and I knew it. Most of my housemates (we were sixteen, living in one small red-brick house with a mother nun) hated philosophy classes and would panic before the examinations. I remember their asking me to review the material with them the afternoon and evening before the midterm and the final and my struggling to make sense of the textbooks for them as we met in the third floor bathroom where we could sneak a cigarette. Most of what I told them was probably all wrong, but when you know your friends are counting on you, you try. Once in a while, one of my housemates would counter my interpretation and a dialogue would begin. But this was very rare. How we ever passed those courses I have no idea! Later, before we graduated, we had to write a short thesis explicating our *own* philosophy. I remember being called to the Castle (the residence of the religious faculty) to talk to a review committee. As I entered the massive, high-ceilinged room and surveyed the semicircle of eight nuns sitting around a thick, antique mahogany conference table, I felt very small and insignificant.

"Ann, have a seat," Mother Superior said to me, indicating a chair at the far end of the table. "We've all read your thesis and find it very different. I might say very original." Mother seemed to be searching carefully for her words. "What we would like to know is where you learned these things? Was it in the philosophy courses you took here at the College?"

"Yes and no, Mother," I responded. "Lovejoy's *Great Chain of Being* did make a strong impression on me. And I always liked going to philosophy class, even though I rarely understood very much. My essay is an attempt to record what I think about such issues as the nature of freedom, persons, time, and the role of love in human life."

"Oh," Mother said, looking in a knowing way at her colleagues seated rigidly around the table. "Well, I guess you realize it is not very orthodox."

"No, I didn't realize that, Mother. To tell you the truth, I never thought about it. I didn't even consider Catholic dogma as a criterion for this philosophical essay."

"It isn't, dear. It isn't."

We did have three very good students in our class who often asked the male professors the most wonderful questions. But they were not in our dormitory, or they, rather than I, would have been helping the others prepare for exams. They were day students. Once the most brilliant of them asked our professor (whom I found almost unintelligible), "Could a woman go on and do a graduate degree in philosophy?"

"I doubt it," he responded quickly, "and I certainly wouldn't advise *you* to try it."

"That was that," I thought. "Betty is so much better in philosophy than I. What chance would I ever have?"

Senior year was very special. A Father Deonard was to come from the University of Louvain and teach us an elective course on Karl Jaspers. A tall, handsome man in white flowing Dominican robes, he appeared on campus in September and introduced himself and his course to the student body.

"You're all welcome," he said in his wonderful accent. "Philosophy is the birthright of each of you. I won't *teach* you anything, but you could gain a great deal. Hopefully, by the end of the course, we'll all realize how much we don't know."

"Isn't he great?" I whispered to my roommate. "Let's get up early and register first thing after breakfast," I added.

"Not for me," she responded. "I already know I don't know anything about philosophy, and I don't need him telling me about it for another year."

I took the course anyway, and I enjoyed every minute of it. Nearing graduation, I ventured the question again. "Father, do you think a woman could do philosophy in graduate school?"

I could tell he was thinking very hard because he took a long time to answer and his brow took on many wrinkles. "I wouldn't advise it for any of you as a professional choice," he said very slowly. "But that's not to say that you couldn't or shouldn't continue to read philosophy and think about the philosophical dimension of your own experience. And there is no reason why you shouldn't come together with your friends to talk about these issues on an informal basis."

"That was that," I thought for the second time.

The very same year, I had studied with a little French priest from the Sorbonne. We had concentrated on the Fourth Gospel, one of my favorite works. Two nights before our last class, he gave a small party at his residence for the seniors. I remember that he ordered a case of French champagne for the occasion. When I entered the living room, he proposed a toast to me, "To the young woman who wrote the marvelous commentary on the Fourth Gospel."

I was thrilled. Here was this expert who knew so much about philosophy and theology telling me that I had done a good job.

"Perhaps I should get his opinion about going on in philosophy," I said to myself.

The party was quite joyous, and Father was the person everyone wanted to speak to that evening, so it took me a while to get near him.

"Father, what would you think about my going on in philosophy?" I ventured.

"Not a good idea, Ann. You're good, quite good, but let's face it, you're a woman. And philosophy is a man's discipline."

"Maybe I'm not good enough."

"That's not it. You're better than some of the men that go into the field."

"What about theology?"

"The same, my child," he said, lowering his head and shaking it from side to side.

I was numb. Even though the priest had not said anything that I did not expect, his very saying it shocked me. It seemed to me that he saw no contradiction in his words at all. As a matter of fact, he followed his remarks by saying, "Now let's not get too serious tonight. Let's have some more champagne and enjoy ourselves. You've been such a source of joy for me this semester." And then he put his arm around me in a comforting manner. And I was sure he cared for me very much.

But all I could think of at the time were six words: "In the beginning was the Word." Obviously, he thought this Word was only for certain people.

And what was that Word?

There are those who have thought it was truth. And others have thought it was meaning, meaning that could make significant difference in the quality of our everyday lives and how we relate to each other and to the rest of the natural world. But one thing is certain: The Word is not restricted to white men! It is for all people. That includes blacks, Chinese, Indians, women, and children. If philosophy is a quest for truth and meaning, then all women and children ought to have the same opportunity to do philosophy, do it well, and, if they so desire, make it the center of their professional lives.

That option was not open to me, so I chose intellectual history. It was the closest I could get in 1963. Since then I have had a few more heroes—all of them women. Margaret Fuller, Simone Weil, Emma Goldman, and Katherine Hepburn. Not one of them was a professional philosopher, with the exception of Weil, who took a degree in philosophy and taught it at a lycée in France for a short time. (Maybe the French priest thought of her as a modern-day Joan of Arc, a saint, rather than a woman!) They were good models for someone who, in 1973, saw a possibility to bring philosophy to the children of the world in such a way that the silencing and exclusion that I had experienced might become a thing of the past. It was in 1973 that I first read the manuscript of *Harry Stottlemeier's Discovery*. It took only one reading for me to realize that here was a vehicle for bringing philosophy to children.

When I say *philosophy,* I mean a quest for self-knowledge, or, better yet, a love of wisdom. It entails good questioning, paying attention to the details of one's experience, dialogue with others, open inquiry, recognition of one's ignorance, and a willingness to follow the inquiry where it leads. It involves the child in a growing commitment to careful reasonable deliberation with others, living a life that is judicious, searching, and honest. It also involves a care for the procedures of inquiry, other persons, and the environment around us. It is this view of philosophy that I found embedded in *Harry Stottlemeier's Discovery*. I can still remember how moved I was on reading Chapter Fourteen on art and ethics and Chapter Seventeen on the community of inquiry, and how excited I was at the prospect of somehow bringing this work to the world of education. (That I completed the first reading very late in the evening did not prevent me from calling the author and talking for hours regarding the significant difference such a work could make to elementary-school children.)

In the last twenty years, we have seen the development of at least three intellectual movements—black philosophy, women's philosophy, and Philosophy for Children—that aim to make unheard voices heard, to give sectors of the population encouragement and a space to speak their own word, to participate in the ongoing conversation that is their birthright. (And one might add that a fourth movement, animal-rights philosophy, is an attempt on our part to voice the concerns of animals for them, to bring their interests and perspectives into the conversation.)

Michael Oakeshott, hardly a proponent of any of these movements, characterized the situation eloquently:

> We are all inheritors neither of an inquiry about ourselves and the world nor an accumulating body of knowledge but of a conversation begun in primeval forest and extended and made more articulate in the course of centuries. It is a conversation that goes on both in public and within each of ourselves. Of course, there is argument and inquiry and information, but wherever these are profitable, they are recognized as passages in this conversation. Education, properly speaking, then, is an initiation into the skill and partnership of this conversation . . . in which we learn to recognize the voices, to distinguish the proper occasions of utterance, and in which we acquire the intellectual and moral habits appropriate to the conversation. And it is this conversation which, in the end, gives place and character to every human activity and utterance.[1]

But what if there are voices that are never heard, Mr. Oakeshott? When they claim the right to be heard and the time is right and they succeed in asserting their right to be heard, they will be part of the conversation, he would respond.

The Hegelian faith that guides the Mr. Oakeshotts of the world makes me very angry, because philosophy then becomes a tool to justify the status quo. It was Paulo Freire, at the other end of the political spectrum, who urged all oppressed people to make their voices heard, to create the conditions that would make it possible for them to take part in the conversation. In his *Pedagogy of the Oppressed*, he describes poignantly what it is to belong to a "culture of silence." Children belong to such a culture. Women belong to such a culture. Often alcoholics and drug addicts belong to this culture. Such individuals view themselves as impotent. They keep their eyes down when the powerful walk by. They know they are outside the real conversation, the conversation that matters. Cut off from the flow of ideas, hopes, and dreams of those in power, the oppressed are powerless to question the assumptions or have a role in defining the concepts that affect their daily lives.

Feminist philosophy and Philosophy for Children were phenomena of the 1960s. One could argue that our readiness now to listen to the voices of children doing philosophy has been prepared by feminist philosophy. This is not to detract from the originality of children's philosophy or to say that it is merely the consequence of the work of the mothers. If we look at the history of both movements, we discover that they developed concurrently. Today, feminist philosophy is more developed, more diversified, and more self-critical. Not only are many different feminist voices heard defending alternative philosophical positions, but feminists like Jean Grimshaw write books questioning the assumptions of some of the loudest, most influential voices:[2] Mary Daly, Simone de Beauvoir, Shulamith Firestone, Susan Griffin, Carol Gilligan, and others.[3] This is a sign of health.

Children's philosophy has not evolved this far. Yet, on the other hand, it has reached more individuals. We can estimate that hundreds of thousands of children have read and discussed *Harry Stottlemeier's Discovery* with their peers in classrooms and have become conscious of what it is to participate in a philosophical community of inquiry. Half of these world children are girls, who have had no problem in making their voices heard not only on ethical concerns but on metaphysical, epistemological, and aesthetic issues, as well as on questions concerned with social justice, philosophy of mind, and philosophy of science. Further, the female children have had no problem in mastering the formal and informal logic in *Harry Stottlemeier's Discovery* nor in employing their reason to question the validity of the female characterization in the novel itself. Because of the rise of interest in thinking skills and critical thinking, Philosophy for Children has had more access to the educational establishment. If it is successful in influencing schools of education in many countries where future teachers are prepared, its effects will be even more far reaching. At this point, however, we have to be on our guard that the movement does not deteriorate into one more course in logic or critical thinking for children to master rather than continuing to provide an opportunity for children to express their own views within the context of the philosophical tradition. But one thing is certain:

> Not exposing children to philosophy would be a shame because philosophy perfects what is a natural capacity in people. It's not like teaching them to learn the violin. It's teaching kids to use their own voices.[4]

As to diversity and self-criticism in Philosophy for Children, it is only a matter of time. Philosophy for Children is now a part of the elementary-school curriculum in twenty-five countries and is growing in acceptance among philosophical societies of the world as a respectable area of philosophical inquiry. At the same time it is continually having an impact on the educational establishment, questioning many current assumptions regarding teaching and learning. As philosophers begin to listen seriously to what children have to say while doing such programs as *Harry Stottlemeier's Discovery*, they will discover motives for developing new materials rooted in the traditions and cultural mores of each nation. Further, philosophers will begin to reconsider their own philosophical positions as they listen to and respond to the views of children in classroom communities of inquiry. To the extent that all philosophy is a search for wisdom and is embedded in the activity of inquiry, to that extent it ought to be possible for philosophers to take seriously the questions, assumptions, and perspectives of children as they enter into philosophical discussions with their peers and with adults.

Feminist philosophy and Philosophy for Children can be seen as a response to the tensions and contradictions of the sixties. Like the rest of the history of philosophy, these two movements must be understood against a social and political backdrop. In this case, the backdrop was the Vietnam War, the student movement, the assassinations of John Kennedy, Robert Kennedy, Malcolm X, and Martin Luther King, the Cuban missile crisis and the Bay of Pigs invasion, the rise of irrational interests from drugs to fringe religious groups to the occult, a back-to-nature trend, and the civil-rights movement. If black people could make their voices heard, if black people could do philosophy well, perhaps women and children could do the same. Perhaps they could discover what they had to say and, in turn, make a difference in how we think about philosophical procedures and substantive issues. Further, perhaps women and children could raise new problems, call issues into question in new ways, and move to the center topics that until now have been on the periphery. Consider the following moves from women's philosophical concerns to those of children:

From	*To*
1. Mothering	1. Being a child of two people
2. Divorce	2. Divorce's effect on childhood development
3. Abortion	3. Not being wanted
4. Pornography	4. Childhood sexuality
5. The reality of femininity	5. The reality of toys
6. Feminist epistemology	6. Children's epistemology
7. An ethics of care	7. An ethics of childhood
8. Relationships between women and men	8. Sibling rivalry
9. Women's rights	9. The child's right to inquiry
10. Discrimination	10. Discrimination
11. Housework	11. The world of play
12. Sexist language	12. Abusing children's language
13. Women and medicine	13. The ethics of doll hospitals
14. Time in the life of women	14. Time in the life of a thumb sucker
15. Fantasy and womanhood	15. Imaginary playmates
16. Love and friendship among women	16. Love and friendship among children

There is a growing consensus among philosophers that much of the history of philosophy would look different if the perspectives of women had been taken into account. Feminist philosophy has helped us see that.[5] Although they are quite different in many ways, feminist philosophy and Philosophy for Children share some similarities. Both aim to make unheard voices heard. Both stress the discovery of meaning and the importance of listening to many perspectives in coming to know and understand. Both pay attention not only to the content under discussion but to how we do philosophy and the epistemological, ethical, and political implications of the process. In Philosophy for Children, the community of inquiry is the pedagogical ideal. In feminist philosophy, something very similar obtains. It stresses working together, building on each other's ideas, and encouraging each woman to speak her own word. Both Philosophy for Children and feminist philosophy see the self as relational, question the Cartesian framework, with its epistemological assumptions and dualist ontology, and use the narrative as an essential tool in doing philosophy.[6]

Feminist philosophy has made the issue of gender in philosophy and the ways in which gender issues influence philosophical positions problematic. In a short time, the issues raised by children doing *Harry Stottlemeier's Discovery* in the classroom will also become a focus of professional philosophy. Once this occurs, philosophical positions will tend to be viewed against the backdrop of explicit or implicit assumptions about childhood ways of knowing, childhood perspectives, and childhood experience. But this will only happen if children continue to do philosophy in a rigorous fashion as a regular part of their elementary-school experience. To the extent that professional philosophers can help children speak their own words, share their philosophical theories, and help each other make sense of the world, to that extent they will contribute significantly to the growing comprehensiveness of the philosophical conversation and to the evolution of the discipline of philosophy itself.

NOTES

1. Michael Oakeshott, *Rationalism in Politics* (New York: Basic Books, 1962), p. 199.

2. Jean Grimshaw, *Philosophy and Feminist Thinking* (Minneapolis: University of Minnesota Press, 1986).

3. Mary Daly has written three important books in the area of feminist philosophy: *Beyond God the Father* (Boston: Beacon Press, 1974), *Gyn-Ecology* (Boston: Beacon Press, 1978), and *Pure Lust* (Boston: Beacon Press, 1984). In many ways it was Simone de Beauvoir's work *The Second Sex* (New York: Knopf, 1952) that triggered the feminist revolution, and although many feminists today question some of her philosophical assumptions her work is all-important. Shulamith Firestone, in *The Dialectic of Sex* (New York: Bantam, 1971), not only brought into question issues concerning relationships between men and women, reproduction, and woman and society but was one of the first feminists to deal with the subject of children's rights and children's position in society in relationship to women's position in the economic world. Susan Griffin, in *Woman and Nature: The Roaring Inside Her* (New York: Harper and Row, 1978), was one of the pioneers in investigating the issue of the environment and feminism. And, finally, Carol

Gilligan's *In a Different Voice: Psychological Theory and Women's Development* (Cambridge, Mass.: Harvard University Press, 1982) posited the thesis that women view relationships and, therefore, moral obligations much differently from men because of the socialization process that they undergo. Gilligan's use of a Kohlbergian framework with regard to moral development has always put her conclusions into question for me.

4. Gerard Vallone, *New York Times* (Education Section, 8 November 1988).

5. With regard to the relations between women and men, see Alison Jaggar and Paula Rothenberg, eds., *Feminist Frameworks* (New York: McGraw-Hill, 1978) and Jaggar's *Feminist Politics and Human Nature* (Totowa, N.J.: Rowman and Allanheld, 1987). On the way women perceive science, see Sandra Harding, *The Science Question* (Ithaca, N.Y.: Cornell University Press, 1986). On friendship between women, see Janice G. Raymond, *A Passion for Friends: Toward a Philosophy of Female Affection* (Boston: Beacon Press, 1986). Nancy Chodorow has written on mothering in *The Reproduction of Mothering: Psychoanalysis and the Sociology of Gender* (Berkeley: University of California Press, 1978). Sara Ruddick has written an important work on *Maternal Thinking: Toward a Politics of Peace* (Boston: Beacon Press, 1989), and Joyce Tribilcot has edited *Mothering: Essays in Feminist Theory* (Totowa, N.J.: Rowman and Allanheld, 1983). If one wants to see what has been done on housework, I would suggest Robert Seidenberg and Karen De Crow, *Women Who Marry Houses* (New York: McGraw-Hill, 1983). On the topic of love and care, see J. Finch and D. Groves, eds., *A Labour of Love: Women, Work, and Caring* (London: Routledge and Kegan Paul, 1983), and Nel Noddings, *Caring: A Feminine Approach to Ethics* (Berkeley: University of California Press, 1984). On epistemology, see Jane Duran's *Feminist Epistemology* (Larsham, Md.: Rowman and Littlefield, 1990). Also see Alison Jaggar and Susan R. Bordo, *Gender/Body/Knowledge: Feminist Reconstruction of Being and Knowing* (New Brunswick, N.J.: Rutgers University Press, 1989), and Sandra Harding and M. L. Hintikka, *Discovering Reality: Feminist Perspectives on Epistemology, Metaphysics, Methodology, and Philosophy of Science* (Dordrecht: Reidel, 1983). On the issue of pornography and violence, see Susan Griffin, *Pornography and Silence: Cultural Revenge vs. Nature* (New York: Harper and Row, 1981); Andrea Dworkin, *Pornography: Men Possessing Women* (New York: Perigee Books, 1981); and Eva Feder Kittay, "Pornography, and the Erotics of Domination," in *Beyond Domination*, ed. Carol Grould (Totowa, N.J.: Rowman and Allanheld, 1983), 145–74.

6. See Jean Grimshaw, *Philosophy and Feminist Thinking* (Minneapolis: University of Minnesota Press, 1986), and Catherine Keller, *From a Broken Web: Separation, Sexism, and Self* (Boston: Beacon Press, 1987). I might also add that women writing on ecofeminism (Karren Warren, "Feminism and Ecology: Making Connections," in *Environmental Ethics* 9 [1987]: 3–21; Carolyn Merchant, *The Death of Nature: Women, Ecology, and the Scientific Revolution* [San Francisco: Harper and Row, 1980], and Val Plumwood, "Nature and Gender," in *Environmental Ethics* 11 [1989]) have expressed deep interest in creating a new curriculum in environmental ethics for elementary-school children. An outline of the curriculum appears in an unpublished manuscript, "International Curriculum in Environmental Ethics," which was submitted as a proposal to UNESCO in February 1990 by the International Council for Philosophical Inquiry with Children.

PART THREE

Metaphysical and Epistemological Problems

The first chapter in this part is Ann Margaret Sharp's "Discovering Yourself a Person." Here she examines Chapter One of Harry Stottlemeier's Discovery. In it, Sharp finds that because the first chapter relies heavily on the analysis of concepts like reasoning, reflecting, falsifying, inquiring, and so on, it is an appropriate place for the discovery (or invention, it might be added) of who and what we are. As one watches the characters in Harry begin the process of inquiry and as one watches them stumble toward the formation of a community, one finds them formulating individual ways or styles of thinking. As they interact with one another around, say, the problem of conversion, they are learning not only a principle of logic but a way of being and thinking in the world. In a similar manner, the children and the teacher discussing the novel are and should be emulating the behavior of the fictional community.

In the course of the chapter, Sharp also considers the relationships of language to a community of inquiry and to the discovery of self. Evidence for her claims, as it typically does in Philosophy for Children scholarship, comes in the form of a transcript of an actual classroom dialogue.

Martin Benjamin and Eugenio Echeverria use a historical analysis to make points about the position of Philosophy for Children. In "Knowledge and the Classroom," they trace classroom assumptions—that there is a set content to be taught, content must be transmitted from teacher to student, students must (passively) receive the content, and so on—to their roots in the Cartesian origins of modern philosophy. Benjamin and Echeverria then work their way forward to the twentieth century and examine the way in which Thomas Kuhn's classic The Structure of Scientific Revolutions has forced philosophers and scientists to rethink Cartesianism and its contemporary heir, scientific methodology. With Kuhn, Benjamin and Echeverria stress the social, or communitarian, nature of scientific practice and discuss the ways in which scientists work toward consensus. Knowledge, then, is not some mirror of reality but the product of an inquiring community. It is that assertion which a community takes as warranted.

When Benjamin and Echeverria bring this pragmatic notion of knowledge into the classroom, they note a number of changes, ranging from the arrangement of the furniture, through an increased valuation of learning as a group endeavor and a redefinition of the role of the teacher, to a significant alteration in the function of language in the classroom.

Philip C. Guin's "Thinking for Oneself" deals with one of the thornier issues in Harry Stottlemeier's Discovery and, in general, in Philosophy for Children—the difference between thinking and thinking for oneself. In part, Guin sees the distinction as revolving around the question of thinking in a discipline and thinking about a discipline. He then goes on to point out how the corrective potential of the community of inquiry enables the formation of the individual's ability to think for herself or himself. In conclusion, Guin gives eight powerful *reasons supporting the claim that thinking for oneself should be an educational objective.*

Michael S. Pritchard, in "Critical Thinking: Problem Solving or Problem Creating?" modestly refrains from giving a definition of critical thinking. Instead, he engages his reader in a thought experiment where he examines the characters in Harry. *Pritchard gives numerous reasons to believe that Lisa is the most creative child one encounters in* Harry, *and then, precisely because she is the most creative, he argues that she is the most critical thinker in the novel. For Pritchard, the critical thinker is as much a problem creator as a problem solver.*

Finally, John C. Thomas, in "The Development of Reasoning in Children through Community of Inquiry," attempts to go beyond the anecdotal sorts of evidence provided by Philosophy for Children practitioners to refute the oft-cited Piagetian claim that children are incapable of formal reasoning until, typically, the ages of eleven or twelve. Thomas examines Piaget's methodology, his statements about child logic, and his theories of the child and of reasoning in the child, and compares them with their analogues in Philosophy for Children.

7

Discovering Yourself a Person

Ann Margaret Sharp

■ ■ ■

> To discover yourself discovering a rule about language and how it
> works is to discover yourself as a person in the world.

BY NOW, I would guess that thousands of teachers and tens of thousands
of children have read and discussed the first chapter of *Harry Stottlemeier's
Discovery*, where Harry discovers the Aristotelian rule of conversion. In all
probability, the children have talked about truth, conversion, discovery, invention, resentment, daydreaming and perhaps the role of Lisa in the discovery of
the conversion rule. More important, with this chapter the students begin to
form a classroom community of inquiry.

UNDERLYING PROCESSES AND ASSUMPTIONS

However, I wonder how many teachers have analyzed with their students the
concepts that underlie the chapter and which, at one time or another, ought to
be clarified by the students themselves. Some of these concepts are thinking,
reasoning, reflecting, falsifying, hypothesizing, theorizing, inquiring, and classifying. They denote processes engaged in by the children in the novel, as well
as those exercised by the students in the classroom. For most of us these are,
at best, fuzzy concepts.

One purpose of thinking should be to become more clear about the concepts that we use in our everyday language. Without contradictions or, at
least, confusion on which to reflect, our intellects would have no task.[1] Our
minds are stocked full with all sorts of confusing ideas from the very early
years. "But as Harry walked home, he still felt badly about not having been
able to answer when Mr. Bradley called on him. Also, he was puzzled. How

had he gone wrong?" Like Harry's discovery, the end products of our thinking are connected to their beginnings in confusion. Chapter One of *Harry Stottlemeier's Discovery* renders a myriad of fuzzy concepts, enough to provide food for thought for years.

However, analysis of the cognitive processes mentioned above is hardly possible without some notion of where the children are, what they are assuming when they speak of thinking or inquiring. In helping children clarify these concepts denoting processes, the assumptions need to be uncovered. Otherwise, there is no anchoring of discussion, nothing to prevent it from becoming a series of question-begging assertions.

Accordingly, in the first chapter of *Harry*, we perceive at least three levels of possible meaning that teachers must help the students appreciate as they read and discuss the story. There is, first, the meaning gleaned from an analysis of the concepts drawn from actual events in the novel—the discovery (invention) of the rule of conversion, the problem of truth (only true sentences follow the rule), the problem of mind ("Harry's mind just wandered off" or "Something in Harry's mind went CLICK!"), Harry's daydreaming and resentment. Second, there are the cognitive processes engaged in by the characters and children in the classroom, their thinking and inquiry. Finally, there are the assumptions behind these cognitive moves, what we are actually doing when we are thinking, theorizing, and inquiring.

Provided we are aware of these levels of meaning, how are we to proceed with Chapter One? The first time around in the classroom, it is appropriate to take the agenda from the students, the way they see the chapter, their sense of interest and perplexity. In most cases, what the children will introduce will have a philosophical dimension, and it is the teacher's job to tease out this dimension and explore it with them in a dialogical manner. There should be an effort to involve as many students in the discussion as possible and to encourage them to listen carefully to what others have to say. Further, the teacher should foster an atmosphere in which the students begin to build on the contributions of each other in such a way that the inquiry grows in comprehensiveness and objectivity.

In the analysis of concepts, we often encounter the mystery and perplexity introduced through careful reflection. On the face of it, "His mind just wandered off" or "Something in his mind went CLICK" seems innocuous enough. But for some children these expressions are laden with difficulty. I remember visiting a class in London composed of a number of children whose first language was other than English. One fifth-grader said he was interested in how the word "mind" was being used in these two expressions. At this moment, the principal, who was observing, interrupted and said, "Oh, it's just an idiom. If you knew English better, you'd understand." The child was persistent. Later, he raised his hand and said, "I'm still confused about the word 'mind.'" There was some more talk about idiomatic usage in English by the adults in the room. At this point, I intervened.

"Can you tell us what you find confusing?" I asked.

"It's being used as a noun," he responded.

"Do you see a problem with that?"

"Yes, I think of 'mind' as a verb," he responded.

"I find that interesting," I replied. "Perhaps we can put the problem on the board and discuss it later," I said, addressing the teacher.

"Yes," the child said. "Just what is 'mind'?"

THE EMERGENCE OF PERSONHOOD

Perhaps it is in the mystery and perplexity aroused by the analysis of concepts that we begin to see the emergence of personhood. The child in the example above has reflected on the use of the word "mind" and has detected what for him is a grammatical error. In his reflection there is the implication of consciousness, self-consciousness, and personhood. Moreover, what has allowed the boy to make this move is his participation in a philosophical community of inquiry discussing Chapter One of *Harry*.

This chapter models not only the paradigm of inquiry but philosophical dialogue itself. Lisa and Harry form a minicommunity, and at times one cannot help but think of the Platonic dialogues. It is in talking with our peers and our teachers that we gain a sense of who we are, a sense of our place in the world, a sense of how things are, and a sense of the relationship between who we are and how things are in the world.[2] It is this perception of connectedness, or relationship, that is essential in the development of a sense of our own personhood.

One of the reasons that *Harry* is a novel rather than a text is that the story form that models dialogue is a more effective pedagogical tool for conveying information in such a way that children can appropriate it for themselves. Further, in order for children to learn they must reenact the process of discovery or creation that the original thinker might have experienced. Dewey points out in *Experience and Nature* that most educators make the mistake of taking the finished product and imposing it on the next generation in a didactic manner, rather than setting the conditions for children to experience the process that the original thinker might have gone through in bringing her or his ideas into consciousness. The novel aims to accomplish this end.

Classes in Philosophy for Children usually begin by reading the text aloud. One wants to create an experience that all can share. Out of this shared experience, students are able to investigate the ideas in the text in a social rather than a private manner. Language is the primary tool for this investigation. In discussing the ideas in the text, perceptions, desires, intentions, implications, and meaning are all articulated.[3] To understand oneself is to understand one-self as one confronts the novel and to receive from it and the community the meanings that are implicit and explicit. It is these meanings that then enter into the funded experience of the community of inquiry. Once the teacher under-stands this, she or he begins to move from a notion of subjectivity to a notion of intersubjectivity or objectivity. Students gradually become free to interpret the reading in a more comprehensive and objective manner, to perceive in the text the meanings that are there. On the other hand, the students become conscious of the power that the work possesses to project itself outside itself, thereby giving birth to a world of shared meanings and experiences.[4]

The philosophical dialogue that ensues among the students both models and practices community. It contains the ethical dimension of taking turns, lis-tening carefully to one another, building on one another's ideas, speaking when appropriate, and making one's contribution at the right time. Paulo Freire, in *Pedagogy of the Oppressed*, makes the point that it is in the dialogue itself that we become persons. Speaking and listening imply a reciprocity, a learning to give and take, a tolerance and respect for each other, as well as a growth in understanding of the issues under discussion. The use of language is a social phenomenon. It enables us to do many things: to distinguish similarities and differences, the present and the absent, the past and the future, the actual and the ideal. It enables us to engage in reflection and communication. Language mediates between us and the world. Becoming a person is not only learning how to use language but how to use it reflectively. To be a person is to be able to respond to others in a self-reflective manner. Persons are thinking creatures who know that they are thinking. Since the views and readings of our class-mates are communicated to us by means of language, it is just this language that eventually becomes the object of our communal reflection. In this way "we become infinitely reflecting mirrors to one another as we live together in community."[5]

WHAT DOES HARRY DISCOVER?

Often the teacher will ask the students, "Just what did Harry discover?" Some children might respond, "The idea that you can't turn a true sentence around without its becoming false." Another might say that Harry discovers class relationships. A third might think that Harry discovered a relationship between logic and language, a relationship between thinking and talking. Still another might say that Harry discovered validity. Someone else might point out that Harry discovers a new way of obtaining knowledge. Often, we think that if we want to learn something or know something we should either observe it for ourselves or read about it in some book. Harry discovers that we can come to know things through reflection, and, in this case, through logical reflection.

And yet another student might say that Harry discovers himself. He comes to recognize himself as a person—a being who can reflect on his own thinking, on how he uses language, and on how the two are connected.

Both R. S. Peters and D. W. Hamlyn have pointed out that to recognize oneself as a person one has to be able to view one's thoughts in a reflective manner, as well as to be able to recognize another's point of view. Hamlyn has further argued that the growth of our understanding of what it is to be a person must be seen as an extension of our vision of what it is to be human. We come to see ourselves and others from a wider point of view, that is, from more and more aspects.[6] We come to know ourselves as persons by sharing experiences with others. These experiences can include sharing thoughts, ideas, and feelings and learning to see each other in a different sense. Unless one takes this interpersonal understanding into consideration, one reduces the recognition of oneself as a person merely to a cognitive skill. The problem with this is that it forces children to stand outside the relationships that they have with others. But it is just these relationships that are a necessary condition for them to come to know themselves as persons.[7] Thus, one might say that although we need a myriad of cognitive skills to know ourselves as persons, cognitive skills are not sufficient. Interpersonal relating is essential.

Chapter One in *Harry* models this well. Harry is embarrassed in front of his peers and his teacher and is perplexed. "How had he gone wrong?" He then has an idea. "A sentence can't be reversed. If you put the last part of a sentence first, it'll no longer be true." He then sees Lisa and wants to share his idea with her. "It seemed to him that if he told her what he'd found out, she'd be able to understand." When Lisa gives him a counterexample to his discovery, he feels resentful. But not for long. "If he had really figured out a rule, it should have worked on stupid sentences as well as on sentences that weren't stupid." Harry is able to share his sense of failure ("I really thought I had it") and to finally recognize with Lisa's help where he had gone wrong. At this point, he is able to go back and restate his discovery. And, just as important, he is grateful to Lisa for her help.

To perceive yourself as a person is to be able to recognize what is expected from you. It is to recognize the importance of the second-person pronoun, "you."[8] The child must come to understand what is meant by phrases like "you promised to meet me here," or "you said you would take care of that," or "you ought to have paid attention." Further, one must be able to take on responsibility for one's actions. Persons are beings who can be held accountable for what they have done.[9] One must be able to see a connectedness between one's actions and oneself. The day must come when we cease blaming our doll, the cat or dog, or our imaginary friend for the naughty things that we do. Paradoxically, however, the understanding of what it is to be a person evolves concurrently with practice in being a person with others, acting and thinking as a person living with others, treating others as persons within the community.[10]

At the end of Chapter One, *Harry* models what it is to take responsibility for one's actions. When he hears Mrs. Olsen insinuating that Mrs. Bates might have a drinking problem, he not only recognizes the gossip but he recognizes her mistake in reasoning. More important, he has the courage to call her attention to it. Thus, the rule that he and Lisa have formulated for themselves is put to use: Harry discovers that it can make a significant ethical difference in how people think and talk about other people.[11] It can make a difference in the kind of world that we as persons create. Once he has made Mrs. Olsen aware of her logical mistake and its ethical consequences, he discovers something else: the relationship between thinking, acting, and feelings. Having acted, he notes that his mother seems very pleased with what he had said to Mrs. Olsen, and he further realizes that he feels "happier than he has felt in days." Through his reflection, his discovery of a rule, and his willingness to act on this rule he has affected his own feelings. He has become conscious of the power of his own reflection and his ability to act on the world in such a way that he can make an ethical difference.

THE DEVELOPMENT OF PERSONS

To teach *Harry Stottlemeier's Discovery* well is to help children form a classroom community of inquiry in which to deliberate about the philosophical and logical issues that are suggested in the novel. In the process, children learn how to think well and how to do philosophy well with others. They learn by doing. It is in this practice that they come to discover themselves as persons who can act on the world in a judicious manner.

A community of inquiry is a group of individuals who come together to deliberate about matters of concern. In the process, the participants learn how to object to weak reasoning, build on strong reasoning, accept the responsibility for making their contributions within the context of others' remarks, follow the inquiry where it leads, respect the perspective of others, and collaboratively engage in self-correction. They come to care for each other as persons and for the procedures that they use to inquire. They come to take pride in the accomplishments of the group, as well as in themselves as persons.

There is no conflict between becoming a person and becoming a participant in a community of inquiry. As R. G. Collingwood points out in the *Principles of Art*, "The discovery of myself as a person is also the discovery of other persons around me."[12] A community of inquiry that is working comprises of human interactions in which all parties concerned display the highest degree of conscious sensitivity to the detailed and specific actualities of one another's positions and feelings. It is these exchanges that most represent interactions between persons.[13] The participants learn how to express thoughts and feelings well and to take other persons' views into account. The group engages in both critical and creative thinking. If the group is functioning well, its actions are reasonable and deliberative, future oriented and self-correcting. Participants grow in a consciousness of their own powers.

CONCLUDING REMARKS

Thus, we can say that if one reads the first chapter of *Harry Stottlemeier's Discovery* carefully, one discovers Harry discovering himself. Harry could have given up after he suffered his initial embarrassment in the classroom. He could have given up when Lisa presented him with her counterinstance. But he persevered and eventually discovered, with Lisa's help, a rule that opened up for him a whole new way of thinking about thinking, language, and himself. What emerges is self-reference. Such self-reference implies that a person has become an object to himself.[14] Such persons have the ability to correct their own thinking and take what other people say into account in doing so. This self-corrective thinking, which can be viewed as the creative aspect of Harry's critical thinking, can make a significant difference in how he acts on the world. Likewise, when students read and discuss Chapter One of *Harry* within the context of a community of inquiry, they also commence the process of discovering themselves as persons inquiring together about their relationship to the world.

What did Harry discover in Chapter One? That he is a person. That he is a person beginning the wondrous development of thinking for himself. To discover yourself discovering a rule about language and how it works is to discover yourself as a person in the world.

NOTES

1. Annette Baier, *Postures of the Mind: Essay on Mind and Morals* (Minneapolis: University of Minnesota Press, 1985), p. 56.

2. On this point of connectedness, see E. M. Forster's novel *Howards End* (London, 1910; reprint, Harmondsworth: Penguin Books, 1984), p. 188: "She would only point out the salvation that was latent in his own soul, and in the soul of every man. Only connect! That was the whole of her sermon. Only connect the prose and the passion, and both will be exalted, and human love will be seen at its highest. Live in fragments no longer. Only connect, and the beast and the monk, robbed of the isolation that is life to either, will die. . . . But she failed. For there was one quality in Henry for which she was never prepared . . . his obtuseness. He simply did not notice things, and there was

no more to be said. He never noticed that Helen and Frieda were hostile, or that Tibby was not interested in currant plantations; he never noticed the lights and shades that exist in the greyest of conversations, the fingerposts, the milestones, the collisions, the illimitable views."

3. Gilles Fauconnier, *Mental Spaces* (Cambridge, Mass.: MIT Press, 1985), chapter 1.

4. Paul Ricoeur, "On Interpretation," in *Philosophy in France Today*, ed. Allan Montefiore (New York: Cambridge University Press, 1983), p. 187.

5. Israel Scheffler, *Of Human Potential: An Essay in Philosophy of Education* (Boston: Routledge and Kegan Paul, 1985). See the chapter on human nature and value, pp. 10–33.

6. R. S. Peters, "Personal Understanding and Personal Relationships," in *Understanding Other Persons*, ed. Theodore Mischel (Totowa, N.J.: Rowman and Littlefield, 1974), pp. 37–65. See also D. W. Hamlyn, "Person-Perception and Our Understanding of Others," ibid., pp. 1–36.

7. J. H. Flavell, "The Development of Inferences about Others," ibid, pp. 66–116.

8. Baier, *Postures of the Mind*, p. 43.

9. David Dennett, "Conditions of Personhood," in *The Identities of Persons*, ed. Amelia O. Rorty (Berkeley: University of California Press, 1976), pp. 175–96.

10. Hamlyn, "Person-Perception", p. 34.

11. Flavell, "The Development of Inferences," p. 79. See also Matthew Lipman, Ann Margaret Sharp, and Frederick S. Oscanyan, *Philosophy in the Classroom*, 2d ed. (Philadelphia: Temple University Press, 1980), and Matthew Lipman, "Ethical Reasoning and the Craft of Moral Practice," in press. For further insights into the relationship between reasoning and morality, see three essays by Matthew Lipman: "Thinking Skills in Religious Education," *Educational Reporter*, January 1985; "Philosophy and the Cultivation of Reasoning," *Educational Leadership*, September 1984; and "Philosophy for Children and Critical Thinking," *National Forum* 65 (Winter 1985): 18–23.

12. R. G. Collingwood, *The Principles of Art* (Oxford: Oxford University Press, 1937), p. 248.

13. S. E. Toulmin, "Rules and Their Relevance for Understanding Human Behaviour," in *Understanding Other Persons*, ed. Theodore Mischel pp. 185–215.

14. Amelia Oksenberg Rorty, "A Literary Postscript: Characters, Persons, Selves, and Individuals," in *Identities of Persons*, ed. Rorty, p. 310. See also Frederick Olafson, *The Dialectic of Action* (Chicago: University of Chicago Press, 1979), and Bernard Williams, "Persons, Character, and Morality," in *Identities of Persons*, ed. Rorty, pp. 197–216. In the same book, consult David Wiggins's essay "Locke, Butler and the Stream of Consciousness: and Men as Natural Kinds," pp. 139–74.

8

Knowledge and the Classroom

Martin Benjamin and Eugenio Echeverria

■ ■ ■

OUR CONCEPTION of knowledge strongly influences our approach to the classroom. What we teach and how we teach, what we expect of our students and how we evaluate them, all presuppose a certain understanding of the nature, origin, and limits of human knowledge.

In what follows we briefly describe the conventional approach to the classroom and the conception of knowledge underlying it. We then criticize this conception and set out to defend an alternative that has far-reaching implications for elementary and secondary education, and for higher education as well. Classroom teaching and learning, we suggest, should be modified so as to reflect this alternative conception of knowledge.

THE CONVENTIONAL CLASSROOM

Much classroom teaching is conceived as the transmission of "knowledge" or "information" from the teacher to the student. The young person's mind is regarded as a largely empty vessel that will soon be filled with beliefs about the world, and it is the teacher's responsibility to ensure that these will be true and important beliefs—that they will accurately represent the world as it is. The teacher therefore takes the most active role in the classroom, and students are required to listen, take notes, memorize, and be able to demonstrate their knowledge by filling in the proper blanks or choosing the appropriate alternative on the test.

Knowledge, in this view, is a set of beliefs that accurately mirrors the world. The emphasis in the classroom is on transmitting these beliefs clearly and precisely. Topics that are ambiguous, uncertain, vaguely understood, controversial, and so on are usually ignored on the ground that they have little to do with knowledge. Student inquiries about such matters are usually discouraged or deflected as idle (sometimes mischievous) curiosity to be taken up at some later point after the "real" knowledge has been transmitted. Rarely, then, is interaction between teacher and student genuinely initiated by the latter. The teacher not only has all of the answers but also all of the relevant questions. Students are not, at least initially, regarded as knowing enough to ask the right questions, that is, questions to which the teacher can give clear and definite answers.

Another important feature of the prevailing conception of knowledge is that teaching is essentially dyadic. The most basic relationship is between teacher and student, and the ideal learning situation involves only a singular teacher (or tutor) and a singular student. Schools teach children in groups only because it is financially impossible to have a one-to-one teacher-student ratio. Although educational efficiency may require that students learn in a group, this is always regarded as second best.

The conventional classroom presupposes a certain epistemology, or theory of knowledge, that has dominated Western philosophy since the seventeenth century. Knowledge, in this view, is acquired passively rather than actively, is more the product of careful observation than of pragmatic exploration. It is also largely individualistic; any singular knower with a properly receptive mind is, in principle, capable of acquiring knowledge of the world by him- or herself. Education, therefore, has two principal aims: first, to transmit all of the important knowledge that has been acquired firsthand by those who have preceded us (what Russell has called "knowledge by description"), and, second, to make sure that the student's mind remains accurately aimed and highly receptive— so that it is itself capable of acquiring "knowledge by [direct] acquaintance."[1]

THE CARTESIAN TRADITION IN EPISTEMOLOGY

Since Plato, Western philosophers have been preoccupied with distinguishing *genuine knowledge* from *mere opinion*. The former was often characterized as timeless, universal, and immutable, while the latter was, in contrast, regarded as ephemeral, parochial, and contingent. In the seventeenth century, this endeavor was strikingly reformulated by René Descartes. Taking account of various advances in science and mathematics, he provided the questions that were to dominate Western philosophy for the next three hundred years: What is the foundation for all genuine knowledge? And what method will allow us to use it as a touchstone for distinguishing true beliefs from false? Philosophers as otherwise different as Gottfried Wilhelm Leibniz, Benedict de Spinoza, John Locke, George Berkeley, David Hume, and Immanuel Kant, as well as their various disciples and intellectual descendants, have followed Descartes in their quest for certainty, foundation, and method. Each seeks an essentially transcultural, historical, indubitable fixed point, or bedrock, from which a more or less foolproof method will trace those appropriately related beliefs that can then be embraced with as much certainty as is the foundation.

Descartes's concern, as Richard Bernstein has pointed out, is not merely intellectual or academic: "It is the quest for some fixed point, some stable rock upon which we can secure our lives against the vicissitudes that constantly threaten us. The specter that hovers in the background of this journey is not just radical epistemological skepticism but the dread of madness and chaos where nothing is fixed, where we can neither touch bottom nor support ourselves on the surface."[2] We are, in this view, confronted with two, and only two, alternatives. Either we identify a foundation for knowledge, a fixed point that will, together with the proper method, allow all human beings, regardless of cultural or historical setting, to more or less mechanically distinguish true beliefs from false, or we succumb to personal confusion and social and political chaos—a world in which neither individuals nor groups can distinguish truth from falsehood.

Given this characterization of the choice, it is perhaps no wonder that so many have embarked upon the Cartesian quest, even though they have set out on paths markedly different from that taken by Descartes himself. And there appears to be wide agreement, at least in the West, that the correct route, if not the final destination, has finally been found in modern science. The scientific method and its employment, not only in physics and chemistry but also in politics, psychology, economics, and even ethics, is regarded by many as the correct response to the Cartesian quest. The idea, rooted in the main project of the Enlightenment, is to find out what nature or the world is *really* like— wholly independent of any of our particular aims or preconceptions—and then to have nature or the world dictate the shape of our individual lives and social, political, and economic institutions. While rejecting the *a priori* rationalism of Descartes, modern science claims to provide the touchstone (sense experience) and the process (the hypothetico-deductive method) for distinguishing true beliefs from false with as much certainty as various subjects will allow.

Underlying the conventional wisdom, as Richard Rorty has emphasized, is a certain metaphor, or picture, that has dominated epistemology since Descartes.[3] This is the picture of the mind as a great mirror containing various representations—some accurate, some not—of nature. It is the task of epistemology to identify the foundation and to provide a method that, when properly employed, will "polish" the mirror and ensure that all that is represented on it accurately reflects, or is true of, the world.

Descartes's own rationalist epistemology was founded on the indubitability of his existence as a thinking thing; all other true beliefs, he maintained, could be derived from this fixed point alone by valid deductive reasoning. While rejecting Descartes's starting point and rationalist (or nonempirical) methodology, the epistemology of modern science tacitly retains his conception of mind as separate from body. Saddled with the question of how the mind so conceived can acquire knowledge of the external world, it then accepts an essentially Lockean conception of "outer space" (the external world) as being represented in "inner space" (the Cartesian mind) by various sense impressions and the correct operation of the mental processes. Although the letter of Locke's account has since been abandoned, the metaphor of mind as a mirror of nature has been retained. The "polishing" is now carried out by the hypothetico-deductive (or scientific) method; the accurate reflections are those that are either directly derived from sense experience or indirectly related to such experience and certified to be so by the correct application of the method.

True beliefs, in the traditional view, are those that *correspond* to a fixed, external reality that is wholly independent of our various plans and projects. And a principal task of epistemology is to provide a *method* that will confront and constrain our untutored beliefs so as to separate the factual (those beliefs that actually correspond to the world) from the fanciful (those that do not). In addition, the acquisition of knowledge is, following Descartes, conceived as an essentially *individualistic* undertaking. Any single person equipped with the correct method is, in principle, capable of sorting out true from false beliefs by him- or herself. Moreover, once the method is placed in operation, the knower assumes the passivity of a *spectator*. Like certain computer operators, knowers monitor the working and results of the method on their own (internal) "screens." Knowing is, on this view, an observational or contemplative endeavor, and we succumb to error, as Descartes puts it, "when the *exigencies of action* . . . oblige us to make up our minds before having the leisure to examine matters more carefully."[4]

Transported into the classroom, this spectator theory of knowledge—with its emphasis on a fixed, external world that can be accurately represented in our individual (Cartesian) minds by the correct application of the right method—governs a large part of what goes on. The passivity of students, the underlying individualism, the assumption of a fixed external reality to which the teacher's beliefs correspond but the students' do not, the emphasis on students' having to be taken through a series of steps that will enable them to replace false with true beliefs, and so on are the legacy of the Cartesian tradition in epistemology. But what if that tradition and the assumptions underlying it are fundamentally mistaken? Indeed, this is just what a number of influential philosophers are currently saying. If they are right, what is now being hammered out in the seminar room may have important implications for what should be going on in the elementary and secondary classroom.

AGAINST THE CARTESIAN TRADITION

We cannot, in the space available, fully convey the depth and complexity of contemporary criticisms of the Cartesian tradition in epistemology.[5] Nor can we examine various attempts to defend it against these criticisms. We can, however, summarize what we take to be trenchant and ultimately unanswerable objections to the Cartesian tradition.

The publication in 1962 of the first edition of Thomas Kuhn's *Structure of Scientific Revolutions* marks an important turning point in debates over the adequacy of the Cartesian tradition.[6] Modern science, as we have noted, has been regarded by many as the culmination of the Cartesian tradition in epistemology. It is said to provide both the foundation (sense experience) of knowledge and the proper method for distinguishing true beliefs from false. It puts us in touch with reality and allows us to determine, in more or less mechanical fashion, which of our beliefs actually correspond to the world and which do not. According to Kuhn, however, this is a conception that bears only a partial resemblance to actual scientific practice; a historical understanding of the workings of science reveals a significantly different picture.

Although there are aspects of science (what Kuhn calls "normal science") that appear to proceed in accord with the conventional wisdom, the deepest questions and decisions in science—those involving choices between competing comprehensive theories, or "paradigms"—do not. Conflicts between competing paradigms cannot be resolved by a more or less mechanical application of determinate theory-neutral criteria. No such criteria were available to those who had to choose, for example, between Ptolemy's astronomical theory and Copernicus's theory, between the oxygen theory of combustion and the phlogiston theory, or between Newtonian mechanics and the quantum theory. When a group of scientists disagree about such matters, Kuhn maintains, "there is no neutral algorithm for theory-choice, no systematic decision procedure which, properly applied, must lead each individual in the group to the same decision."[7]

This is not to say (as Kuhn's overstatements occasionally imply and his critics uncharitably infer) that rationality has no role to play in deciding between competing comprehensive theories. This would be so only if such a choice could not be regarded as rational unless it were the outcome of the computational application of a standardized set of fully determinate, wholly consistent, theory-neutral criteria. But *a priori* commitment to this highly idealized conception of scientific decision making, Kuhn points out, reduces to absurdity. The actual practice of good science, he maintains, provides our best model of scientific rationality.[8] And this practice, when carefully examined, reveals that choices among competing comprehensive theories are not the product of a more or less mechanical application of a set of theory-neutral criteria. Thus, he concludes, if an abstract, philosophical conception of rational decision making is not embodied in the actual practice of good scientists doing good science, it is the philosophical conception, and not the actual practice, that must give way.

How, then, *do* scientists choose between competing comprehensive theories? If they do not and cannot appeal to an algorithmic decision procedure to fully resolve their differences, and yet are said to choose rationally, how do they reason? Kuhn does not deny that there are standard criteria for evaluating the comparative adequacy of competing comprehensive theories. Accuracy, consistency, scope, simplicity, and fruitfulness, he agrees, all "play a vital role when scientists must choose between an established theory and an upstart competitor."[9] But two sorts of difficulties arise when we assume that these very useful and important criteria provide a mechanical decision procedure for choosing between competing theories. First, when taken separately, they are *imprecise:* "Individuals may legitimately differ about their application to concrete cases." Of two competing theories, for example, one might be more accurate in one respect, the other more accurate in another. Second, when taken together, these criteria "repeatedly prove to *conflict* with one another; accuracy may, for example, dictate the choice of one theory, scope the choice of its competitor."[10] Thus:

> When scientists must choose between competing theories, two men fully committed to the same list of criteria for choice may nevertheless reach different conclusions. Perhaps they interpret simplicity differently or have different convictions about the range of fields within which the consistency criterion must be met. Or perhaps they agree about these matters but differ about the relative weights to be accorded to these or to other criteria when several are deployed together. With respect to divergences of this sort, no set of choice criteria yet proposed is of any use.[11]

Rather than construing accuracy, consistency, scope, simplicity, and fruitfulness as rules that fully determine choice, Kuhn suggests we regard them as values that influence it. As a set of mechanical or computational rules, accuracy, scope, and so on underdetermine theory choice, but as values they frame the arguments and debates and help to shape and support the judgments that scientists make that one theory is, on balance, better than another.

The exercise of *human judgment* in choosing between competing, comprehensive scientific theories is therefore, according to Kuhn, inescapable. But judgment is not to be confused with mere preference or expression of taste. Judgments, as opposed to expressions of taste, are "eminently discussable" and need to be backed up by reasons, even if these reasons (e.g., "greater accuracy," "more consistent," "wider scope," etc.) do not function as determinate criteria and thereby "dictate" choice. Judgment, as Kuhn understands it, falls somewhere between algorithmic, or computational, decision procedures, on the one hand, and mere expressions of preference or taste, on the other. It is rational without being narrowly (and often vacuously) rationalistic.

Although Kuhn's thesis is not strikingly original—it is heavily indebted, for example, to the work of Ludwig Wittgenstein and others—*The Structure of Scientific Revolutions* has had enormous influence. A number of philosophers have subsequently combined Kuhn's insights with those of others (e.g., W. V. Quine, Wilfrid Sellars, Donald Davidson, and Hans-Georg Gadamer) in order to develop a more explicit and comprehensive critique of the entire Cartesian tradition in epistemology.[12]

Underlying Kuhn's account of scientific change, Rorty has pointed out, is an acknowledgment of the "ubiquity of language," the recognition that it is impossible "to step outside of our skins—the traditions, linguistic and other, within which we do our thinking and self-criticism—and compare ourselves with something absolute."[13] We *know* the world only through language and cannot, as it were, "get outside" our particular languages (natural and scientific) to examine the extent to which they mirror The World As It Really Is. Language, as Rorty puts it, ought to be seen

> not as a *tertium quid* between Subject and Object, nor as a medium in which we try to force pictures of reality, but as part of the behavior of human beings. On this view, the activity of uttering sentences is one of the things people do in order to cope with their environment. The Deweyan notion of language as tool rather than picture is right as far as it goes. But we must be careful *not* to phrase this analogy so as to suggest that one can separate the tool, Language, from its users and inquire as to its "adequacy" to achieve our purposes. The latter suggestion presupposes that there is some way of breaking out of language in order to compare it with something else. But there is no way to think about either the world or our purposes except by using language. One can use language to criticize and enlarge itself, as one can exercise one's body to develop and strengthen and enlarge it, but one cannot see language-as-a-whole in relation to something else to which it applies, or for which it is a means to an end.[14]

The reference to John Dewey in this passage is revealing. It is to the legacy of the great pragmatists—Charles S. Peirce, William James, and Dewey—that we must turn if we are to acquire a more adequate understanding of the important relationships between language, knowledge, and practical judgment and the implications of these relationships for the classroom.

IN PLACE OF TRADITION

If, as Kuhn maintains, "there is no neutral algorithm for theory-choice, no systematic decision procedure which, properly applied, must lead each individual [scientist] in the group to the same decision,"[15] what are the grounds of a rational choice among competing theories? How can one *know* that one theory is better than another? And what can we mean here by "better," if not a *more accurate representation* of The World As It Really Is? The short answer to this network of questions is broadly pragmatic. The competing theories constitute different vocabularies, or "tools," for contending with (parts of) the environment. After varying amounts of debate and discussion, those who must employ them may eventually *judge* that one of them is, for the purpose at hand, more *useful* than the other. The favored vocabulary allows those who employ it to achieve certain desirable concrete results that are either unattainable with the competitor or attainable only at the cost of a number of cumbersome ad hoc adjustments. Practicing scientists regard one theory as *better* than another, then, not because they have been able to determine that it more accurately represents the world, but because it is, with regard to the things that they find themselves *doing,* "more useful." The emphasis is on action rather than contemplation, theories as tools rather than as representations.

Let us note, in this connection, the essentially social or communitarian nature of scientific practice. Contemporary scientists are members of communities bound by more or less common languages and upbringings. The problems that engage them, the methods they employ, and the standards to which they appeal are all determined by a consensus of their respective (scientific) communities. The Cartesian picture of the ahistorical, solitary inquirer employing a more or less mechanical method in the search for timeless truth bears little resemblance to the Peircean "community of inquiry" of modern science. It is an informed critical consensus of members of the relevant community, and not the application of a linguistically, historically, and culturally neutral set of criteria, that provides the actual test of scientific validity. And what is true of scientific knowledge in this respect is true of knowledge generally: Knowledge in any domain is essentially social and the product of a community of inquirers, rather than the outcome of a singular mind properly programmed to sort out those impressions and ideas that actually mirror the world from those that do not. Knowledge, on this view, is best understood as the social justification of belief, not as accuracy of representation—what Dewey called "warranted assertability," not the Cartesian fantasy of direct (or culturally, linguistically, and historically unmediated) "contact with reality." [16]

This pragmatic conception of knowledge is not the product of a startlingly new definition. The pragmatist defines knowledge quite conventionally: Knowledge is "justified true belief." What is distinctive about the pragmatic conception is its appreciation of the extent to which both justification and truth are social rather than individualistic, normative rather than descriptive, rooted in action rather than observation, and inescapably linguistic. Consider, first, justification.

To justify a belief is to support it with one or more *other beliefs*. It is to make a judgment that the latter provide adequate grounds for the former. "How then do we justify these justifying beliefs?" The answer is fairly obvious; we justify them through other beliefs. "And what of these still other beliefs? How are they to be justified?" Through still other beliefs, and so on. "But isn't this circular?" Yes, but not viciously so. Justification, insofar as it is essentially linguistic (i.e., endorsing some propositions or sentences on the basis of our acceptance of others), is inescapably holistic. We can only know the world through language, sentences, and propositions, and we can only justify certain (linguistically structured) beliefs through other (similarly structured) beliefs. Justification, therefore, depends on the *coherence* of some of our beliefs with other beliefs, not on directly demonstrating the *correspondence* of some of our (linguistically structured) beliefs with The World As It Really Is (i.e., the world as it is wholly independent of human language, perception, or understanding). There is no such thing as knowledge of The World As It Really Is, if we construe knowledge as *justified* true belief. For to justify a belief is to give *reasons* for it, and reasons are essentially linguistic. Thus, insofar as these justificatory beliefs are linguistically structured and language is socially determined, justification is a matter of conversation and social practice.

"But," our interlocuter may now ask, "how do we know when to stop? If justification is as you say—if there is no absolute bedrock or foundation for knowledge—won't the process go on forever and to no conclusion?" No, not if we regard knowledge, like language, as a tool for making our way in the world. Knowledge is important to us because we are agents and we realize that our actions will be more likely to have the consequences we desire if they are based on justifiable true beliefs (i.e., knowledge, and not "mere opinion"). And the chain of justification comes to an end where we determine that continued "why" questions will have little or no bearing on our actions or that the (practical) costs of further questioning outweigh the benefits of acting on the basis of the current level of justification. It is thus that justification may be said to be rooted in human activity—our particular commitments, plans, and aspirations as agents—as well as being linguistic, social, and normative.

The same may now be said, more briefly, about truth. To characterize a certain belief as "true" is, most generally, to commend it: to say that, given our particular plans, commitments, and aspirations, and our desire for their success, it would be good for us to endorse this belief.[17] It is also to say that it is quite likely that anyone else with the same sort of background understanding and practical interests and concerns would come to the same conclusion. Thus, as Rorty points out, the line between a belief's being true and its being justified is very thin; for by "true" we mean roughly "what we can defend against all comers."[18] Apart from this, there is little to be said about truth or true beliefs in general. We can, of course, note more interesting things about how we determine the truth of particular beliefs in, say, certain areas of physics, psychology, history, ethics, art, religion, or politics; or how we determine whether certain beliefs about our own personal history are true. But there is no overarching Theory of Truth that will be of much help in dealing with these matters. For the justifications of such beliefs will depend on various context-dependent standards. And each of these standards will be determined in part by particular linguistic, social, normative, and practical considerations. A belief is true if it can be shown to *cohere* with other well-grounded beliefs, not if it can be shown to *correspond* with something that is wholly independent of human language, history, or culture—what we have dubbed The World As It Really Is. Repeated efforts to explain what the latter would amount to—how, that is, we could demonstrate apart from linguistic reference to *both* signifier *and signified* that the former is true of (or "corresponds with") the latter—have ended in failure.[19]

This, however, is not to say that the world is the creation of our beliefs. Most of the world is, as common sense would have it, wholly independent of our beliefs. But the *truth about the world* is not. Truth is a feature not of the world itself, but rather of certain sentences or descriptions of the world. And sentences are elements of human languages and human languages are human creations, rooted in various human activities.[20] If, then, we conceive of knowledge as justified true belief it cannot be separated from the languages and activities of particular groups or communities of human beings.

Thus what Kuhn and others have revealed about scientific knowledge is true of knowledge in general. Knowledge is inescapably linguistic and inseparable from human activity and various concerns, nearly all of them social. It is a product of practical reasoning (what Aristotle termed *phronesis*). Even what is often called "theoretical" or "contemplative" knowledge is the product of social practice. It differs from "more practical" kinds of knowledge not in being independent of practical or social concerns but rather in being bound up with practical and social concerns of a certain kind. There is, moreover, no reason to grant any sort of exalted status to theoretical or contemplative knowledge. The value of any sort of knowledge will be context dependent. The special knowledge of a theoretical physicist will pale by comparison with that of a sensitive family counselor if, for example, the physicist's marriage is falling apart and preserving his relationship with his wife now means more to him than his work in the laboratory.

In short, knowledge is not, as the Cartesian tradition assumes, simply a matter of aiming a highly polished mirror at the world and then passively and more or less mechanically ticking off the way things "really are," wholly independent of various practical concerns, both social and personal. It is, on the contrary, a linguistic, and therefore social, activity and, as such, inseparable from various practical concerns. Furthermore, given the holistic nature of justification—the impossibility of basing our linguistically structured beliefs on anything but other linguistically structured beliefs—knowledge is always a matter of practical judgment. There is no algorithm or criterion independent of various practical concerns that will tell us when we have arrived at an adequate justification. The acquisition and retention of knowledge, therefore, can never be passive or mechanical.

"But," it might now be objected, "how can this conception of knowledge account for progress? If we can never step outside the network of our beliefs to determine their adequacy, to make direct comparisons between our beliefs about the world and The World As It Really Is, how can we ever improve upon the set of beliefs that we were brought up with?" A plausible response is suggested by a metaphor attributed to Otto Neurath. Our task, according to Neurath, is like that of a mariner who must rebuild his ship bit by bit, plank by plank, on the open sea. The mariner cannot destroy or abandon his ship and start from scratch. But neither is he stuck with the ship as it is. As the mariner can improve upon his ship, can make it more suited to his purposes, while continuing to stand on its deck, so too can we improve upon some of our beliefs— that is, deepen and expand knowledge in certain areas—while continuing to rely on others. But no belief or set of beliefs is immune from scrutiny. It is just that we cannot, as Descartes assumed, criticize them all at once and from the top down.

We turn now to the classroom. If we replace the Cartesian conception of knowledge with the foregoing alternative, we will have to alter our approach to elementary and secondary education. The conventional classroom presupposes the validity of the Cartesian conception of knowledge. What, then, should teaching and learning look like if knowledge is regarded as a product of dialogue among a community of inquirers actively engaged in making their way in the world and seeking to determine which beliefs are true, because socially justified, and which not?

THE CLASSROOM AS A COMMUNITY OF INQUIRY

A classroom based on the foregoing conception of knowledge would differ from a conventional classroom in a number of ways. Physically, the most striking feature would be the arrangement of the furniture. The rows of student desks facing the desk of the teacher in the traditional classroom would be replaced by one or more sets of desks, usually arranged in circles. That the students would, as a rule, now be facing each other as well as the teacher would emphasize that learning is in large part a social activity.

There is an important difference between students learning *in* a group and learning *as* a group. Students in conventional classrooms learn in groups largely because financial considerations make it impossible for each student to have his or her own tutor. The emphasis is on the transmission of "knowledge" from active teacher to passive student, and the (financially prohibitive) ideal is a one-to-one teacher-student ratio. In contrast, the sort of classroom we envisage— what we characterize as a "community of inquiry"—regards group learning as essential to education. Members of a class who work *as* a group learn to see themselves as active participants in the discovery, analysis, and justification of claims to knowledge. As such, they constitute a model of the nature and structure of knowledge as it exists outside of the classroom. The emphasis is on dialogue, interaction, and a joint cooperative undertaking guided by a skilled and sensitive teacher who is him- or herself an interested inquirer.

Such teaching should begin in the earliest grades by establishing an atmosphere in which children are encouraged to ask questions and to develop the personal characteristics necessary for membership in a community of inquiry. The classroom should foster trust, a willingness to explore a wide variety of possibilities, being a good listener, mutual respect, and a readiness to offer and request reasons for various beliefs. The best way to develop these characteristics is for the teacher to model them; students will be influenced far more in this connection by what the teacher *does* than by what he or she says. Moreover, these characteristics cannot be cultivated in a vacuum. They must be reinforced in a context of conversations about matters that *mean* something in the lives of the students. The conversations must, therefore, be such that their outcomes are likely to have some practical effect on how the students live (at least within the context of the school). For younger children this means that the focus should often be upon *their* world—the world of the playground, the classroom, and the home.[21] As years pass and the student's world is extended, both spatially and temporally, the subject matter will naturally become more historical, global, and abstract. But the connections to the student's life—her interests, judgments, and activities—will remain. As the student grows older her world expands, as does the size and complexity of her community of inquiry. She is soon "conversing" with the dead as well as the living (through her study of history and the classics) and with people from all over the globe (through her study of geography, area studies, current events, and so on).

Dialogue is at the center of the classroom conceived as a community of inquiry, but it is dialogue in a significantly enriched sense. It involves not only dialogue among students and dialogue between students and teacher(s) but also dialogue between students and the authors of what they listen to, read, and view. The student becomes an active, critical listener, reader, and viewer, one for whom presentations, books, or films generate questions as well as provide answers. Listening, reading, and viewing all become conversational. Another kind of dialogue fostered by a community of inquiry is *internalized* dialogue, or dialogue with oneself. As a student engages in various kinds of dialogue with others, she will become aware of herself from the outside as well as from within. This new way of viewing the self will occasionally generate conflicts between the internal and the external standpoints, which will in turn lead to the kind of dialogue with oneself that is a mark of self-examination and reflective living. This conversational conception of knowledge and community has been eloquently characterized by Michael Oakeshott:

> As civilized human beings, we are the inheritors, neither of an inquiry about ourselves and the world, nor of an accumulating body of information, but of a conversation begun in the primeval forest and extended and made more articulate in

the course of centuries. It is a conversation which goes on both in public and within each of ourselves. Of course there is argument and inquiry and information, but wherever these are profitable they are recognized as passages in this conversation. . . . Education, properly speaking, is an initiation into the skill and partnership of this conversation in which we learn to recognize the voices, to distinguish the proper occasions of utterance, and in which we acquire the intellectual and moral habits appropriate to conversation. And it is this conversation which, in the end, gives place and character to every human activity and utterance.[22]

Empirical research reinforces these philosophical considerations about the importance of dialogue for cognitive development. Lev Vygotsky, for example, suggests that social interaction and philosophical dialogue enhance and develop the child's cognitive capacities.[23] Yet Douglas Barnes's studies of verbal inter-action in the classroom concluded that what little dialogue occurs deals largely with matters of fact and closed (rather than "open") questions. Students were seldom offered the opportunity to engage in the sort of open-ended dialogue that encourages and supports higher-order reasoning and prepares them to engage in the "conversation of mankind" identified by Oakeshott.[24]

Of course, even in a classroom structured as a community of inquiry, there will still be a need to learn certain factual information, memorize the multipli-cation tables, and so on. But these tasks will, when possible, be prefaced with an explanation of their status and pragmatic value. For example, historical and scientific factual information will be accompanied by an account (the sophisti-cation of which is made relative to the student's particular grade level) of the extent to which each is contingent and interpretive. And learning things like correct spelling and the multiplication tables will be justified instrumentally. For example, "As you can see, it will be important for you to be able to do X, and if you want to be able to do it quickly and well, it is very useful to learn (or memorize) Y and Z." Rather than being presented as the essence of knowl-edge, Y and Z will be regarded as useful means to a personally important end. Thus, by showing the connections between what one must arduously commit to memory and its place and value in personally important knowledge-related ac-tivities, the teacher gives meaning to the act of memorization and reduces the likelihood of its leading to an alienating and philosophically misleading Cartesian epistemology.

CONCLUSION

The contrast between the classroom as a community of inquiry and the tra-ditional classroom is as sharp as that between the pragmatic conception of knowledge outlined above and the Cartesian conception. Students in a commu-nity of inquiry are encouraged to ask questions and to be active participants in learning, not simply passive recipients or spectators. There is less emphasis on memorization of a large (and not particularly well connected) number of "facts," and more on acquiring the ability (temperamental, as well as intellectual) to reason well and to think for oneself. Students whose classrooms are structured as communities of inquiry will come to regard knowledge as social, bound up with human interests and projects, and therefore contingent or provisional (though none the less *useful* for this). They are likely to be more tolerant of complexity and ambiguity than students in conventional classrooms, though this will not incapacitate them. As pragmatists, they will recognize that the justification of belief is rooted in human activity and that the human condition often requires well-grounded, provisional commitment to one or another belief or course of action in the face of uncertainty.

There is, of course, much more to be said about the classroom as a community of inquiry. But most of it will have to come from those who actually become involved in guiding and observing the day-in, day-out activity of developing such classrooms. Our concern has been to show that we must now add epistemological considerations to whatever other reasons have been offered for preferring the community-of-inquiry conception of the classroom to the conventional conception.

NOTES

1. Bertrand Russell, *The Problems of Philosophy* (London: Oxford University Press, 1946), pp. 46–59.

2. Richard Bernstein, *Beyond Objectivism and Relativism* (Philadelphia: University of Pennsylvania Press, 1983), p. 18.

3. Richard Rorty, *Philosophy and the Mirror of Nature* (Princeton, N.J.: Princeton University Press, 1979).

4. René Descartes, *Philosophical Works of Descartes*, trans. Elizabeth S. Haldane and G.R.T. Ross, vol. 1, *Meditations* (Cambridge: Cambridge University Press, 1969), pp. 198–99.

5. See, for example, Bernstein, *Beyond Objectivism and Relativism*, and Rorty, *Philosophy and the Mirror of Nature* and *Consequences of Pragmatism* (Minneapolis: University of Minnesota Press, 1982). Also see Richard Rorty, *Contingency, Irony, and Solidarity* (Cambridge: Cambridge University Press, 1989), and *Objectivity, Relativism, and Truth* (Cambridge: Cambridge University Press, 1991).

6. Thomas S. Kuhn, *The Structure of Scientific Revolutions*, 2d ed., enl. (Chicago: University of Chicago Press, 1970).

7. Ibid., pp. 199–200.

8. Thomas S. Kuhn, "Notes on Lakatos," *PSA 1970, in Memory of Rudolf Carnap*, ed. Roger C. Buck and Robert S. Cohen. Boston Studies in the Philosophy of Science, No. 8 (Dordrecht: D. Reidel, 1971), p. 144.

9. Thomas S. Kuhn, "Objectivity, Value Judgment, and Theory Choice," in *The*

Essential Tension, ed. Thomas S. Kuhn (Chicago: University of Chicago Press, 1977), p. 322.

10. Ibid. Our emphasis.

11. Ibid., p. 324.

12. Rorty, *Philosophy and the Mirror of Nature*, and Bernstein, *Beyond Objectivism and Relativism*.

13. Rorty, *Consequences of Pragmatism*, pp. xix, xxxix.

14. Ibid., p. xviii f.

15. Kuhn, *The Structure of Scientific Revolutions*, p. 199 f.

16. Rorty, *Philosophy and the Mirror of Nature*, p. 176.

17. William James, "Pragmatism's Conception of Truth," in James, *Pragmatism* (New York, 1907; reprint, Indianapolis, Ind.: Hackett, 1981), pp. 91–105.

18. Rorty, *Philosophy and the Mirror of Nature*, p. 308.

19. Rorty, *Consequences of Pragmatism*, pp. xxi–xxvii.

20. Richard Rorty, "The Contingency of Language," *London Review of Books*, 17 April 1986, p. 3.

21. See, in this connection, the novels comprising the Philosophy for Children curriculum devised by Matthew Lipman and Ann Margaret Sharp of the Institute for the Advancement of Philosophy for Children at Montclair State College, Upper Montclair, New Jersey.

22. Michael Oakeshott, "Poetry as a Voice in the Conversation of Mankind," in Oakeshott, *Rationalism in Politics* (New York: Methuen, 1962), p. 199.

23. Lev Vygotsky, *Mind in Society*, ed. Michael Cole et al. (Cambridge, Mass.: MIT Press, 1962).

24. Douglas R. Barnes and Frankie Todd, *Communication in Small Groups* (London: Routledge and Kegan Paul, 1977).

9

Thinking for Oneself

Philip C. Guin

■ ■ ■

IN THIS CHAPTER, I will attempt to unravel some of the complexity of understanding "thinking for oneself." Though the expression figures throughout *Harry Stottlemeier's Discovery*, little elucidation is to be found there, presumably in order that children will have the opportunity to discuss its significance without prejudice. The claim is made that thinking for oneself is the product of community effort rather than an individualized achievement. Therefore, attributing thinking for oneself to an individual entails acknowledging the community of inquiry to which she or he belongs. I discuss the following topics: a sample of how children often view thinking for oneself; a contrast between thinking for oneself and thinking; the notion of a community in making thinking for oneself possible; and whether thinking for oneself should be an educational objective. I will make intermittent reference to *Harry* in an effort to unpack how thinking for oneself is used in the novel.

HOW CHILDREN VIEW THINKING FOR ONESELF

Harry Stottlemeier's Discovery is replete with the demands of children that they be allowed to think for themselves. Asked what thinking for oneself means, pupils will correctly insist that "one *always* thinks for oneself." And surely it is a truism that, whether thinking as others would have us think or thinking most vigorously and creatively, whether imparting the products of indoctrination or tendering unseasoned hypotheses, we necessarily think for ourselves. The *decision* to turn our thinking over to others only proves the point.

That this interpretation becomes strained under the force of further inquiry will be suspected, and children soon find themselves searching for answers elsewhere. Often they seem to want to substitute "for oneself" with "about oneself." In these cases we find twitches, pains, and desires, in short, the vicissitudes of life, as the objects of reflection. Coupled with the truism, this retreat into subjectivity yields a surprising contention. As Arthur tells us, "Everyone says Madge is so dull. But I find her interesting and attractive."[1] "Sure Arthur is thinking for himself," children concede, "but so what, it's only the way *he* feels, his opinion." Therefore, even if thinking for oneself is a worthwhile educational objective, children do not seem to see it as such.

What is required, we assume, is further inquiry. In the face of so many counterestimations, Arthur might be persuaded to provide reasons in defense of his judgment. Further discussion might give way to children's appreciation of Arthur's resolve to reflect, to be consistent, his allegiance to evidence, fidelity in drawing inference, disposition to examine presuppositions, and willingness to trace consequences. By spelling out contexts in which Arthur can thoughtfully consider Madge, children come at least to understand how he feels, how he sees the world. Even so, children in the end retort, "But it's his opinion, not ours."

THINKING AND THINKING FOR ONESELF

Having reached an impasse, insofar as thinking for oneself terminates in the obvious, the idiosyncratic, or both, we are still left with the uneasy feeling that something is askew, and that a better reading is to be gleaned from actual occurrences in *Harry*. Witnessing their struggle throughout the novel to reach their goal, we would hope that Harry and friends, in the sequel, will have the opportunity to think for themselves. In *Harry*, Mark's lament that in school, although "we do learn to think . . . we never learn to think for ourselves,"[2] suggests a path we might follow. Assuming there is a distinction to be made, assuming the children are not on a benighted quest, one thing is abundantly clear: Thinking for oneself is not so much revealed in judgments as in the characteristic way in which judgments are reached. This is no trifling matter, inasmuch as children all too often attribute thinking for himself to Arthur for no other reason than that he is different. But Arthur's confession offers no clue; we still look to his reason, motives, and attitudes to support the judgment. Given the latter, are we not convinced that Arthur is thinking *and* thinking for himself? What more could possibly be required?

The case of the bank burglar is instructive. By his admission, banks are burglarized, not because of a breakdown of moral scruple, but matter-of-factly, "because the money is there." We laugh as we realize the many prior questions unanswered in the burglar's straight-faced confession. Still, we credit him with proficient thinking within the discipline of burglary. Whether his effort translates into thinking for himself is another question. The discipline of burglary calls for expertise, compliance with rules and canons adding up to proficiency— in these matters we have a virtuoso. However, the sort of question we want to have addressed goes beyond mere proficiency: "What difference does it make that the money *is* in the bank?" To the extent the burglar is willing and able to entertain the question with the analogous effort with which he has proven himself successful within the discipline, we might, if his deliberations and reasons are convincing, feel obliged to grant that he is thinking for himself. Our question invites the burglar to be critical not only *within* the discipline but also *about* the discipline. We want him to come to terms with both his desire for money and his compliance with the desire. A more comprehensive examination of this profession inspires us to believe the burglar is beginning to think for himself. In his newly found appreciation of consequences, in his examination of assumptions, in his dispassionate concern for procedure—his impartiality and respect for persons and evidence—we detect the marks of thinking for himself.

We may, nevertheless, be dubious in regard to Arthur. The burglar, after all, enjoys a fairly well defined discipline, in which thinking is evaluated according to criteria that satisfy. In turn, we surmise the discipline and its accompanying requirements become the objects of thinking for oneself. In extolling Madge, Arthur does not seem to have the burglar's prescriptive advantage, nor does there seem to be a clear way to distinguish his personal and possibly prosaic view from thinking, let alone thinking for himself. In fact, one might urge that Arthur's judgment of Madge *is* personal, and that it is perverse of us to question it further. But supposing Arthur is willing and able to defend his judgment, is prepared to persuade rather than bully us, should there not be some reasons that fare better than others? On the one hand, naturally suspect are self-regarding avowals of states over which Arthur has no control, which stand alone without critical scrutiny—"Madge makes me tingle." On the other hand, we would be obdurate to withhold thinking for himself from Arthur, if the reasons given begin to hang together to form a coherent and consistent picture. That being the case, Arthur's audience may come to question its own estimation of Madge—"Perhaps we have made a mistake."

THE ROLE OF COMMUNITY IN THINKING FOR ONESELF

Whether he wins or loses, what stands out is the social context wherein Arthur focuses and examines his point of view. As a member of a community, albeit a dissonant community, Arthur has heard his detractors and they have heard his reply. We allow that Arthur is thinking for himself, not because of some rarity of private thought, but because of the corrective potential of the community. Sensitized to the points of view of others, Arthur's judgment is highlighted, as it is exposed as disputational as well as given. Stripped of this corrective potential, his judgment has little more cognitive merit than a capricious glance. Consequently, we would hold that, even though Arthur might arrive at his judgment for the best possible reasons, independent of the community, he cannot in principle be said to be thinking for himself.

This conclusion is itself controversial. In the ultimate chapter of *Harry*, the children have reached the point of decision, whether or not to continue their deliberations next year. By now the reader appreciates Harry and friends as exemplifying a community of inquiry with a rich variety of views. As Fran points out to Mr. Spence, "here I am, sitting in the back of the room, and you're up there at the front of the room. And what do you see? You see faces. And what do I see? I see the backs of people's heads."[3] In turn, Anne takes Fran's observation as a statement of the subjectivist position—"I think Fran's right. I think each of us lives in his own world that's different from other people's." Harry reacts with a corrective—"if she [Fran] were to go up front, she would see only faces, and if Mr. Spence were to go to the back of the room, he would see only backs of heads."[4] In this way the children give voice to the dissolution of subjective barriers through community effort.

In holding that the community of inquiry is in a position to overcome subjectivism, does it follow that it *must* be in place to produce thinking for oneself? Karl Popper has given a plausible argument in favor of the latter position, insofar as scientific inquiry is concerned. Popper asks us to imagine Robinson Crusoe on his island, replete with scientific laboratories and astronomical instruments. Regardless of his findings, regardless of how attentive and scrupulous he is in his investigations, Crusoe fails to convince us:

> There is an element of scientific method missing. . . . For there is nobody but himself to check his results; nobody but himself to correct those prejudices which are the unavoidable consequence of his peculiar history. . . . What we call "scientific objectivity" is not a product of the individual scientist's impartiality, but a product of the social or public character of scientific method; and the individual scientist's impartiality is, so far as it exists, not the source but rather the result of this socially or institutionally organized objectivity of science.[5]

If, as Popper contends, the scientist's objectivity draws its support from an institutional or social background, can we demand less of Arthur? Granted that unexamined feelings persist behind Arthur's judgment, still, thinking for himself emerges in proportion to this willingness to discuss the matter openly. Only in this way are we assured of Arthur's impartiality, as well as his partiality. That is to say, Arthur's *best* reasons must bear the burden of social criticism to be *understood* as supporting his judgment, not only by his audience but by himself. Supposing we could reserve thinking for oneself for oneself, a kind of reflexiveness, what residual guarantee of success is possible other than our rock-bottom feelings that we are right? Indeed, what agency would ever inform us should we be wrong? Granted that there is a difference between the scope and character of the respective communities to which they submit their views, still, by subordinating his view to his detractors, Arthur is like the scientist in insisting, "Let *us* get to the bottom of this."

An objection might be raised that Arthur could be wrong, yet thinking for himself, independent of the community. Even though the proponents of phlogiston and the luminiferous ether were mistaken, were they dunderheads as well, unable to think for themselves? But here, following Popper, the answer lies clearly with the verdict of the community of scientific inquirers. Certainly one could be wrong and still be thinking for oneself. In Arthur's case, so poignant with feelings, we are not likely to interfere unless we detect feelings and motives so utterly self-serving, so false, as to compel us at least to warn Madge—if not Arthur. As Charles Peirce reminds us:

> It is terrible to see how a single unclear idea, a single formula without meaning, lurking in a young man's head, will sometimes act like an obstruction of inert matter in an artery, hindering the nutrition of the brain, and condemning its victim to pine away in the fullness of his intellectual vigor and in the midst of intellectual plenty.[6]

Since the scientist's claim is etched more vividly by virtue of its institutional bearings, questions of truth and falsity do arise. In Arthur's case, wrongheadedness is not likely to become a factor unless harm to others or to himself becomes evident. But as harm emerges, it necessarily becomes social, and thinking for oneself becomes a possibility.

Peirce also reminds us that the interests of the community often figure before our own. In fact human beings are not nearly so selfish as has been widely assumed:

> The constant use of the "*we*"—as when we speak of our possessions on the Pacific—our destiny as a republic—in cases in which no personal interests at all are involved, show conclusively that men do not make their personal interests their only ones, and therefore may, at least, subordinate them to the interests of the community.[7]

A correlative is to be found in *Harry*. At one point Mr. Partridge, the principal, condescends to hear student arguments. They argue well, and Partridge is compelled to try to divide them by suggesting that each of their individual concerns issues from selfish motives. He concludes by chiding Mickey with an invidious analogy between accepting bad-tasting medicine and accepting adult authority—"just as you'll be a healthier person for swallowing the medicine, so you'll be a better person for accepting what I've told you." Harry sees through the ruse, and he points out to Partridge that "Mickey and Tony weren't asking you to do what was better just for *them*, . . . they were asking you to do what would be better for everyone."[8] Harry's universalization stands in contrast to Partridge's attempt to trivialize the children's arguments. Harry sees that so long as the singularity of the children's replies are taken to task, one by one, the concerted work of the group will be lost. Harry's appeal is not directed at the freedom for children to do as they please, but "that kids need to be free to think for themselves just as much as grownups do, maybe more so."[9] And the upshot must be that children need the community of their peers in order to think for themselves.

THINKING FOR ONESELF AS AN EDUCATIONAL OBJECTIVE

Although Harry feels that thinking for oneself is a need, whether children should be enabled to do so remains an open question. If thinking for oneself is indeed a legitimate need, the answer would seem to follow in the affirmative. Certainly the classroom can be turned into a community of inquiry, children listening and talking to their peers, and teachers can be trained to facilitate meaningful discussions. Nevertheless, there will be those who will contend that such an enterprise is wasteful of time, if not dangerous. Time is valuable, they will argue, and to spend it in dubious discussion with no guarantee that the product will be important in children's development would be irresponsible. Moreover, a danger lurks in assuming that children can profit from discussions with their peers. After all, children lack the experience and tools necessary to deal with substantive issues, whereas teachers have wisdom and subject-matter competency. It is the teacher who should be on center stage, judiciously and expeditiously imparting knowledge to children. The diffuse dialogue will never be a substitute for the structured lesson plan. Left to their own devices, children cannot be expected to move much beyond mere anecdotal material or the recounting of titilating experiences. In short, thinking for oneself should not be a priority in the classroom because children, in their innocence and ignorance, *need* to be told, Harry's admonition notwithstanding.

This attitude is common enough to warrant proposing some counterpossibilities. My own classroom experience has indicated at least the following eight possibilities as a result of a well-functioning community of inquiry, in which thinking for oneself has been demonstrated.

Thinking for oneself fosters the development of the autonomous child. In the community of inquiry, children do learn to cherish independent thought. The nonintimidating character of the community, where all serious beliefs and proposals are entertained, encourages children to generate a rich variety of original ideas.

Thinking for oneself ensures personhood. Because the community of inquiry promotes rapport and trust, children are secure in expressing thoughts and feelings. The shy or reticent child learns to take risks, while the vociferous child learns to listen. In this manner, expressing and listening, children are enabled to better understand themselves and others.

Thinking for oneself strengthens the tools of inquiry. The community provides the corrective: Cherished opinions are continually subjected to possible counterinstances, possible consequences of proposed actions are proffered, inconsistencies and contradictions are exposed, and reasons given are evaluated as being better or worse. Through practice in the classroom community, children come to appreciate rational procedures and the skills necessary to make them possible. Extensive testing has corroborated this point.

Thinking for oneself fosters tolerance and concern for others. As the community develops, children learn that their individual need for meaning or significance requires that each member be treated as a potential source of information. Children soon learn that it is to their advantage to be kind to their peers, to treat them as coinvestigators. Children thus find that they have a vested interest in cooperation.

Thinking for oneself counters autocratic and totalitarian tendencies. In the community, children come to reject undefended pronouncements. Consequently, no individual in the community will stand out as being exempt from the corrective potential of the group.

Thinking for oneself vouchsafes democratic ideals. Insofar as democratic institutions require members possessed of ideas that can be defended with good reasons and arguments, the classroom community of inquiry is a perfect setting in which children come to appreciate the power of group action. Whether or not they can label it as such, the community of inquiry is a democratic institution.

Thinking for oneself promotes the search for knowledge and truth. Because the group is self-correcting, children are constantly aware of their individual fallibility. Moreover, children learn that consensus is at best a prelude to further inquiry.

Finally, thinking for oneself promotes happiness. Having enjoyed membership in a community of inquiry, children have come to discover both serious and invigorating work. Membership has provided the conditions for honesty and fulfillment—honesty for those who thought they knew it all, fulfillment for those who felt they had nothing to offer. Children find great satisfaction in belonging to the community.

Whether one appreciates these possibilities will depend on dispositions and assumptions. For some, thinking for oneself as an educational objective is a frightening idea. For others, it is an ideal long neglected in the classroom. All would agree that we want the best for children, and this, of course, is the loaded goal needing unpacking. In descriptive terms, educational agencies, though there are exceptions, continue to harbor suspicions regarding both the alleged need and right of children to think for themselves. If we look at the alternatives, we find that at one extreme conditioning and indoctrination are welcomed as being the expedient and safe alternative. At the other extreme, a kind of benign attitude reigns suggesting that practically anything goes. Neither alternative is likely to result in much thinking for oneself. But even if most educators abjure both extremes, it is not clear that they are willing, in turn, to espouse straight-away thinking for oneself as an educational given. Consequently, if we wish to examine thinking for oneself in relation to what is best for children, perhaps we could reflect on a question: Provided that one thing best for children is that they be enabled to learn, can they learn from discussions with their peers as well as from textbooks and teachers? The possibilities I have outlined would suggest that they can.

NOTES

1. Matthew Lipman, Ann Margaret Sharp, and Frederick S. Oscanyan, eds., *Philosophical Inquiry: An Instructional Manual to Accompany* Harry Stottlemeier's Discovery, 2d ed. (Lanham, Md.: University Press of America, 1984), p. 133.

2. Matthew Lipman, *Harry Stottlemeier's Discovery* (Montclair, N.J.: First Mountain Foundation, 1982), p. 24.

3. Ibid., p. 93.

4. Ibid., p. 94.

5. Karl R. Popper, *The Open Society and Its Enemies*, vol. 2, *The High Tide of Prophecy: Hegel, Marx, and the Aftermath* (New York, 1945; reprint, New York: Harper and Row, 1963), pp. 219–20.

6. Charles S. Peirce, *Selected Writings*, ed. Philip P. Wiener (New York: Dover, 1966), p. 118.

7. Charles S. Peirce, *Collected Papers*, ed. Charles Hartshorne and Paul Weiss (Cambridge, Mass.: Harvard University Press, 1965), vol. p. 355.

8. Lipman, *Harry Stottlemeier's Discovery*, p. 47.

9. Ibid.

10

Critical Thinking: Problem Solving or Problem Creating?

Michael S. Pritchard

■ ■ ■

FOR SOME TIME NOW I have been puzzling over what we really have in mind when we say that the schools should be doing a better job of helping students develop their critical-thinking abilities. Although most educators agree that something should be done, there is no consensus on how to go about it. I suspect that this is partly because there is no consensus on what critical thinking is. I offer no definition. But I do have some reflections that, I hope, will contribute to our understanding of critical thinking.

I will begin with a thought experiment. Imagine Harry Stottlemeier and his classmates materializing and showing up as fully matriculated fifth-graders in a school in your area. Imagine also that, although they know nothing about IAPC's Philosophy for Children programs, the fifth-grade teachers in this school express serious concern about the critical-thinking skills of their students. They are disturbed by the national trend toward lower scores on standardized reading and math tests, and they are keenly interested in programs designed to aid their students in "problem solving."

Among Harry and his classmates, who would these teachers identify as the best test taker and problem solver? I suspect the overwhelming choice would be Tony. He is bright, quick, analytical, very good in math, and highly motivated to find answers. Who would they identify as the most imaginative thinker? This would be a more difficult choice, but I would place Lisa, Suki, and Ann near the top of the list. Who would be identified as the best critical thinker? If test scores and demonstrated problem-solving skills are the marks of critical thinking, Tony would be the likely choice.

However, my choice is Lisa. My fear is that far too many teachers and administrators would pick Tony. It is generally acknowledged that we do not have machine-graded tests that are a good measure of creative thinking. If critical and creative thinking are quite distinct, it might be thought, as many apparently do, that machine-graded tests can be a good measure of critical thinking. My view, however, is that it is precisely Lisa's creative thinking that gives her the edge over Tony in critical thinking. Furthermore, critical thinkers like Lisa may sometimes have greater difficulty with machine-graded tests and problem-solving tasks than the Tonys of this world. Lisa is as much a problem *creator* as a problem *solver*. This is a mark of her philosophical turn of mind.

Virtually all educators agree that we need to do a better job of helping students develop their critical thinking. IAPC contends that its Philosophy for Children program is well suited to meet this objective. I agree that it is. Lisa would feel more at home than Tony in classrooms that model IAPC objectives. Would this be true in other classrooms that claim they are trying to improve the critical thinking of their students? In this age of accountability and testing, the reverse might well be the case.

While accountability and testing are important, critical thinking of the kind exemplified by Lisa should also be encouraged. My worry is that this is not widely enough acknowledged or appreciated. I will now try to spell out some of my concerns in greater detail.

WHAT IS CRITICAL THINKING?

Robert Ennis offers the following succinct definition of "critical thinking":

> "Critical thinking," as I think the term is generally used, means *reasonable reflective thinking that is focused on deciding what to believe or do*.[1]

A positive feature of this definition, as Ennis points out, is that it does not exclude creative thinking:

> Formulating hypotheses, alternative ways of viewing a problem, questions, possible solutions, and plans for investigating something, for example, are all creative acts that come under this definition.[2]

However, even with this inclusion of creative thinking, Ennis's definition may be too narrow. Certainly critical thinking can be used to decide what to believe or do. But it can also be used to make sense of what one reads, sees, or hears, to make inferences from premises with which one may disagree or about which one has no particular view, and so on. Of course, this can eventuate in making decisions about what to believe or do, but this need not be the primary focus.

For example, consider the following pair of sentences recently discussed in E. D. Hirsch's *Cultural Literacy*:

1. Three turtles rested *beside* a floating log, and a fish swam beneath them.
2. Three turtles rested *on* a floating log, and a fish swam beneath them.[3]

In an experiment by J. R. Barclay, J. D. Bransford, and J. J. Franks, subjects presented with the first sentence consistently, but mistakenly, recalled their original sentence to be:

3. Three turtles rested on a floating log, and a fish swam beneath *it*.

Subjects who were originally presented with the second sentence did not recall their sentence as:

4. Three turtles rested beside a floating log, and a fish swam beneath *it*.

Understanding the differences among these sentences, including the inferences that can or cannot be made from the original pair, requires critical thinking. But the primary focus is on understanding meanings rather than on deciding what to believe or do.

Ennis's taxonomy of critical-thinking skills is actually broader than his definition of "critical thinking" would suggest.[4] For example, it includes dispositions to seek clear statements of questions, to be open-minded, to seek as much precision as the subject permits, to think in an orderly manner, and to be sensitive to the feelings and level of understanding of others; and it includes abilities such as focusing on the context of an argument, detecting unstated assumptions, clarifying arguments, making inferences from premises, and interacting with others in a reasonable manner.

But, as Ennis observes, critical thinking is commonly associated with problem solving.[5] And he does not warn the reader that this association might be too narrow. My experience has been that many teachers do think of critical thinking too narrowly in terms of problem solving. This explains some of the resistance many have to Philosophy for Children—which could be thought of as problem *creating* as much as problem solving. Highly developed critical thinking frequently poses more questions than answers. It opens up new avenues for inquiry and, in this sense, is creative as well as critical.

This is not to deny the value of critical thinking in problem solving, even though, as I will soon argue, problem solving does not always involve critical thinking. However, the exercise of critical imagination that sometimes creates more problems than it solves (at least in the short run) should be encouraged; and it is here that Philosophy for Children flourishes.

PROBLEM SOLVING AND CRITICAL THINKING

To explore relationships between problem solving and critical thinking, let us consider a math problem:

20 is to 30 as 10 is to (a) 5; (b) 10; (c) 15; (d) 20; (e) 25[6]

If John answers (c) 15, does he display critical-thinking skills? Not necessarily. This depends on how he arrived at this answer and, perhaps, why other answers were not selected. Suppose he reasoned this way: "This is obviously a question about ratios. I've seen problems like this before. 20 is ⅔ of 30. 10 is ⅔ of 15. So, 15 is the right answer." But what is it about the problem that led him to view it as a problem about ratios? If this occurred to him only because of its familiarity, problem-solving skills were used; but it is not clear that any critical thinking was required.

Suppose Amy selects (d) 20. (This answer is frequently selected by teachers to whom I present this problem.) She reasons: "In each case the difference between the first and second number is 10." She might not have noticed that 20 is ⅔ of 30. Instead, she might simply have noticed that 30 is 10 greater than 20. Is this answer wrong? It might well be marked wrong on a standardized test. But it is not at all clear that it should be marked wrong. Although Amy's procedure might not be what the test makers had in mind, it could be objected that they should have made their intentions more clear. As far as critical thinking is concerned, neither John nor Amy seems to have employed really striking critical-thinking skills, although Amy might be given the edge in creative thinking.

Now suppose that a third student, Mark, circles both (c) 15 and (d) 20. He does this because he thinks that both answers are acceptable and he circles both as a way of indicating that the question lacks precision. This response (which would be machine graded as wrong) does exemplify an important critical-thinking skill—as does Mark's refusal to opt for one "best" answer.

Many teachers commenting on this problem suggest that, since the test makers probably had (c) 15 in mind as the correct answer, they should not have included (d) 20 as a possible choice. That is, they object that this is a poorly constructed problem. Well, let us replace (d) 20 with (d) 30.

Susan now answers: "I think that 20 is to 30 as 10 is to 10." On the face of it, this answer seems so absurd that we might suspect that Susan either is not taking the problem seriously or she needs a math lesson. However, she explains: "If you add ten to each of the second numbers, the first number will be ½ of the second new number."

Anyone who can offer this explanation also has some understanding of ratios. But, obviously, not everyone who understands ratios will take such an imaginative approach to the problem. Suppose Susan now playfully adds: "I see that 15 would work. But so would 10. I chose 10 because it wasn't so obvious. I had to think harder to come up with that answer. I like challenges like that. Besides, it was supposed to be a *problem*, wasn't it?" Here we can see critical imagination at work—but only because Susan is given an opportunity to explain her thinking.

To prevent "clever" responses like this from ruining a test (or Susan's score), we might drop (b) 10 from the possible choices. Let us replace (b) 10 with (b) 60. So now the problem reads:

20 is to 30 as 10 is to (a) 5; (b) 60; (c) 15; (d) 30; (e) 25

Kevin now says: "I think 20 is to 30 as 10 is to 5. If you add 20 to each of the second numbers, the first number will be ⅔ of the second." He adds: "Of course, 25 could be right, too. After all, 20 is smaller than 30 and 10 is smaller than 25. 30 and 60 would work, too."

At this point one might object that the problem needs to be "disambiguated"—if it is stated with greater precision, such answers will clearly be inappropriate. Here is an attempt:

This is a problem in ratios. Consider ²⁰⁄₃₀. If 10 is the numerator, what denominator should be selected if the ratio is to match ²⁰⁄₃₀? [Note: Do not add or subtract from the denominators.]

(a) 3; (b) 7; (c) 15; (d) 23; (e) 31

This way of stating the problem seems reasonably clear. (If necessary, we could add: "No 'clever' answers allowed!") But this clarity comes with a stiff price. The need for critical-thinking skills in solving the problem is minimal.

Of course, we do want students to be able to understand and solve problems with ratios. But we also should want students to detect ambiguities, explore alternative possibilities, and at least occasionally come up with unconventional approaches to problems.

Unfortunately, there seems to be much that conspires against the exercise of critical thinking—both in the schools and in ordinary adult life. I still vividly recall our daughter Susan, then eleven, declaring at the dinner table, "You can't get away with being philosophical in school." One of her illustrations was being told that her alternative way of extending a number series was incorrect. She was asked to provide the next three numbers in the series: 1, 4, 9, 16. . . . She correctly supplied: 25, 36, 49. But, rather than getting these numbers by squaring 5, 6, and 7, she noticed that the differences between numbers in the series were 3, 5, 7, 9, and so on. So, she solved the problem by addition. Susan's reward was being told that she was wrong—rather than being told that her method was interesting, even though not what her teacher had in mind. Rather than being encouraged to explore why her method matched the results of the squaring method, Susan was given the message that only the "tried and true" path was worth pursuing.

This message is not only for children. A short time ago all administrators at my university were required to take a PLATO computer course on affirmative action and equal employment opportunities. The intent of the program was to increase our understanding of and sensitivity to legal and moral concerns in these areas. Unfortunately, the software program permitted no departure from what was literally stated in the accompanying textual materials. For example, the text on sexism stated that curricula have contributed to sexism. A reasonable inference from such a statement would be that the homework issuing from curricula can also contribute to sexism. However, since this inference was not made in the text, that choice was "incorrect" on the multiple-choice test. Ironically, rather than enhancing the sensitivity of readers to important and complex issues, the PLATO program encouraged a mindless adherence to a rather unimaginative text.

The current effort to raise the speed limit on freeways has reminded me of some difficulties I had many years ago with the written driver's exam for the State of Michigan. At that time the speed limit was 70 M.P.H. One question asked whether one should slow down and check the oncoming traffic before entering a freeway or speed up to match the speed of the oncoming traffic. I opted for slowing down, on the grounds that my Volkswagen Beetle could not match up with the cars moving at 70 M.P.H. Furthermore, since a high percentage of cars were traveling well in excess of the speed limit, I concluded that I would be violating the law if I were to try to match the speed of oncoming traffic. I attempted to explain my choice to the person who administered the exam. She tersely replied, "They just want the most logical choice!"

Apparently the "most logical choice" is one that does not allow for significant exceptions (inherently slower vehicles)—and it disallows the contextual discretion and judgment essential to competent driving. The purpose of the exam, it might be replied, is to determine whether drivers have *general* knowledge of the rules of the road and good driving practice. No doubt some such knowledge is important, but equally important is critical judgment—something such tests are neither designed to measure nor encourage.

The moral of these stories is mixed. On the one hand, critical thinking can sometimes impede test taking. Successful test taking is important, and critical thinkers are not always rewarded for exercising their critical capacities. On the other hand, successful test taking is actually only a small part of one's life. Of more permanent significance is one's ability to engage in flexible, reflective thinking. If we are to truly encourage the development of such thinking, we must be prepared to accept "trouble"—occasional unconventional answers, times when more questions than answers surface, and occasional challenges to the assumptions of teachers. I think we should welcome such "trouble"—it is part of what makes teaching a worthwhile and exciting profession. A worry is that the association of critical thinking with problem solving will predominate at the expense of a more balanced view that includes problem creating. Only if the latter is accepted can we expect philosophy to have a significant place in the classroom—and only then will we have critical thinking at its best.

LISA AND TONY AGAIN

Earlier I indicated that, if asked to select a model critical thinker from *Harry Stottlemeier's Discovery*, my choice would be Lisa. Lisa's critical thinking is invariably creative, as illustrated in several passages.

It is Lisa in Chapter One who upsets Harry's discovery. Harry is convinced that if true sentences are reversed, they become false. If she had understood more precisely what Harry wanted and followed his lead, perhaps she would have provided him with more "confirmations" of his discovery. Instead, she comes up with a stunning counterexample: "No eagles are lions." This leads Harry and Lisa to rethink his discovery. Notice, however, that it is Harry who makes the revision: "That's it! If a true sentence begins with the word 'No,' then its reverse is also true. But if it begins with the word 'All,' then its reverse is false" (p. 4). Lisa is silent. Perhaps her thoughts here are similar to those she has later when discussing some syllogisms with Fran:

> "Fran, I don't think we can say for sure yet that what we've done is right. There may be cases like the one I gave you before where the conclusion turns out true instead of false. Maybe we just haven't tried enough different types yet and maybe there are some rules we don't know yet." (p. 77)

It is clear in Chapter Three that she does have reservations about Harry's rules. After dreaming that all animals are catlike, Lisa concludes:

> "So all animals aren't cats, but in make believe they can be! And in dreams they can be. I can imagine what I please, and when I do, Harry's rules won't apply." (p. 12)

For the moment she is satisfied. However, it is quite consistent with Lisa's inquisitiveness that later she might wonder if, in some sense, Harry's rules apply even to "make believe." Final closure on complex issues is not something we can expect from Lisa.

It is also Lisa, in Chapter Four, who has trouble with Mrs. Halsey's suggestion that students write a paper on the topic "The Greatest Thing in the World." Lisa points out that "greatest" could mean "biggest" or "most important." In Chapter Eleven, Lisa recalls looking at herself in the mirror after being told she looks like a Pekinese. Now she reflects:

> "But the other day Grandma said, 'Never judge a book by its cover,' and it occurred to me that books and people *are* alike in one respect: they're both full of thoughts. I wonder if that's silly? Anyhow, one thing I know for sure is that mirrors lie; they don't show you as you really are.

Shortly after this insightful piece of self-reflection, Lisa turns her attention to the conflict between her school and the religious convictions of Dale Thompson and his family. She wonders why none of the students talk about Dale now that he has left school. She suggests that they are ashamed:

> "Because we didn't do anything to help him?" Harry asked.
>
> "Yes, I suppose so—although honestly, Harry, I don't know what we could have done. No, I think we're ashamed of the way we think about things; because if people could have realized the awful results of thinking the way they do, they might not be so ready to do bad things." (p. 57)

Lisa's critical thinking has now enriched her social understanding by providing a deeper explanation.

Finally, although she has been one of the major contributors to the development of logical ideas in *Harry*, in Chapter Seventeen, Lisa challenges the value of talking about reasoning in class. She recalls a poem her father read to her:

> "It said the thoughts in our minds are like bats in a cave, and these ideas go flying about blindly, keeping within the walls. But then, in the last line, the poem says that every once in a while, 'a graceful error corrects the cave.'" (p. 95)

Tony asks Lisa if she is suggesting that they should all learn to make "fancy mistakes":

> "I'm just saying," said Lisa, "that you should keep an open mind, and don't think you know it all because you've figured out a few rules of thinking." Lisa looked for a moment more at Tony, and then glanced across the room at Harry. "I'd like to keep working on it, I really would. It was fun. And it does seem to work with the way we talk. But I don't think it works with the way we imagine, or the way we feel about things, or the way we dream. . . ." (p. 95)

So here we have Lisa's critical thinking at its best—modestly embracing what can be firmly established, while remaining open to the possibility that human understanding may require other ways of thinking as well.

Lisa says that Tony thinks everything is very simple: "Like he has one number, he adds a second to it, and then he figures out what the third one is—it's the sum of the first two—you know, like seven plus three make ten. So he thinks that if you take one sentence, and you add another one to it, you should be able to get a third sentence which is the result of adding the first two together" (p. 75). Tony wants answers. Where clear, decisive answers are available, he is probably a delight to his teachers.

However, if Tony really does think that everything is very simple, I will have to agree with Lisa, who often finds things to be complex and confusing. In any case, if we were choosing sides, Lisa would be my first choice for a critical-thinking team. I will illustrate why with a final example.

Irving Copi presents this "brainteaser" in his *Informal Logic*:

> Mr. Short, his sister, his son and his daughter are fond of golf and often play together. The following statements are true of their foursome:

a. The best player's twin and the worst player are of the opposite sex.

b. The best player and the worst player are the same age.

Which one of the foursome is the best player?[7]

Tony would assume that there *must* be an answer to this problem, and he would quickly and efficiently work it out. Lisa might look at the problem and say that it cannot be solved because we cannot assume that the unnamed twin is a member of the foursome.

The irony here is that critical thinking seems to be the loser. By making an unwarranted assumption, Tony is able to come up with an answer. Perhaps the consolation would be if Lisa were to go on to say: "Of course, if we *could* assume that both twins are members of the foursome, the best player would obviously be the daughter."

At this point Harry might repeat a contrast he draws between Tony and Lisa in Chapter Seventeen: "He can show how he proceeds, and you can't." However, Lisa might repeat her reply: "What makes you think I can't?"

I would still choose Lisa.

NOTES

1. Robert Ennis, "A Conception of Critical Thinking—With Some Curriculum Suggestions," in *Newsletter on Teaching Philosophy*, American Philosophical Association, Summer 1987, p. 1.

2. Ibid.

3. E. D. Hirsch, Jr., *Cultural Literacy* (Boston: Houghton Mifflin, 1987), p. 38.

4. Ennis, "A Conception of Critical Thinking," p. 2.

5. Ibid.

6. This problem was inspired by problem no. 5 of the WASI Test in Arthur Whimbey and Jack Lockhead, *Problem Solving and Comprehension*, 3d ed. (Philadelphia: Franklin Institute Press, 1982), p. 4. The WASI problem does not provide 20 as a possible answer, thus making it more likely that 15 will be selected. However, as the discussion above shows, 5 and 10 could be selected, and they are among the WASI choices.

7. Irving Copi, *Informal Logic* (New York: Macmillan, 1986), chapter 1.

11

The Development of Reasoning in Children through Community of Inquiry

John C. Thomas

■ ■ ■

JEAN PIAGET must be counted among the most influential scientists of our time. Were it not for his work, the field of developmental psychology and our understanding of the child would be far different. His theories and his experimental results have inspired a generation of admirers who have attempted to advance the field of study he pioneered. Even those who arrive at a different conception of the child often are able to do so only because of Piaget's contribution to that understanding. Yet his conclusions are not without problems, nor have they gone unchallenged. The Philosophy for Children program is founded upon a concept of the child that in some important ways deviates from the Piagetian view.

This chapter will look at the work of Piaget on children's reasoning and compare it to that of the Philosophy for Children program. The primary reason for doing so is a very pragmatic one. The program is often faced with criticism by "Piagetians," or "constructivists," as they sometimes seem to like to call themselves, on the grounds that it does not take into adequate account the developmental level of the children involved. How can one have a reasoning program for young children when Piaget proved that children are incapable of reasoning until the age of eleven or twelve? No doubt that is a good question. Many practitioners of Philosophy for Children will find it easy to give personal testimony and anecdotal evidence that children do reason at a very early age, but what is wanted is something more. No doubt a confrontation of sorts between Philosophy for Children and Piaget is due. This chapter is intended to be an attempt at that.

There are three points to be considered. First, does Piaget's methodology give us confidence that his conclusions are warranted? In fact, the methodology had serious flaws and would not pass scrutiny for its scientific basis. I will leave this for now, since showing that Piaget's conclusions may not be scientifically warranted is not the same as demonstrating that they are false or inadequate. I think this can be shown by comparing it with a more adequate methodology—namely, that of Philosophy for Children.

Second, what did Piaget actually say about what he called "child logic," and why did he say what he did? Indeed, we discover that he did not think that young children could reason. He apparently came to this conclusion on three grounds:

By the time Piaget began to look at reasoning in children, he had already established that they go through a series of unalterable, biologically fixed developmental stages. It seemed almost impossible for him to recognize counterinstances to his own theory. This led him at times to either ignore instances of child reasoning that did not fit his scheme or fail to follow up on what the children were saying when he had an interpretation of their responses that fit his theory.

Piaget had a very narrow understanding of what constitutes reasoning. For him, reasoning is the recognition of the necessary relationship between the premises and conclusion of a deductive argument. Given this narrow definition, and his reluctance to pursue the responses children made to his questions, it is no wonder that he concluded that they could not reason.

Piaget thought that children were "egocentric" and hence unable to see from outside of their own point of view and their own narrow frame of reference. This naturally made them incapable of assessing premises and conclusions from any other perspective than their own interests. The logical relation between premises and conclusion is, however, independent of circumstances and personal preference. Hence, the naturally egocentric child is incapable of seeing the logical connectedness of things.

The third point to consider is the importance of a direct comparison of Piaget's concepts of the child and of reasoning in the child with those of Philosophy for Children in light of their value for education. Piaget's theory was not explicitly developed for educational purposes, but it has had an enormous impact on educators and hence on curricular matters. Hence, it is imperative that Philosophy for Children, which was specifically developed with an educational agenda in mind, confront Piaget. This discussion is concerned with the last two of these three points.

Young children, in Piaget's interpretation, are rife with contradiction. They can have no sense of one or more propositions leading to another, and they cannot form any consistent idea of a general principle operating in the world. They are at the mercy of the immediate, and reasoning is at best a "logic of action but as yet [not a] logic of thought." Philosophy for Children takes a quite different view. It is able to do this because the program conceives of "reasoning" in a much broader sense than Piaget was willing to do. According to Matthew Lipman, Ann Margaret Sharp, and Frederick S. Oscanyan, logic has three meanings in philosophy for children. It means *formal logic* [à la Piaget], with rules governing sentence structure and connections between sentences, and it also stands for *giving reasons,* which includes seeking and evaluating reasons for something said or done. Finally, logic means *acting rationally,* and concerns standards for reasonable behavior.[1]

Clearly, if not in the first meaning then in the other two, the concept of reasoning, or "logic," described here is a richer one than that of Piaget. Children *give reasons* and for that can be said to have reasoned. If "giving reasons" or "acting rationally" is to have any meaning, it must include the idea that children can think and act with consistency. In other words, to give a reason is not to connect propositions together in an arbitrary and incoherent manner, but to recognize that there is a connection between the propositions given as reasons and the proposition that is supposed to be (logically) connected to them. Of course, children can be mistaken about this connection, just as adults frequently are. That does not mean that they are illogical or irrational or incapable of reasoning any more than it means that for an adult. Children *may* not be so good at giving reasons as adults, but that does not demonstrate that they are not able to reason. It simply means that they make more mistakes than adults. But making mistakes is part of the process of learning. Children will learn to make fewer mistakes if they are engaged in the process of giving reasons. Their development will be one in facility, not in capacity. It is this position that marks out the incompatibility between Philosophy for Children and Piaget. Practitioners of either educational methodology will come to quite different conclusions about what reasoning is and what children are capable of. Piagetians will tend to see reasoning as a late development to be put off until age eleven or twelve. They will also tend to see reasoning, or logic, as the acquisition of a set of skills— reasoning skills, or "thinking skills," as they are popularly called. Philosophy for Children practitioners will tend to see reasoning as a process of thinking possible for even young children. And they will not see reasoning in terms of "thinking skills" but in terms of "being reasonable." What this means will have to be adumbrated in due course.

It might seem at this point that Piaget and Philosophy for Children have no common ground. This would be a mistake. There are at least two fundamental notions that Piaget and Philosophy for Children share, constructivism and the idea of the social origins of reason.

To deal briefly with the first, Philosophy for Children agrees that children construct meanings. They are not given them nor do they discover them already formed within themselves. In other words, Philosophy for Children adheres to neither the Platonic notion of innateness nor the Lockean, empiricist notion of the tabula rasa, or passive mind. Here is one way in which Lipman, Sharp, and Oscanyan express the idea of constructivism:

Meanings cannot be dispensed. They cannot be given or handed out to children. Meanings must be acquired; they are *capta,* not data. We have to learn how to establish the conditions and opportunities that will enable children, with their natural curiosity and appetite for meaning, to seize upon the appropriate clues and make sense of things for themselves. Many teachers will say that they are already doing this, and no doubt they are. But the educational process, from schools of education where teachers themselves are trained on through to the actual school classroom, does not operate in this fashion. Something must be done to enable children to acquire meaning for themselves. They will not acquire such meaning merely by learning the contents of adult knowledge. They must be taught to think and, in particular, to think for themselves. Thinking is the skill *par excellence* that enables us to acquire meanings.[2]

This idea of "thinking for themselves" will be taken up as a crucial notion soon, but notice how the authors claim that meaning is constructed through the process of the child thinking and trying to make sense of things. They say "meanings must be acquired," so they are not innate. But this statement clearly does not indicate that these meanings are acquired by getting them from somewhere else: "Children . . . acquire meanings for themselves." In other words, it is *their* meaning, and they acquire it because, to them, it is *meaningful.*

So far, then, Philosophy for Children and Piaget are in agreement. There is another fundamental idea that they have in common, but it is the difference in how they use it that shows just how their "constructivism" diverges. This common idea is the "social origins of reason." Piaget sets it out at the very beginning of *Judgment and Reasoning in the Child*:

It is chiefly because he feels no need to socialize his thought that the child is so little concerned, or at any rate so very much less concerned than we are, to convince his hearers or to prove his point.

If this be the case, we much expect childish reasoning to differ very considerably from ours, to be less deductive and above all less rigorous.[3]

It is odd that Piaget can say this and yet not recognize the implications that this might have for his experimental results. Indeed, a little later in the same work, he tells us that

the decisive factor in causing a child to become conscious of himself [and therefore capable of reasoning] was contact and above all contrast with the thought of others. Before society has administered these shocks, the child inclines to believe every hypothesis that comes into his head, feeling no need for proof and incapable if he did feel such a need of becoming conscious of the motives which really guided his thought.[4]

It is not surprising that children will not develop a facility for reasoning if they experience no need to do it, but this is true of adults as well. Although adults have learned through experience to internalize the process of social reasoning to a great extent, we have also developed impressive traditions and institutions to capture the utility of reasoning's social aspect. One only has to think of the conferences and symposia occuring throughout the world and the abundance of scholarly and scientific journals. These are not only a means of transmitting information but a testing ground for ideas, forums for entering into dialogue, and communities of inquiry. Piaget sees the importance of the social dimension but fails to see that a community of inquiry, where reasonableness is the standard, is what is missing from the children he labeled as nonlogical. Piaget himself unknowingly makes an eloquent case for Philosophy for Children and its idea of developing communities of inquiry in the classroom: when he says:

> But as soon as thought becomes socialized, a momentous factor comes into play; imitation and assimilation are transformed, solidarity is established between them, and thought becomes increasingly capable of reversibility. For the capacity for leaving one's own point of view and entering into that of other people robs assimilation of its deforming character, and forces it to respect the objectivity of its data. The child will henceforth attempt to weave a network of reciprocal relations between his own point of view and that of others. This *reciprocity* of viewpoints will enable him both to incorporate new phenomena and events into his ego, and to respect their objectivity, *i.e.* the specific characters which they present. Gradually, this same reciprocity of view-points will accustom the child to the reciprocity of relations in general. Henceforth, imitation of reality will find its completion in assimilation of reality by the mind.
>
> Social life, by developing the reciprocity of relations side by side with the consciousness of necessary implications, will therefore remove the antagonistic characters of assimilation and imitation, and render the two processes mutually dependent. Social life therefore helps to make our mental processes reversible, and in this way prepares the path for logical reasoning.[5]

Why did Piaget fail to see the natural implications for community of inquiry in these ideas? The answer to this is complex, too complex to be dealt with in detail here, but there are a couple of points that can be made. First, Piaget seemed to be compelled, whatever subject he studied with children, to make it conform to his stage theory. So it is not surprising that in studying reasoning in the child Piaget found exactly the same fixed structures at work. Second, Piaget's theory of egocentrism led him to discount the idea that children could enter into social relations in a manner that was relevant to the formation of logical thinking, that is, taking the other person's point of view. As children never fully shed this limitation until eleven or twelve years of age (according to Piaget), there is no way they would be able to reason logically before then. Therefore, the community of inquiry is an anomaly at any age before formal operational thinking. The viability of the idea of egocentrism has already been seriously undermined by writers such as Margaret Donaldson in her *Children's*

Minds. Clearly, if Piaget's concept of egocentrism falls, then the community of inquiry makes good educational sense. And this seems to be the way it is.

The idea of the community of inquiry is the cornerstone of Philosophy for Children, and it separates the program's idea of the sociality of reason from that of Piaget. It is not too much to say that it is the most fundamental idea for the entire Philosophy for Children methodology—one might even say that it *is* the methodology. In some ways the idea of "community of inquiry" is analogous to Piaget's notion of "egocentrism," with this difference: For Piaget, "egocentrism" is a means of explaining why children *cannot* do something; in our case, it explains why they cannot reason. "Community of inquiry," on the other hand, is an idea by which Philosophy for Children is able to show what they *can* do—reason, even at the earliest ages.

There is one more piece to fit before the picture comes into clear view. In a properly constituted community of inquiry, three things are present that are not found in Piaget's methodology: the socially constituted situation in which the problem to be considered emerges; the dialectic that forces the movement of thought and is not content with initial utterances; and, finally, the felt *need* to solve the problem. (Piaget would perhaps relate it to the need to establish equilibrium.)

It is because the community of inquiry has this three-fold nature that reasoning and the construction of meaning become conjoined.

It is the sense of the *meaningfulness* of the problem as a *need* that urges one toward the creation of the *meaning* in the situation. Children find meaning where there is meaningfulness. They learn to reason when they have a motive to do so. This is the crux of Donaldson's discovery of the capacity of very young children, perhaps even infants, to "decenter," that is, to escape their egocentric predicament. Donaldson makes this point clearly in reporting on an experiment that runs counter to Piaget's experimental results on egocentrism:

> The point is that the *motives* and *intentions* of the characters [in the experiment] are entirely comprehensible [unlike Piaget's questions], even to a child of three. The task requires the child to act in ways which are in line with certain very basic human purposes and interactions (escape and pursuit)—it makes *human sense*. Thus it is not at all hard to convey to the child what he is supposed to do: he apprehends it instantly. It then turns out that neither is it hard for him to do it. In other words, in this context he shows none of the difficulty in "decentering" which Piaget ascribes to him.[6]

Community of inquiry, as conceived by Philosophy for Children, comprehends five basic elements:

1. Involving the children in the process by starting from their interests (this matches Donaldson's findings).

2. Discussion, talking, and listening (the dialectical and social element in the reasoning process).
3. Giving and expecting reasons for what one says (the process of becoming reasonable through giving reasons).
4. Respecting oneself and others (this is the ethical dimension and is the foundation for acting rationally).
5. Thinking for oneself. This is the essence of what it means to be a reasonable person (in this sense, being reasonable, reasoning, is a concept far above the relatively sterile idea of "thinking skills" and formal logic).

How these are intimately connected with Philosophy for Children in general and community of inquiry in particular should be easy enough to deduce. In order to bring the whole picture together, I will spell out what is embedded in the idea of "thinking for oneself." Up to now, I have made a case for the Philosophy for Children program as a better alternative to a Piagetian approach on the grounds that it provides for the existence and growth of reasoning in children from the earliest ages. The main thrust of this argument has centered on the idea of community of inquiry. But community of inquiry is only half the story. Though it may be good for some reason to "speed up" the process of reasoning, that in itself may not be sufficient grounds to do it. One might argue to the contrary that "children grow up too fast anyway—let them develop naturally." Of course we could point out that we begin teaching them to write long before they can demonstrate anything like calligraphy. We do it because the process of writing itself has valuable educational objectives beyond mere penmanship. So too with reasoning. That is where "thinking for oneself" as a concept comes into play in the Philosophy for Children model for education.

What I propose to do now is to tie together much of what has been said explicitly and implicitly throughout this discussion. To begin with, let me make the following assumption, which I will not try to justify:

A world inhabited by reasonable people is better than one that is not.

What does it mean to be a reasonable person? The answer is implicit in the preceding discussion. Suffice it to say for now that being reasonable means something more than having reasoning skills. Educators who are interested in putting reasoning into the curriculum are making a mistake if they believe that they are teaching reasoning when they are teaching "thinking skills." There is no contradiction in saying that someone can be a very fine logician but not be a reasonable person. Being a reasonable person is a matter of character; in Aristotelian language, we might say that it is a "virtue." One who is reasonable has internalized the practice of reason and adopted it as a fundamental *value* for herself or himself.

Gareth Matthews has shown us the intrinsic value of doing philosophy with children,[7] and this is accepted by the Philosophy for Children program. But the doing of philosophy has another role to play—developing reasonable human beings. If Aristotle was at all near the mark when he defined the human as a *"rational* animal," then, so far as philosophy promotes reason, it is the paragon of the humanities. Minimally, we can say that the development of reasonableness as a matter of character is facilitated by the practice of philosophy.

Matthews has shown, without a shadow of a doubt, that children are natural philosophers. It is part of their impetus to make meaning out of the world. This is something that all children have in common. It is something they will eagerly do if they find the encouragement and the environment for it.

Philosophy provides the center of interest that we have seen to be so vital to the development of reasoning in the child. Furthermore, it is a center of mutual interest among children, and it therefore provides the crucial social dimension of interest we have also seen to be vital for reasoning to happen. Through the mutual exploration of philosophical whimsy (to use Matthews's phrase), children learn not only to enjoy their own playful wonderment about the world but also come to learn the difference between satisfactory and not-so-satisfactory responses to it. What they begin to realize, especially if they are encouraged by a sympathetic adult who is sensitive to the processes of philosophizing, is that the difference between satisfactory and not-so-satisfactory responses is a matter of reasonableness. Hence they will begin to value the reasonableness of thinking—both in themselves and in others. In learning to value it, they learn to think for themselves.

Stubbornly adhering to an idea in spite of good reasons for changing it (not necessarily abandoning it) is not what "thinking for oneself" means: It means to be able to understand why one's idea is a reasonable one to hold and to be able to explain that reasoning to oneself and to others. If one is involved in a community of inquiry, then thinking for oneself will be a characteristic shared by all its members (at least the community will be working in that direction). It follows that thinking for oneself in a community of inquiry necessarily leads to the understanding that others may have different ideas but may have good reasons for maintaining them. The give-and-take of the community of inquiry leads to a dialectical spiral in which each individual comes to construct a more coherent meaning out of his or her wonderment at the world. In encountering the diversity of thought to which reasoned thinking can lead, the child comes to see the members of the community of inquiry (which may include adults) as equals in the business of constructing meanings. Thus children are led inexorably to develop an environment of mutual respect. This is the true meaning of thinking for oneself. Its outcome is people who value and respect themselves and others. Put differently, the community of inquiry is fundamentally an *ethical* community, one founded not upon rights but upon respect for persons (including oneself). With this respect comes the capacity for "thinking for oneself."

If the creation of such individuals is a worthwhile educational goal, if education should bring us closer to the ideal of a world inhabited by reasonable people, then we cannot afford not to believe that children can reason. If reasonableness is to enter into the character of our people, we must begin by developing the habits of reasoning, the respect for reasoning, and the value of reasoning in the youngest child. It is that vision that the Piagetian model cannot support and that the Philosophy for Children model takes as its foundation.

NOTES

1. Matthew Lipman, Ann Margaret Sharp, and Frederick S. Oscanyan, *Philosophy in the Classroom*, 2d ed. (Philadelphia: Temple University Press, 1980), p. 131.

2. Lipman, Sharp, and Oscanyan, p. 13.

3. Jean Piaget, *Judgment and Reasoning in the Child* (London, 1928; reprint, Totowa, N.J.: Littlefield, Adams, 1976), p. 1.

4. Ibid., p. 24.

5. Ibid., p. 180.

6. Margaret Donaldson, *Children's Minds* (New York: Norton, 1979).

7. See Gareth Matthews, *Philosophy and the Young Child* (Cambridge, Mass.: Harvard University Press, 1980).

PART FOUR

Logical Issues

Logic, in particular formal, Aristotelian logic, serves as the backbone of Harry Stottlemeier's Discovery. *Laurance J. Splitter, in "A Guided Tour of the Logic in* Harry Stottlemeier's Discovery," *takes the reader through the seventeen chapters of the novel, showing how the logic evolves from a beginning in conversion to the development of categorical and hypothetical syllogisms. Splitter provides a justification for the choice of Aristotelian logic over others. In addition, he looks at the development of a good deal of the informal logic that occurs throughout the novel.*

In "Standardization," Clive Lindop examines the assumed (assumed by the children in Harry) equivalence of six expressions—"each," "every," "any," "a," "if–then," and no modifier at all—with the quantifier "all" and shows, arguing from Zeno Vendler's Linguistics in Philosophy, *that, at least in some cases, the equivalence is merely apparent. By focusing on the problems of translation in standardization, Lindop prepares the novice practitioner for the sorts of novel examples and counterexamples young children are prone to give as they go about the business of standardization. Indeed, standardization provides a model of how the translation process can be rule governed. This fits in with the premise of Philosophy for Children—translation skills are as important as concept-formation skills.*

Lindop's chapter "Relationships" offers an admittedly problematic definition of "relationship" and then explains the traditional characterizations of the term: symmetrical, asymmetrical, and nonsymmetrical; and transitive, intransitive, and nontransitive. Lindop carries his discussion backward to the problem of conversion, which is the opening one of Harry Stottlemeier's Discovery, *and forward to the formation of the syllogism. By spotlighting relationships, Lindop calls our attention to a fundamental aspect of the Philosophy for Children approach that emphasizes the relationship that holds among things.*

Philip C. Guin offers this conclusion from Charles Glock and his colleagues' epochal study, Adolescent Prejudice: *"Prejudice is nurtured especially among youths who have not developed the cognitive skills and sophistication to combat it." Guin, in "Countering Prejudice with Counterexamples," then goes on to show how the development of certain skills and sophistication, in this case sensitivity to the rule of contradiction, can aid in the growth of tolerance and concern for other persons. He argues that the community of inquiry is best suited to this kind of development.*

12

A Guided Tour of the Logic in Harry Stottlemeier's Discovery

Laurance J. Splitter

■ ■ ■

(These comments are intended as a companion to "Minimal Re-
quirements for Thinking Skill Instruction via *Harry Stottlemeier's
Discovery*" and to *Philosophical Inquiry: Manual to Accompany* Harry
Stottlemeier's Discovery. References to the novel are indicated with
N, those to the manual with *M.*)

LOGIC FORMS the backbone of the *Harry* syllabus, although it is by no means
the only philosophical theme that arises there. However, the logical discoveries—exemplified by the persistence and single-mindedness of the central character, Harry—constitute a recurring theme that weaves its way through the
overall story, and thereby into the thought and talk of the classroom community
of inquiry. For it is logic that holds our thinking together—the rules and principles of logic provide criteria for distinguishing better thinking from worse. It
is logic in language that makes reasoning possible.

The contextual approach to the teaching of logic, as illustrated in the *Harry*
syllabus, deserves further comment. It is deplorable but undeniable that the
systematic teaching of thinking and reasoning in schools has been conspicu-
ous by its absence. No doubt one part of the explanation for this sad state of
affairs (sad when one reflects on the potential of such teaching to provide students with a range of indispensable intellectual skills) lies in the inadequacies
of teacher education and the subsequent lack of teacher expertise. At all grade
levels, teachers have traditionally been more concerned with surface errors in
spelling and punctuation than with more profound errors of reasoning.

Some educators have defended the lack of specific logic programs in the
school curriculum on the ground that logic in isolation is too dry and abstract
to engage the interests of children. Better, they say, to teach logical thinking

within the context of traditional disciplines. There is some merit in this position. Nevertheless, teachers who are tempted to take such a line of retreat should ask themselves why traditional school subjects have failed to prepare students in the areas of reasoning and inquiry skills. Perhaps they will find an answer in the propensity of these subjects to *assume* rather than teach these skills. As it turns out, the traditional discipline of philosophy provides an eminently suitable context for teaching elementary logic to children.

A word of caution to teachers of *Harry*. The novel and manual (together with other activities and strategies that teachers may wish to incorporate) help to provide a rich context for the logical principles and ideas about to be described. It follows that this guide is *not,* in and of itself, a substitute or short-cut approach to the syllabus.

The logic in *Harry* is known as traditional, or Aristotelian logic because it leads up to, and focuses on, the syllogism. What follows is a rough step-by-step guide to this system of logic as it develops in the syllabus.

Traditional logic is not the only system of logical principles, and many philosophy departments prefer to teach alternatives that are richer in both syntax and semantics. But traditional logic has one special feature that should make it attractive to teachers and children: It is couched in ordinary language and does not involve symbols or other technical apparatus. In *Harry*, the development of the logical rules is intended to complement the growth of cognitive skills in children of from ten to thirteen years of age. Philosophy for Children does not subscribe to the view that logic—which involves abstract reasoning (as does philosophy generally)—is beyond the reach of the young. But it does seek to avoid imposing adult frameworks on children or confronting them with logical systems beyond their capacities.

[*Notes:*

1. In the interests of continuity and clarity, discussion of a number of logic-related topics that arise in the *Harry* syllabus has been abbreviated in these notes when I felt that such topics did not bear directly on the system of syllogistic logic being developed. Nearly every chapter contains some treatment of induction, concept formation, detecting sound reasons, using the mind to "figure things out," and the like. The absence of detailed discussion in regard to these issues is based on pragmatic considerations and should not be taken to imply that the tools of good thinking are purely deductive or syllogistic.

2. Each chapter in the manual ends with some suggested answers and guidelines, as well as some questions aimed at self-evaluation. Teachers should not ignore these, but they are free to disagree with the answers given. Of course, many philosophical questions are open ended and do not admit of clear answers.

3. One philosophically central topic that recurs throughout all the novels in the Philosophy for Children syllabus is the idea of treating one another as *persons* and not as things or objects (in *Harry*, see N11–12, 24, 31–33, Ch. 9, 53–55,

60–61, 69–74, and Ch. 17; M35–36, 60–65, 132–34, 169, 177–79, 229–31, 278–80, 291, 298–99, 316–17, 365–73, and 437–44). This idea is a crucial aspect of personal development and self-esteem, and teachers should take every opportunity to discuss it carefully with their students.]

CHAPTER ONE

This section considers the basic logical structure of sentences beginning with "all" and "no" (N2–4; M11–12):

ALL [noun phrase] ARE [noun phrase], and
NO [noun phrase] ARE [noun phrase].

Obviously, few sentences in ordinary English are naturally expressed in this way, but we can encourage students to treat this procedure as a game. Take an ordinary English sentence and see if it can be paraphrased in one of the above forms (called "standard form"). Sometimes the paraphrase will involve some loss of meaning, but students can judge this for themselves.

In logic, the noun phrase before "are" is called the *subject term,* and the one after "are" is called the *predicate term.* This terminology does not quite fit what some of us once learned in grammar classes, but it has the advantage of isolating the verb "are."

Harry's discovery (it is a discovery from his point of view) is that sentences with the above logical form (i.e., sentences with "two kinds of things" in them, as Harry puts it) cannot be reversed; or, rather, they can be reversed, but if the original is true the reversed sentence is false (N2–4; M12–16).

[*Notes:*

1. "Reversing" a sentence in this context means exchanging the subject term with the predicate term.
2. Reversing only works when sentences are in standard form. So, for example, Harry's original example involving planets has to be paraphrased before reversing. Students may take some time to appreciate this; let them discover it in their own way. Alternatively, we might point out that in order to play the logic game by the rules "All planets revolve around the sun" has to be paraphrased as "All planets are things that revolve around the sun" (the word *things* introduces a dummy noun phrase without changing the meaning).

   No doubt some children will try and reverse the original sentence to obtain something like "All suns revolve around the planet." The class may sense that this is a fairly strange sentence—it is not clear what it means, let alone whether it is true or false. Rather than make a dogmatic ruling here, teachers might suggest that the class put this example aside for the time being and come back to it after considering other kinds of sentences (like "All dogs bark").
3. The rule that Harry initially gets so excited about does not always work: Some sentences starting with "all" can be reversed (M14; teachers need not worry

if no one thinks of this, but in fact many children do). More important, all sentences beginning with "no" can be truly reversed: If As and Bs do not overlap, then neither do Bs and As. No one in the story discovers the first kind of exception, but Lisa guides Harry to the second when she gives him the example "No eagles are lions."

4. The issue of truth is immensely important in language, reasoning, and, more broadly, in our dealings with one another. It arises in Chapter One because Harry implicitly chooses sentences that are true to begin with in order to test what happens to their truth value when they are reversed. (In fact, depending on the sentence chosen, the reversal may remain true, but in most cases it is false.) Logic is very much concerned with the preservation of truth. In other words, in building up a collection of logical rules, we are interested in finding out which kinds of linguistic alterations or inferences preserve truth and which kinds do not. But this means that we should begin with true sentences rather than false ones. Or—and this is a better way of making the point—when playing the logic game, we pretend that our starting sentences are true, even if they are not.

5. Throughout the novel, situations arise in which Harry and his friends are able to apply the logical rules that they are discovering (see, for instance, N4, 8, 13–14; M16, 34). Drawing the attention of students to such practical applications and encouraging them to come up with their own helps them relate rules of thinking to their experiences outside the classroom.]

CHAPTER TWO

This chapter provides further practice in paraphrasing sentences into standard form. The children in the novel discover that a number of words or modifiers are more or less synonymous with "all"; for example, "each," "every," and "any." (They are not strictly synonymous: Look at "all/each/every one/any of you may now step forward to receive an award." "Each" suggests one at a time, and the meaning of "any" depends very much on context.) More puzzling for some children are the words *a* and *the,* which may have either a singular or a plural sense, depending on the context.

[*Note:* Rather than talking about whether certain words ("all," "each," "every," etc.) are synonymous, it makes more sense to talk about whether the sentences containing these words (in this case, the standard-form sentences) are synonymous.]

The familiar modifier "only" has some curious logical properties. Basically, "only" effectively reverses an "all" sentence. Thus: "Only those who work hard are eligible for promotion" may be restated as "All those eligible for promotion are hard workers" (M31–32b; see also M416).

There are also various kinds of sentences that can be expressed in the form "No . . . ," using such words as "never," "none," and "not any."

CHAPTER THREE

The nature of thoughts and thinking (a recurring topic) is considered here—hence inferring, reasoning, "figuring things out" (N10; M48–51). Induction and faulty reasoning ("jumping to conclusions") are also discussed (N11; M60–62). Induction is treated in more detail in later chapters, especially Chapter Five.

The main point of Lisa's image involving the catlike animals (N12; M66–69) is that in fantasy we can break the rules of logic and reason. In her dream, the sentence "All cats are animals" can be truly reversed (although some students deny that zebras and giraffes can be cats, even in a dream). The power of imaginative thinking is an important educational tool, but it is vital that children understand that fantasy and reality are different and should not be confused with one another. (See also M433 and Lisa's views at N95.)

Tony and his father discover a geometrical reason for Harry's rule of reversibility (N13–14; M70–72). "All jim-jams are mungos" can be represented as two circles, the class of jim-jams inside (or maybe coinciding with) the class of mungos. Incidentally, the other standard-form sentences can also be represented using class-membership diagrams. Those students who are more adventurous, artistic, or mathematically inclined might like to explore this topic. The diagrams bring out the connection between our standard-form representations and the general subject of classification (M70).

CHAPTER FOUR

This chapter looks at ambiguity and vagueness (M87–89) and introduces the quantifier "Some" (N17–20; M93–96). Thus we end up with four kinds of logical sentences (N19):

All . . . are . . .
No . . . are . . .
Some . . . are . . .
Some . . . are not . . .

[*Notes:* Working out how these four types of sentences are logically related is fairly complex, but, depending on the interests and abilities of the students, this can be an exercise. Suppose we take a true sentence starting with "All." Will the corresponding "No," "Some . . . are," and "Some . . . are not" sentences be true or false? (See also Chapter Twelve.)

In ordinary English "some" usually refers to an amount between "none" and "all." So, for example, "one apple," "a few apples," and "most apples" all standardize as "some apples," and "all apples" is compatible with "some apples," as the manual points out (p. 93—it is worth reading through these explanatory sections). If you specifically want to rule out "all," use two sentences: For example, "Nearly all the students in the room are Australian" would be paraphrased as "Some students in the room are not Australian." Obviously, there is some loss of meaning here, but in the paraphrase we have only used the standard-form sentences.

The Standardization Chart on M94 provides good practice for teachers and students.]

CHAPTER FIVE

The logic briefly explored here is inductive logic, which (although the manual does not make this clear) includes both generalization and analogical reasoning (N21–22; M111–21, see also M266–67). Until this point, the logical system we have been working with has been deductive logic. When we reason inductively, we are allowing for the possibility that the conclusion might not be true, even though we are accepting the premises as true; in deductive reasoning, this possibility is excluded.

The basic problem of induction arises in situations where we simply cannot observe all the possible cases—we are forced to judge that the objects we cannot see are going to be similar in relevant respects to those we can observe. Even though induction is less "certain" than deduction it is just as indispensable to our ordinary ways of thinking. As David Hume pointed out, our most mundane actions and beliefs depend totally on inductive processes. For example, I eat a sandwich for lunch in the belief that it will nourish but not poison me. This belief—which is about a future and hence undetermined event—is based on all past experiences of sandwich eating. The implicit inductive reasoning goes something like this: "Whenever I have eaten a sandwich in the past, it has nourished me, so it is likely that it will do so in the future." (The use of polls to test public opinion is a good practical example of inductive thinking.)

In the novel, Harry realizes that a sample of brown chocolate does not fix the color of the unseen chocolates. Maria is wrong to insist that if some are . . . , then some are not. . . . Consider another example. As a visitor to a school, I see a group of children in the playground behaving badly (suppose these are the only students I see). I can say "Some students are hooligans," leaving it open as to whether "All students in this school are hooligans."

Of course it would be equally wrong to infer from "Some are" that "All are." I may have witnessed the behavior of a small group who are not at all representative of the whole school population.

To sum up: We cannot make any sound inference from "Some are" to "All are," or from "Some are" to "Some are not." To make the first move is to commit the fallacy of false generalization, whereas the second involves what might be called the fallacy of false exclusion.

The difference between inductive and deductive reasoning becomes clearer when syllogisms are introduced. Syllogisms are examples of deductive reasoning because they involve inferences that are meant to be absolutely certain.

CHAPTER SIX

The main topic here is the nature of the mind, and the manual contains some interesting exercises plus a section for teachers on different theories of the mind (M150–51). The exercises on detecting assumptions in a Logic Review (M157–59) are tricky and should be examined and discussed by teachers beforehand. The topic is important, though, because many errors in reasoning occur through a failure to detect dubious assumptions.

CHAPTER SEVEN

The subject is differences of degree versus differences of kind (N31–32; M173–80). The discussion of this topic is important partly because children need to understand this difference (even if it is hard to define exactly) and partly because it leads into the topic of relationships.

By becoming familiar with the many words in ordinary language that express relationships, children will be better prepared to look at some logical rules involving this topic of relations and relationships, and, later on, at the nature of syllogisms (Chapter Eight).

The notion of "turn-around" (or symmetric) relationships is discussed in this chapter (N33–34; M181–84). Most relationships can be classified as follows (M183):

1. the sentence expressing the relationship remains true when turned around (e.g., "Jeff *is the same height as* Joan"),
2. the sentence always becomes false when turned around (e.g., "Joan *is the mother of* Jeff"), and
3. the turned-around sentence may be true or false depending on the circumstances (e.g., "Jeff *is fond of* Joan").

Students should be encouraged to explore why some relationships are type 1, others type 2, and still others type 3.

CHAPTER EIGHT

After further discussion of turn-around relationships (N38), Harry discovers that certain relationships "carry over" (N39–40; M207–13: these are sometimes called transitive relationships). In brief, this means that where A relates to B and B relates to C, then A relates to C. Relationships of degree (taller than, faster than, warmer than, etc.) usually carry over. They are examples of type 1 relationships. As before, others may be type 2 (never carry over) or type 3 (sometimes do and sometimes do not—one cannot tell just from the relationship itself).

[*Note:* Relationships that turn around or carry over in particular circumstances may nevertheless be type 3, rather than type 1. If four people are all fond of each other, the relationship "fond of" will turn around and carry over as long as we restrict it to these four people. But we can easily imagine applying this relationship in circumstances where it does not turn around or carry over. So it is a type 3 relationship in both cases.]

Type 1 carryover relationships give us the basic pattern for the syllogism. Notice that the "middle term"—*B* above—drops out in the final sentence, but it occurs once in the first sentence and once in the second. So overall, each term (*A, B, C*) is mentioned twice (see Chapter Fourteen for more detailed discussion of the middle term "dropping out").

If we think of the word "are" as expressing a relationship, namely, "belongs to the class of," then we can construct arrangements of sentences that have the following pattern:

All *A*s are *B*s.
All *B*s are *C*s.
Therefore, all *A*s are *C*s.

The horizontal line means that from the first two sentences (called "premises") taken together (and assumed to be true) we can infer the third (called the "conclusion"). An *argument* can be defined as a collection of premises leading to a conclusion. Arguments that fit the above pattern are called *syllogisms*. And because the inference or reasoning will always be correct when this particular pattern is present, these syllogisms are described as *valid*. Teachers should go through M211–13 very carefully before discussing this topic in class. And they should encourage students to come up with their own examples.

[*Notes:*

1. The concept of validity is so fundamental in deductive logic that it defies straightforward definition. Validity is that feature of arguments that makes them "work," logically speaking. It describes the connection between premises and conclusion that permits us to infer the latter from the former. And it is tied to the concept of truth, as the following definition brings out: An argument is valid if, and only if, whenever we assume or pretend that the premises are true the conclusion *must* thereby be true. The importance of "must" here should be clear from the following (obviously invalid) example:
      All spaniels are dogs.
      All cats are mammals.
      Therefore, all apples are fruits.
   Here, the premises and conclusion all happen to be true. But we can imagine a situation in which the premises remain true and the conclusion becomes

false (for instance, that apples are a kind of reptile), and this confirms that the argument is not valid.

Whereas logical inference is fundamentally concerned with the preservation of *truth,* it is—at this introductory level at least—not concerned with the preservation of *meaning.* (So inferring is not the same as translating.) Later on (N75–76), the children realize that drawing a conclusion from premises is not like equating numbers in arithmetic: The conclusion follows from the premises, but it does not (usually) have the same meaning.

2. The particular pattern discussed in *Harry* is only one kind of valid syllogism. Remember that there are three other kinds of standard-form sentences ("No *A*s are *B*s," "Some *A*s are *B*s," and "Some *A*s are not *B*s"), and these can all be combined to yield syllogisms, some valid and some invalid. But this is a topic for more advanced study (although some students may bring it up, and, if they do, they should be encouraged to explore it). Most textbooks on logic will contain a more detailed treatment of syllogistic (or traditional) logic.]

CHAPTERS NINE, TEN, AND ELEVEN

These chapters contain no further development of our logical system, but they highlight the importance of thinking logically and clearly—especially when the situation is one in which emotions run high. We can examine the reasons we offer for our beliefs and actions and realize that some reasons are much better than others (M253–58). Examples of "bad reasoning" that come up in these chapters include: reasoning based on majority opinion (N44; M236–37); reasoning based on appeals to alarm or fear (N49; M259–60); and reasoning based on appeals to authority (N49; M261–62).

Further examples of fallacious reasoning include: personal ("ad hominem") attack, equivocation (exploiting ambiguous terms), appeals to pity or emotion, begging the question (circular reasoning), ignoring the point at issue, and assuming that wholes are always just the sums of their parts and vice versa (see also N66; M329–31).

These chapters present an opportunity for teachers to help their students develop a sensitivity to different forms of fallacious reasoning. Regrettably, these notes are not adequate in helping teachers develop the same sensitivity. Most introductory logic textbooks contain a discussion of fallacious reasoning (refer to sections under "informal fallacies").

CHAPTER TWELVE

The concept of contradiction is the main topic here, although the novel contains a brief discussion of sentence reversal, this time involving sentences beginning with "Some" (N58). It turns out that "Some . . . are . . ." sentences (like "No . . . are . . .") remain true when reversed, but "Some . . . are not . . ." sentences (like "All . . . are . . .") do not necessarily remain true.

On to contradiction (N58–62; M306–12). Intuitively, to contradict is to assert the opposite, or the negation, of something. To contradict a simple sentence like "Fred is fat," we can say "Fred is not fat." If a sentence is true, then its contradictory must be false, and vice versa.

[*Note:* The sentence used in the previous paragraph is not a standard-form sentence and, as such, does not really belong to our system of logic. However, as the manual points out (M308), any coherent sentence can be contradicted by another sentence, which we call its opposite, or negation.]

Now consider our four logical sentences involving quantifiers and noun phrases. To deny or negate "All pirates are criminals," it is not necessary to assert that "No pirates are criminals." Rather, we can say that at least one pirate is not a criminal—"Some pirates are not criminals." So this last sentence is the genuine contradictory of the original. The point is that it only takes one exception to falsify an "All" sentence.

Similarly, to deny "No pirates are criminals" is to assert that at least one is—"Some pirates are criminals." Similar reasoning reveals that the contradictory sentences for "Some pirates are criminals" and "Some pirates are not criminals" are "No pirates are criminals" and "All pirates are criminals," respectively. This should become clearer if one thinks carefully about the logical meaning of "some" and if one looks at a few examples. The situation is summarized at N59 (see also M307). Notice that the episode involving Luther and his bike (N61–62) illustrates the idea of contradicting an "All" sentence. "All cars stop at the intersection" is contradicted by "Some cars don't stop at the intersection," as Luther found out when just one car did not stop.

The novel (p. 60) introduces the traditional abbreviations or nicknames for our four types of sentences: $A, E, I,$ and O (see M312). So, in summary, A and O contradict each other, as do E and I.

[*Note:* Some students (and teachers) will insist that the contradictory of "All pirates are criminals" (A) is indeed "No pirates are criminals" (E); they will hold the same position for "Some pirates are criminals" (I) and "Some pirates are not criminals" (O).

The following observations might clarify this issue. If an A sentence is true, then the corresponding E sentence must be false. But if an A sentence is false, the corresponding E sentence *may not be true* (so A and E are not genuine contradictories, because genuine contradictories could never both be false at the same time). Also, if an I sentence is false, the corresponding O sentence must be true. But if an I sentence is true, the corresponding O sentence *may not be false* (so I and O are not genuine contradictories, because genuine contradictories could never both be true at the same time).]

As the manual points out (p. 306), it is important that students grow up with some understanding of contradiction, if only so that they can strive to avoid contradictions (and hence be consistent) in their reasoning.

CHAPTER THIRTEEN

Although there is no further development of the logical system, this chapter explores some key logical concepts that teachers and students should find interesting. These include causes and beginnings (N64–66; M328–29), parts and wholes and fallacious reasoning involving these (N66; M329–31), and possibility (the difference between possibility and truth and the "four possibilities": N66–68; M332–40).

[*Note:* As the manual points out, the notion of possibility is central to the ideology of Philosophy for Children. Philosophy itself is as concerned with what is possible as it is with what is true. Many wonderful and exciting ideas can spring from considering what might be (or might have been) true. By encouraging children to explore the realm of the possible, we are urging them to examine the very boundaries of thought (including the notion that some things are genuinely impossible or self-contradictory). To borrow from the manual (p. 332), "The idea of possibility can be truly liberating."

Teachers should make use of the logic reviews (M345–49) for themselves and their students.]

CHAPTER FOURTEEN

The first part of this chapter (N69–73; M354–75) is one of the richest sections in the Philosophy for Children syllabus. It has a number of themes relating to aesthetics, ethics, and personal growth.

The development of syllogisms continues at page 74 of the novel (M376) with the principle that in a valid syllogism the middle term (i.e., the one mentioned twice in the premises) "drops out" of the conclusion. Further, the subject term in the conclusion is also the subject term in one of the premises and that the predicate term in the conclusion is the predicate term in the other premise (N75–78; M376–80). One point of caution: In the examples raised on N75–76, the premises are swapped (as compared with the examples from Chapter Eight). This makes no logical difference but may cause some initial confusion.

One other issue raised in this chapter concerns another kind of fallacious reasoning: When one constructs a syllogism that does not have the pattern described in the previous paragraph, it may *not* be valid (in the language of the manual, pp. 378–79, it is not a *reliable* arrangement). This means that in a real-life example, the conclusion may not be true even though both premises are true (N76–77; M378–79). Here is an example:

    (a) All funnel-web spiders are poisonous. (True)
        All tiger snakes are poisonous. (True)
        Therefore, all funnel-web spiders are tiger snakes. (False)

Notice that in this example the middle term ("poisonous," or "poisonous things") does drop out of the conclusion, but the argument is not valid because in the premises this term occurs in the predicate position twice (it would also be invalid if, in the premises, the middle term occurred in the subject position twice). In a valid syllogism, the middle term appears *diagonally* in the premises and then drops out of the conclusion.

[*Note:* The following syllogisms are also invalid. Can you see why?

(b) All computers are machines.
All machines are breakable (things).
Therefore, all breakable things are computers.

(c) All Fords are automobiles.
All vehicles are machines.
Therefore, all Fords are machines. (from M377)]

There is another important development on these pages. Unreliable (i.e., invalid) reasoning arrangements can have true premises and a true conclusion. Recall this example from earlier on in these notes:

(d) All spaniels are dogs.
All cats are mammals.
Therefore, all apples are fruits.

If anyone is bothered that (d) has too many terms to be thought a plausible argument, consider another example:

(e) All dogs are animals.
All mammals are animals.
Therefore, all dogs are mammals.

This argument is not valid either, yet it has true premises and a true conclusion. So validity is not the same as truth—recall the "definition" of validity that was suggested earlier:

An argument is valid if, and only if, whenever we assume or pretend that the premises are true the conclusion *must* thereby be true.

In (e), as in (c) and (d), the conclusion happens to be true, but its truth is not entailed or brought about by the truth of the premises. Observe what happens to (e) if one makes a simple change, substituting "snakes" for "dogs":

(f) All snakes are animals.
All mammals are animals.
Therefore, all snakes are mammals.

Syllogisms (e) and (f) are so similar in shape or form that one would expect them to be either both valid or both invalid. But (f) is clearly invalid because it has true premises and a false conclusion. So, by this reasoning, which relies on an analogy, (e) is invalid as well.

What we are beginning to discover here is that the logical value of an argument (i.e., its validity or invalidity) depends not on the actual terms or words used, but on the structure, pattern, or form of the argument. Here is one argument structure:

(g) All *A*s are *B*s.
All *C*s are *B*s.
Therefore, all *A*s are *C*s.

We can see that this is the "skeleton" of arguments (a), (e), and (f) above. Because it is an invalid form, we can expect that all arguments that have this structure will themselves be invalid.

I have mentioned that (f) is clearly invalid because it has true premises and a false conclusion. After all, logic is about preserving truth through reasoned argument (inference). So in a valid syllogism the combination of true premises and false conclusion is impossible, for otherwise we could logically pass from truth to falsehood—and that is the one move that logic must exclude.

At N77–78; M379–80, one finds a practical application of the novel's discovery concerning reliable or valid syllogisms and further examples of arguments that have the shape of (g) above. Such practical uses of the rules of reasoning should help students to appreciate the value of logical thinking. On the other hand, as the manual points out, topics such as those discussed in this chapter may be beyond the comprehension of some students (M376, 378). It is the teacher's responsibility to help students decide whether to explore an issue further or defer it (this topic is taken up in the *Lisa* manual), or even dropping it altogether. In the United States, *Harry* is part of the grade-five syllabus; in Australia, it is usually not begun before grade six.

Exercise: Using (g) as a guide—
1. find other invalid forms for syllogisms; and
2. find the one form (involving sentences beginning with "all") that is valid.

CHAPTER FIFTEEN

Again, there is no further development of the logical system, but this chapter contains some interesting conceptual material. Its main subject is causality and related concepts (action, explanation, description, and reasons). These themes are central to the philosophy of science, and part of the chapter is taken up with examples from science class. Not all, though: Harry's discussion with his father on "what comes first," and his own reflections about causes and effects, are models of philosophical activities that do not depend on science or the teacher.

The distinctions that feature in this chapter are important and (once one starts to think about them) puzzling: laws that describe versus laws that prescribe (N81; M393), causes versus effects (the entire chapter in the novel and manual, but especially M394–401), explanations versus descriptions (N81–82; M402–3), and causes versus reasons (N83; M404–5). Science teachers should find much in this chapter to stimulate them and their students. Indeed, science courses that are so content oriented as to discourage children from puzzling over these issues are largely responsible for the distorted view of science that prevails in the general community.

CHAPTER SIXTEEN

In this chapter, the pattern of the syllogism is extended to what is called hypothetical (or conditional) reasoning, that is, to arguments in which one (or both) of the premises is hypothetical. A hypothetical statement is one that has the form "If . . ., then . . .," where the gaps are to be filled in by ordinary statements that are either true or false (N84–89, M414–19). The logical term "if–then" is a very important tool in reasoning, and this brief discussion gives an indication of its power. In the novel, the rules for hypothetical arguments develop, almost inevitably, as a result of the children reflecting on their own and their friends' experiences.

In order to understand the nature of hypothetical reasoning, it is important to realize that in a single hypothetical statement there are actually three statements to consider (M414):

1. the one that occurs after "if" and before "then" (the antecedent),
2. the one that occurs after "then" (the consequent), and
3. the whole hypothetical statement.

[*Note:* In ordinary English, we often replace the word "then" with a comma. Also (and this can be misleading) we often reverse the order of antecedent and consequent. For example, the statement "You will pass the exam if you work hard" is equivalent to "If you work hard, then you will pass the exam." The moral here is always to write the hypothetical statement in its standard form before using it in arguments. (This reminds us of the distinction between "if" and "only if." See M32–32b, 416.)]

In hypothetical reasoning, we usually begin with the assumption that the hypothetical statement itself is true. So, we can take it as our first premise. The second premise can be any one of four statements, according to the following possibilities:

(i) antecedent true,
(ii) antecedent false,

To borrow an example from the manual, let us take as our first premise a hypothetical statement which we shall assume always to be true. If the Australians are winning, then the New Zealanders are close behind. There are four possibilities, according to (i) through (iv) above:

(i) If the Australians are winning, then the New Zealanders are close behind.
The Australians are winning.
Therefore, the New Zealanders are close behind.

This is the basic form of hypothetical reasoning: When the antecedent of a true hypothetical statement is true, we may validly infer the (truth of) the consequent (compare the "Monday" case on N86). This rule is so basic that it is hard to justify, except to insist that it cannot be doubted by anyone who understands the English expression "If . . . , then . . .".

What of the other three possibilities?

(ii) If the Australians are winning, then the New Zealanders are close behind.
The Australians are not winning.
Therefore, the New Zealanders are not close behind.

This inference is fallacious: The New Zealanders might still be close behind even though the Australians are not winning. Moreover, this scenario is quite consistent with the truth of the first premise (compare the "Tuesday" case on N86). In other words, when the antecedent of a true hypothetical statement is false, we can make no valid inference as to the truth or falsity of the consequent.

[*Note:* The second premise is true because it is the *negation* of the antecedent which is assumed to be false.]

(iii) If the Australians are winning, then the New Zealanders are close behind.
The New Zealanders are close behind.
Therefore, the Australians are winning.

This inference is also fallacious: The Australians might not be winning even though the New Zealanders are close behind. This scenario, as we have already observed, is consistent with the truth of the first premise (compare the "Wednesday" case on N86). In other words, when the consequent of a true hypothetical statement is true, we can make no valid inference as to the truth or falsity of the antecedent.

(iv) If the Australians are winning, then the New Zealanders are close behind.
The New Zealanders are not close behind.
Therefore, the Australians are not winning.

Just as (ii) and (iii) are invalid for the same reason, so (i) and (iv) are valid. When the consequent of a true hypothetical statement is false, we may validly infer that the antecedent is false (in other words, that the negation of the antecedent is true—compare the "Thursday" case in N86). To see that (iv) is valid, let us first agree that (i) is a reliable form of reasoning. Then, if the conclusion in (iv) were false, it must be true that the Australians *are* winning. But this step takes us back to argument (i), from which we may validly infer that the New Zealanders are close behind. However, this statement directly contradicts the second premise of (iv), which we have assumed to be true. So the conclusion in (iv) must follow and thus (iv) is reliable (valid).

[*Note:* The pattern of reasoning employed in the previous few lines is very close to the hypothetical pattern that we have just been discussing! In fact, hypothetical reasoning comes naturally to most of us: We do it all the time without being aware of it. Unfortunately, some of us also employ invalid forms of reasoning just as naturally, and this is one reason a critical examination of our thinking patterns is so valuable.]

The manual observes (M415) that when we affirm the truth of a hypothetical statement we do not thereby affirm the truth of either the antecedent or the consequent. Indeed, we commonly use hypothetical statements when we know that the antecedent is false ("If the moon were made of green cheese, then . . ."—a counterfactual statement) or when we have no idea whether it is true or not ("If you get caught, then . . ."). Such statements invite us to explore possibilities and imaginary situations that are still logical, even if not actually true. (This reminds us of Lisa's claim that Harry's rules do not apply when we are imagining or dreaming. See N12, N95; M66–69, M433.)

The two valid and two invalid patterns involving hypothetical statements are examined at length in both novel and manual. Teachers may need to look at a number of examples and discuss the topic with others before all these patterns become familiar. Hypothetical reasoning is not an easy topic, and teachers will have to gauge whether or not to emphasize it in class. As always, we should be guided not so much by what we understand (or do not understand) as by what our students do or would find interesting or puzzling.

HUNCHES AND HYPOTHESES

It is no easy matter to give precise definitions of imprecise concepts. A hunch is a kind of guess, but one supported by "a certain feeling" (N85, 90; M413). Hypotheses, on the other hand, come into their own when we are faced with a problem for which no clear solution presents itself. To put forward a hypothesis is to propose a possible solution or way of understanding the problem (N90; M420–21, 424–25; and recall Chapter One). Hypotheses purport to explain, and the best hypothesis (when more than one is available) is the one that explains best. But what does "explains best" mean? A hard question to answer, and one that threatens to take us too far afield. One answer is that the best hypothesis is the one that survives after all the others have been discarded. The illustration offered below should cast some light on this idea.

It is important for students to appreciate that the skill of proposing and then testing hypotheses is a fundamental feature of our lives because we are creatures who learn through experience (put another way: This skill allows us to perform certain kinds of inductive procedures). Scientists propose and test hypotheses in their attempts to comprehend natural phenomena, but this technique is just as much a tool of trade for historians, psychologists, linguists, politicians, philosophers, and others. Students who have some grasp of this skill and its usefulness are likely to have a better understanding of the nature and scope of human knowledge.

Incidentally, the relevance of this topic in the present chapter is quite easy to explain: Hypotheses function, typically, as antecedents in hypothetical reasoning. Consider the following illustration:

I am driving across Sydney Harbor Bridge on a hot day during peak hour. The traffic is moving at a snail's pace. Suddenly, my car gives a cough and a stutter and stalls right in the middle lane.

I am an amateur mechanic and could probably fix things quickly if only I knew what went wrong. I formulate several hypotheses:

    (i) The car has run out of gas.
    (ii) I have a flat tire.
    (iii) My firm's opponents have sabotaged the car so that I would be late for an important appointment.
    (iv) The engine has overheated.
    (v) Those gremlins are at it again!

In proposing (i), for example, I am implicitly arguing as follows: "If the car has run out of gas, *then* this would explain why it stalled on the bridge."

Your task is to select the best hypothesis based on the evidence—not just the one most likely to be true, but the one that would offer the best explanation of the facts. If you feel that one or more of the above hypotheses should be rejected, be clear as to your reasons. To make things more interesting, try adding various bits of information to the original data, and pay attention to the reasoning that you then use. (For example: I filled the car's tank with gasoline just a few minutes before it stalled; therefore, hypothesis [i] is false if we assume that my gas tank is not leaking.)

Hunches deserve separate discussion. One important point is that a hunch may be dangerous even when it turns out to be correct. We should not ignore our feelings—especially when they prove to be reliable time and again—but neither should we ignore the process of careful inquiry that such programs as Philosophy for Children attempt to highlight.

CHAPTER SEVENTEEN

One further logical concept—that of tautology—is raised here (N93; M434–35). Tautologies are statements whose truth is so self-evident as to render them virtually pointless. The classic form of a tautology is "*A* is *A*," "All *A*s are *A*s," and the like. Note the manual's observations that the negation or opposite of a tautology is a contradiction (recall Chapter Twelve) and that tautologous statements sometimes have an idiomatic meaning ("Rules are rules," for example; recall N50).

However, this final chapter is fundamental for a quite different reason: It allows the children, both fictional and real, to reflect on the crucial distinction between subjective and objective points of view. It is worth spending some time trying to grasp the views of the different characters in this chapter. For example, Tony and Lisa are representatives (though not all the time) of the step-by-step and the intuitive ways (respectively) of thinking. Fran appreciates that they might both be right because they are reflecting different points of view or perspectives. But Harry takes this a step farther when he realizes that, although we often do see things differently from one another, we can—with effort—see things from those other points of view. This insight is fundamental to all genuine inquiry: It represents a balance between extreme subjectivism ("Whatever I believe must be true") and extreme objectivism ("My beliefs and opinions count for nothing"). It is at the very heart of both ethics and education.

Lisa has the last word, in one sense. However we choose to understand her poem (N95; reprinted in full at M439), she interprets it as a caution: In our quest for greater understanding and wisdom, making mistakes can be a more fruitful enterprise than being "certain" of the truth.

The value of dialogue and inquiry—those aspects of teaching and learning that are so strongly emphasized in this program—depends upon these remarkable facts. In a community of inquiry, where children learn to listen to, empathize with, and respect, one another's thoughts and ideas, they can begin to move toward a mutual understanding of different perspectives, and hence toward a more objective understanding of the world and of themselves (M436, 442).

It is the challenge of seeking, and perhaps finding, objective knowledge and understanding from the seeds of our own subjective perceptions and ideas that Philosophy for Children offers.

13

Standardization

Clive Lindop

■ ■ ■

A THEME is standardization of sentences originating from Harry's idea that, just as there are many different ways of making the number ten, there are all sorts of other sentences that could be *changed* into sentences beginning either with the word "all" or the word "no."[1]

Mr. Spence agrees to let the class work on this idea and they come up with a list of six expressions that mean the same thing as "all," namely: "each," "every," "any," "a," "if–then," and no modifier at all. The equivalence of "all" with these expressions is taken for granted, and the examples they use reinforce the idea. But, as teachers of philosophy, we must ourselves be clear about what we are doing if we are to do it well. Also, pupils will come up with some sentences using these other expressions that somehow seem odd or improper. The children may comment on this and want to know why. As teachers, we cannot know everything, but as educators we should want to encourage curiosity about our own language and its marvelous forms. So some idea of the reasons for some of the oddities and improprieties of certain forms of expression can only be helpful, as well as stimulate curiosity about language and literature.

As a matter of fact, the meaning of "all" is not entirely carried across into these "equivalent" expressions. What follows is an exposition of Zeno Vendler's 1967 essay, "Each and Every, Any and All," in which he explores the equivalence of these expressions.[2]

Ordinary language has many devices for expressing general propositions of the form "All *s* are *p,*" and Harry's class lists these. The trouble is, however, that these devices are not freely interchangeable: Some are general or collective in scope ("every/each kid in this class . . ."), extending over the whole set; others are more specific or distributed in scope ("a kid in this class . . ."). Vendler undertakes a systematic study of the variants EACH, ANY, and EVERY of ALL to exhibit their similarities and differences, so revealing that treating them as equivalent can obscure important philosophical issues concerning the type, reference, existential import, truth value, and lawlike form of general propositions.

EVERY and EACH are always followed by the singular form of the verb "to be," while ANY (sometimes) and ALL (nearly always) are followed by the plural. Vendler argues that this difference is not merely a caprice of grammar but an indication of a difference in the meaning of these terms. Let us consider some examples.

Timmy offers a bag of candies to Tony, saying, "Take all of them," or you offer a packet of cigarettes to a colleague, saying, "Take all of them." Both you and Timmy could legitimately express surprise if your friend (or Tony) started to pick them out one by one. "No, take them all (together)!" you might exclaim. Had you (or Timmy) initially said, "Take every one of them," their picking them out one at a time would not be out of line: The invitation holds no implication about how to take them, provided *none* are left behind. Had you (or Timmy) initially said, "Take each of them," your friend (or Tony) could well reply, "And do what with them?" The invitation is incomplete. If a magician fanned a set of cards and said, "Take each of them," you would probably complete the sentence yourself as ". . . and examine them." Here you (and Tony et al.) are expected to take them one after another, not missing any, and do something (examine) with them.

Your first invitation, "Take all of them," nicely illustrates the *collective* nature of ALL; it includes the lot. "All of the kids in this class are American" refers to the whole group and therefore calls for the plural verb form "are." The other two forms, "Take every one" and "Take each," are both distributive in reference, but with a different emphasis. EACH directs attention to the individuals as they appear, one by one for some sort of scrutiny—we have to do something with each of them. EVERY stresses the completeness or exhaustiveness of the set—it serves to sum up the distributive character of EACH. Grammatically, "every of them" sounds odd, but "each of them" is correct. EACH suggests or implies the singular ONE, so that in "each one of them" the "one" is redundant, but in "every one of them" it is correct. EVERY does not suggest the singular ONE. This is not merely a matter of grammatical style, for not only the reference (collective or individual) but also the truth value of the expression is affected. Compare "Every kid in the class has $2" and "Each item in the shop costs $2." This does not mean that all the kids in the class (taken together) have only $2 (among them), or that all the items in the shop (taken together) are worth only $2. These examples illustrate that ALL implies collectivity, EVERY and EACH distributivity. That is why ALL calls for the plural, while EACH and EVERY take the singular verb form.

Suppose Mr. Partridge asks Mr. Spence to send all the kids in his class to the office. Would Mr. Spence be complying if he sent any of them? ANY is not equivalent to ALL here, for ANY is indifferent to the number or size of the reference, that is, the reference is incomplete. Mr. Spence can send any one, two, three, and so on to the office, but if he has sent everyone except say, Harry, he still has not sent all of them. So "All of the children are to report to the office" is not the same as "Any of the children are to report to the office."

Had Mr. Partridge asked Mr. Spence to send any of his class to the office, he could comply by sending one of them, or some of them, or any number up to one less than the total number in the class. ANY implies freedom of choice as to which child and how many (but not all). In other words, ANY never amounts to EVERY. In this respect ANY is like SOME rather than ALL.

Lisa's announcement that "if we're all Americans here, then ANY one of us you choose will turn out to be American" (pp. 6–7) brings out the incompleteness of reference to both particular members (freedom of choice) and to size of the set—this has to be mentioned, "any ONE of us." More interestingly, it also emphasizes that ANY functions as a blank warrant for conditional predictions. Anyone who is a member of the class is an American: If one picks any of the members of the class, then one will find that she or he is an American—one chooses whomever one will, one decides how many to check. Nor does it matter if the class, or set, is empty, for the conditional claim has no existential import. Notice also that Lisa's claim, the ANY formulation, unlike the ALL form, focuses attention on the condition of being a member of the class, or set, in question and on the consequences of fulfilling that condition, of being a member: If one is a member, then one is American, regardless of one's identity. ANY does not identify individuals; in this respect, it remains indefinite and open.

While ANY lacks existential import, EACH and EVERY always connote existence; ALL by itself, however, does not. ANY and ALL may occur in the same sense when they lack definite reference and existential import, as in "All visitors to the school must first report to the office." In such cases the translation is equivalent.

Enough has been done to show that the translation of everyday uses of EACH, EVERY, and ANY into ALL sentences may not carry over the entire meaning and, in some cases, may no longer be true. But at least now we know why.

NOTES

1. Matthew Lipman, *Harry Stottlemeier's Discovery* (Montclair, N.J.: First Mountain Press, 1974).

2. Zeno Vendler, "Each and Every, Any and All," in *Linguistics in Philosophy* (Ithaca, N.Y.: Cornell University Press, 1967).

14

Relationships

Clive Lindop

■ ■ ■

WHEN JILL PORTOS tries to tell Lisa and Harry about her father's theory of mind in Chapter Seven, all she can remember is the distinction between differences of degree and differences of kind. Harry is excited by this idea; he links it with his rule, discovered earlier, about turning sentences around. He now realizes that his rule exemplifies certain kinds of relationships between things. Since they occur again and again throughout the story in different guises, it is important for us to understand the nature of these relationships. Furthermore, comprehending these relations will help us to explain why his rule about reversing sentences actually works, as well as to understand how his initial discovery leads to an exciting application in deductive argument.

Relations are easy to illustrate but difficult to define. Philip Wheelwright contends that "relation," like "meaning," is too broad to be defined, inasmuch as any attempt to do so would presuppose at least one instance of it.[1] Morris Cohen and Ernest Nagel give an operational definition: An object is said to be in a relation if, in our statement about it, explicit reference must be made to another object,[2] which nicely illustrates Wheelwright's point about supposition. A relation must be at least dyadic, in that it connects at least two things—the *referent*, FROM which the relation goes, TO the *relatum*, that which it connects. "Jack kisses Jill" illustrates a dyadic relation: Jack (the referent) and Jill (the relatum) are linked by "kisses," the relation between them. "Father O'Toole blesses Jack and Jill" is a triadic relation in which three terms, "Father O'Toole," "Jack," and "Jill," are connected by "blesses." "Jack is a boy" is dyadic. "Jack delivered eggs to the store for Farmer Brown" is tetradic because four terms are joined by the relation "delivered." Other polyadic relations are possible, but relations with more than four terms are not common. Note, however, that the dyadic relation "Jack is a boy" conforms to Aristotle's form of a categorical proposition—two terms, a subject (Jack) and a predicate (a boy), joined by a copula, the verb "to be." The copula, then, is simply a special type of dyadic relation. The examples Harry initially used in forming his rule are all of this type.

However, there is a more practically significant way of classifying relations than merely noting the number of terms joined together in the proposition. Two lines of classification of logical importance are those of symmetry and transitivity, each of which contains three types, which bear on Harry's rule and are illustrated somewhere in the story.

If, say, the proposition "Jack is the son of John" is true, it expresses a relationship between Jack and John in which exchanging the referent (Jack) with the relatum (John), turning the sentence around, as Harry calls it, renders the proposition false. "John is the son of Jack" cannot be true in this instance. Likewise with "mother of," "wife of," "larger than," "darker than," "heavier than," and other unequal comparisons (including differences of degree, which Mr. Portos introduces in this episode). In all relationships such as these, the referent bears a relation to the relatum that the relatum cannot bear to the referent. If such propositions are true, their converse, formed by exchanging the referent and the relatum in the sentence, is false. Such relationships are called *asymmetrical*.

When the subject term (the referent) and the predicate term (the relatum) of a true proposition are also true, the relationship is said to be *symmetrical*. For example, if Lisa is the same age as Harry, then Harry is also the same age as Lisa. Likewise with "equal to," "as tall as," "near to," "far from," and any equal comparison: The referent bears the same relation to the relatum as the relatum bears to the referent. All identity statements are of this type: "Mr. Bush is the current president of the U.S.A." and "The current president of the U.S.A. is Mr. Bush" are both true.

But there is another class of relations, in which the truth of the proposition holds no implication whatsoever about the truth of its converse. That Jack loves Jill, for example, gives no clue as to whether Jill loves Jack or not. From the truth of the proposition, we cannot tell either way whether its converse is true or false. Relations expressed by "loves," "likes," "thinking about," "envies," and so on are neither symmetrical nor asymmetrical, so they are called *nonsymmetrical*. They seem to be typical of psychological relationships we have with others. So just because Bill Beck is mad at Harry, we cannot tell Jill whether or not Harry is mad at Bill.

The symmetry of propositions asserted by sentences has consequences for the conversion (reversal of subject and predicate terms) of categorical propositions. Categorical propositions—those with a subject term and a predicate term joined by a copula, the verb "to be"—can be analyzed from either an intensional or an extensional point of view.[3] From the former standpoint, "All oaks are trees" can be interpreted as meaning that "tree-ness," or "being a tree," is one of the attributes that define "oak." From the latter (extensional) point of view, the proposition means that objects called oaks belong to the class of things called trees, or, in other words, "oak" is included in the extension or denotation of the term "tree." In traditional logic, Cohen and Nagel point out, it is the extensional interpretation that figures in the analysis of propositions. This being so, we find that the conversion of categorical propositions depends on the symmetry of the class-inclusion (or exclusion) relation expressed in the proposition.

We can now explain why Harry's initial discovery—that true sentences beginning with "all," when reversed, become false—works. Reversal, or conversion, in which the converse of a proposition remains true, is only possible when the relation between subject and predicate is symmetrical. In Harry's examples ("all oaks are trees," for instance), the class of things denoted by the predicate term (tree) is always larger than that denoted by the subject term (oak): The extension, or class inclusion, of the predicate class always includes the subject class or group of things. Since the two classes, or sets, are of different sizes, they cannot be identical; and since they are not mutually exclusive because one includes the other, the relationship between them cannot be symmetrical. Thus, the converse of the proposition (all trees are oaks) must be false. This is also true of what Tony's father calls part-whole relationships.[4] It can be illustrated using circles to represent the sets, or classes, of things denoted by the subject and predicate terms.

It is otherwise with Lisa's discovery that a true sentence beginning with "No," when reversed, remains true. Her examples, such as "No lions are eagles," are all examples of mutual exclusion: No lions are to be found in the class, or set, of eagles, and no eagles will be found in the class, or set, of lions, either. This relationship is symmetrical and hence can be converted without negating the truth. This notion of the symmetry of a relationship also explains why the other sentences that Harry and his friends formulate, those that talk about a class, or set, of things named by the subject term (namely, those starting with "some"), are reversible. If it is true, for example, that some boys are brave, it is also true that some brave things are boys. In other words, the class of brave things partially includes the class of boys, and vice versa: The two classes, or sets, overlap. Such symmetry allows for the conversion of this type of proposition. Partial inclusion, like total exclusion, is a symmetrical relationship.

The exceptions to Harry's rule, identity statements, unlike the other sentences that take the form "all As are Bs," are symmetrical. Hence total inclusion of one class of things in another, as expressed by "all As are Bs," covers two different cases: those in which the two classes are identical and those in which one class is contained inside the other. For this reason Cohen and Nagel classify the relationship of total inclusion as nonsymmetrical. Depending on the case, it can be either symmetrical (the identity relation) or asymmetrical (the part-whole relation). From the proposition *alone,* it is not always possible to decide whether the two classes mentioned in it are identical in extension. In the case of "all police are brave," even if true, we bring in outside information (e.g., that some firefighters are brave; that some dogs, we want to say, are brave) in denying that the converse, "all brave things are police," is true. If we did not have this extra knowledge, we might well allow that the converse is true, thus assuming a symmetrical relation of identity between "police" and "brave."

In this episode, Mr. Portos makes a distinction between differences of degree and differences of kind. The former, as we have seen, are asymmetrical relationships. What of the other, the differences of kind? Since no dimensions of length are dimensions of weight, and the converse is also true, it seems that differences of kind represent a case of total exclusion: As such, their relationship or difference is symmetrical. One can doubt whether this "symmetry" can be maintained in all cases. For example, "no yellow is heavy," if expressing the point that the color yellow is not the sort of thing that can have weight, is true. The converse that no heavy thing is yellow is not true. Likewise, it is not true that no dimension or measurement of weight is, or can be, yellow, for lengths of timber sometimes have their ends daubed with different colors to indicate their lengths. So differences of kind cannot always be regarded as mutually exclusive. Since they can sometimes be asymmetrical and sometimes be symmetrical, we may conclude that they are nonsymmetrical.

We have explored one way of classifying relationships—according to their symmetry—and have noted three types of turnaround relationships, as Harry calls them, and their implications for the types of inferences we are entitled to draw from each. In the manual that accompanies *Harry Stottlemeier's Discovery,*[5] they are called merely type 1, type 2, and type 3, but they correspond, in order, to symmetrical, asymmetrical, and nonsymmetrical. For the sake of completeness, I will now look at the other way of classifying relations—according to their transitivity.

Harry does not explore the notion of transitivity until later in Chapter Eight when he realizes that some sorts of relations "carry over," so that on the basis of just two true sentences' information or propositions he is able to carry over the relationship and arrive at a third proposition on the basis of information contained in the first two *alone.* Since Fran is taller than Laura and Laura is taller than Jill, Harry sees that "taller than" carries over, so that Fran bears the same relation (taller than) to Jill that she does to Laura. Such a relation is called *transitive,* for it transfers, or carries over, from one proposition or pair of propositions to another. Examples include "equal to," "older than," "warmer than," "east of," "heavier than," "richer than," "implies," and other conventional relationships and comparisons limited by measurement and other qualification. In all such cases, if A bears a certain relation to B and B bears this same relation to C, then A must bear this same relation to C as well. However, when A bears a relation to B that B bears to C, but A cannot possibly (in logic) bear that same relation to C, the relation is called *intransitive*. Examples of intransitivity are "father of," "daughter of," and such limited comparative relations as "two inches taller than" and "twice as rich as." If, when A bears the same relation to B as B does to C, and it is logically indeterminate whether A bears this relation to C, the relation is *nontransitive*. If Jack likes Jill and Jill likes Tom, nothing is logically implied about the relationship between Jack and Tom. Jack may or may not like Tom; from the information given in the first two propositions, we cannot tell whether Jack likes Tom or not. Our feelings and emotions toward others typically involve nontransitive relations.

So we have now distinguished six types of relations, three of symmetry and three of transitivity, that when combined give nine possible types of relations:

transitive symmetrical (e.g., "as old as," "equal to")
transitive asymmetrical (e.g., "taller than," "ancestor of")
transitive nonsymmetrical (e.g., "not older than")
intransitive symmetrical (e.g., "spouse of")
intransitive symmetrical (e.g., "father of," "wife of")
intransitive nonsymmetrical (e.g., "nearest blood relative of")
nontransitive symmetrical (e.g., "cousin of")
nontransitive asymmetrical (e.g., "employer of")
nontransitive nonsymmetrical (e.g., "lover of")

It is the symmetrical, asymmetrical, and transitive relations that make possible what is called immediate reference: If New York is near Montclair, then Montclair must be near New York; if these shoes are too small for my feet, then my feet are too big for them; and if Jill is the daughter of Mary, then Mary is the parent of Jill. However, such simple operations are not usually of much argumentative importance. Transitive relations, on the other hand, make extended reasoning or argument possible: The syllogism is the paradigm argument form of this sort. The validity of such categorical syllogisms as

All cats are carnivores.
Carnivores are dangerous.
Therefore, all cats are dangerous.

depends on the transitivity (carryover) of the relation of class inclusion. If the class of cats is included in the class of carnivores and carnivores in the class of dangerous things, the class of cats must be included in the class of dangerous things too. The relation "is included in" is transitive; it carries right through the argument form to include "cats," the subject term of the first proposition (or premise), into "dangerous," the predicate term of the second premise.

Similarly with what Cohen and Nagel call relational (*a fortiori*) syllogisms: Their validity also depends on the transitivity of the relations. Thus, since Fran is taller than Laura, and Laura is taller than Jill, then since "taller than" carries through, the conclusion that Fran is taller than Jill must be true.

It is the same with such hypothetical syllogisms as

> If the weather is fine, I will go to the ball game.
> If I go to the ball game, I will spend at least $7.50.
> Therefore, if it is fine, it will cost me at least $7.50.

Each of these three propositions asserts an implication, or entailment (if–then), relation. If the first two are true, then the third must be true; this truth is carried over by the transitive entailment relation. If this relation were not transitive, the third proposition could not be validly deduced from the first two. Notice, however, that the validity of the argument does not guarantee that I will actually go to the game. The deductive argument does not say what will happen in an actual case, only if both premises are true; insofar as they are true, the truth of the conclusion, without reference to a particular instance, must follow. The validity of the argument or chain of reasoning depends entirely on the transitivity of the relation of entailment by which it proceeds. For if the truth of proposition p entails the truth of proposition q, and if the truth of q entails the truth of proposition r, then it must necessarily follow that the truth of p entails the truth of r. And this chain of reasoning, which depends upon the transitivity of the entailment (if–then) relation, forms the basis of all syllogistic-argument forms and of deduction in general.

However, the abstract relation of entailment and the mental act of reasoning (inference), by which we pass from accepting certain premises to accepting the conclusion that they entail, are different in kind. Whereas it is correct to say that one proposition, or pair of propositions, entails another, it may not necessarily be the case that anyone actually makes this inference. The two premises, taken together, that Lisa is trustworthy and that all trustworthy people are law abiding, entail that Lisa is law abiding; but it may or may not be the case that anyone thinks of these two propositions in one context and employs them as premises to infer the conclusion from them.

Sometimes the process of thinking works in the reverse order. One may begin with the proposition one wants to establish logically and may seek a pair of premises that will logically justify it. What one is after here is a justification or explanation for the conclusion. And this is often done in explaining or justifying a conclusion to the others. Often in such cases the full explanation is not given—a single premise, usually the minor (particular), is enough, the major premise (universal) is left unstated and taken for granted as accepted by all. "This production will be good" (conclusion). "The critics raved about it" (minor premise) leaves unstated the major premise that what the critics rave about is good. We usually call this process or argument "giving the reasons." Technically, such arguments are called enthymemes.

Thus we see that Harry is embarking on an even more exciting and practically significant journey of discovery than he realizes. Tony's "So what?" from early in the story will soon be given a more powerful answer than the immediate reference realized at the end of Chapter Two. Harry, and those who work with the novel, in realizing the nature and role of the relationships of turnaround (symmetry) and carryover (transitivity), are beginning to get logical explanations for the efficacy of the rules discovered earlier and are being prepared for development of their skill in deductive (syllogistic) reasoning and explanation. Chapter Eight is truly a pivotal stage of the program.

NOTES

1. Philip Wheelwright, *Valid Thinking* (New York: Odyssey Press, 1962), p. 27.

2. Morris R. Cohen and Ernest Nagel, *An Introduction to Logic and Scientific Method* (New York: Harcourt Brace, 1934), p. 113.

3. Ibid., p. 33.

4. Matthew Lipman, *Harry Stottlemeier's Discovery* (Montclair, N.J.: First Mountain Foundation, 1974), p. 14.

5. Matthew Lipman, Ann Sharp, and Frederick S. Oscanyan, *Philosophical Inquiry*, 2d ed. (Lanham, Md.: University Press of America, 1984), p. 183.

15

Countering Prejudice with Counterexamples

Philip C. Guin

■ ■ ■

IN THIS CHAPTER I intend to accomplish three major objectives. I will show that sensitivity to the rule of contradiction can be useful in the lives of children, especially in combating prejudice and discrimination. Sensitivity to the rule encourages children to seek counterexamples to universal judgments. Second, I will argue that sociological models that attempt to delineate the roots of prejudice can be complemented by an understanding of the rule of contradiction. Here I am concerned with the phenomenon, cited by such models, of assimilating relative differences among groups, which in fact may be true, to overgeneralizations that allege natural or inherent group traits. Finally, I will argue that the pedagogical forum best suited to promoting sensitivity to the rule is the community of inquiry. In the community, counterexamples stand as the most forceful devices challenging cherished beliefs and opinions.

CHILDREN'S DIALOGUE: THINGS AND PERSONS

Some years ago I was working with a class of seventh-grade children at Union City, New Jersey. We had just read the first part of Chapter Five of *Harry Stottlemeier's Discovery*, the episode on induction. Maria introduces the problem of induction through her insistence that "in fact . . . if some courses are *un*interesting, then it must be that there are other courses that are *interesting*."[1] Maria, of course, is assuming no more than most of us do when we use "some are" or "some are not," namely, that the entire class membership under discussion is known to us. Harry readily nails down the point with his example of the bag of candies. The issue is a familiar one: On the basis of a selected sample, what can one safely *infer* in general? Harry concludes that "if all you know is that *some* of the candies in the bag are brown, you can't say what color they *all* are, and you certainly can't say, because some *are* brown, that some must *not* be!"[2] The Union City children were delighted with Harry's example and a lively discussion ensued.

"Suppose," I asked, "if each of you had five dollars would you bet that the next piece of candy removed from the bag will be brown?" It did not take long to establish, in this case, that most of the children had a fairly high utility for risk, most having bet their five dollars by the tenth piece. A critical distinction was made, however, when the example was changed from candy to people. "How many members of an ethnic group would you need to know before you'd say all the members of the group are alike in some special way?" Now the children hesitated, and many would not bet at all. "What's the difference here between candy and people?" I asked. A girl summed up the majority view by explaining that "with the candy there's no change—the pieces just lie there. With people you can never tell, because they do change—they're not the same." This reply, and Maria's obverse comment in the novel, "but people are always jumping to conclusions,"[3] indicate the direction of this discussion.

THE REAL SITUATION AND ITS LOGIC

There is an important difference between my questions to the children and Harry's conclusion above. Whereas my questions address the probability of the situation, Harry's conclusion addresses its logic. Harry is of course correct. We cannot *infer* from the fact that if some of the candies are brown, without knowing the contents of the bag, that some are not brown, or that all are brown. Yet by putting the world into his logical straitjacket, perhaps Harry has exceeded the situation. After all, in the real world, we do bet on the next piece of candy, we do make inductive generalizations (some proper and useful, others painful and dangerous), and we do stereotype and jump to conclusions. Moreover, we are all accustomed to the ease with which we jump to conclusions about persons and things. We learn how calming and cleansing it is to take refuge in universal judgments, how easily they dispatch unpleasant thoughts and confrontations. Universal judgments relieve us of the burden of further deliberation—Why bother if we can round off the world with a resounding "All" or "No," "Yea" or "Nay," Them versus Us? Harry's logic would appear impotent in the face of the real world.

Still it could be argued that Harry's logic does caution restraint, a kind of safety valve shutting down the system should we go too far. Certainly the children in Union City did not go too far. I marveled at their restraint. I wondered what experience or set of experiences, what process of thought facilitates this ability to distinguish substantively between candy and humans, things and persons, the unchangeable and the unpredictable. Was it just sensitivity to the profusion of intervening variables in the latter as opposed to the former case? Or was it Union City savvy, an ethnic empathy for others like themselves, possible victims of prejudice and discrimination? Could there be a connection between Harry's logic and the real world as experienced by these children? In another place and time, where fear, the influence of others, custom, and mental sloth stand behind judgments, children might not exercise Union City restraint.

COGNITIVE AND MORAL SOPHISTICATION

In their compelling study of adolescent prejudice, Charles Glock and his colleagues conclude that without prior cognitive change there will be little chance of lessening prejudice, "that prejudice is nurtured especially among youths who have not developed the cognitive skills and sophistication to combat it." [4] Moreover, as I have already stressed in my remarks on jumping to conclusions, overgeneralization is the real culprit:

> Stereotypes of group differences that make relative differences absolute are false overgeneralizations, however true the relative differences that inspire them. . . . That cognitive failure is a necessary, if not sufficient, ingredient for such overgeneralization is an initial assumption we are as disposed to make as we are to suggest that cognitive sophistication is necessary to guard against such overgeneralization. (*AP*, p. 165)

But what complexity of cognitive growth will suffice? In offering suggestions for educational input, the investigators cite first that "instruction in the logic of inference is called for so that youngsters can come to recognize when group differences are being falsely accounted for" (*AP*, p. 176).

There we have it. Cognitive sophistication spelled out in sensitivity to the logic of inference will be a potent answer to the problem of overgeneralization. However, where the investigators offer examples of the logic of inference, "the notion of causality," or "the rules of evidence," they imply a broadly conceived approach, one that might not set well with the logician. Furthermore, overgeneralization is treated less as an inductive affair than a misreading:

> Why black teenagers are less successful in school and why Jewish teenagers and their parents are prone to clannishness, for example, have to be explained so that their historical roots are understood and the social forces making for their persistence in contemporary society comprehended. (*AP*, p. 176)

What seems operative here is that *perceptual* rather than *logical* inferences, such as Jewish clannishness (relative difference), ought not to be interested in terms of Jewishness (overgeneralization), but in terms of antecedents to be explained causally. And surely this sociological model is important, for it challenges the thesis that innate traits, rather than relative and historical factors, account for group differences. Nevertheless, it might be that logical inference construed in the logician's sense can also serve children in making judgments.

Or to put the matter another way: Can Harry's logic assist children in mediating perceptual inferences in an effort to avoid overgeneralizations?

A thread of logical inference runs throughout *Harry Stottlemeier's Discovery*. In the first chapter, the characters Harry and Lisa discover the rule of conversion covering universal affirmative and negative sentences. Since overgeneralization can be couched in the language of universal sentences, we may find here a clue to the practical application of Harry's logic. Concentrating on universal affirmative sentences, we learn that the conversion of a true sentence is false. Thus, if it is true that "all cucumbers are vegetables," it is false that "all vegetables are cucumbers." However, since the rule does not ascertain whether a generalization is an overgeneralization—in which case the sentence would be false to begin with and not subject to the rule—it is not directly helpful in combating overgeneralization. It does provide a hint though, for if it is true that "all elves are mischievous," it does not follow that "only elves are mischievous," the converse of the former being false. Accordingly, the indiscriminate employment of prejudicial predicates, especially as they are erroneously thought to imply "only," cannot guarantee impunity, since even one's own shortcomings are bound to be exposed. This is deftly brought home in the novel:

> And Laura O'Mara said, "And I still remember about how you can't turn a sentence around that begins with the word 'All,' like the other day when Randy said to me, 'All girls are finks,' and I said to him, 'Well, maybe so, but it doesn't follow that all finks are girls, because I know at least one who isn't!' "[5]

THE IDEA OF CONTRADICTION

Though conversion does not provide the entire picture, it does suggest what is needed. Supposing that conversion deals with the *products* of deliberation, then what is needed is a rule that deals with the *process* of deliberation, a powerful covering rule that will monitor our beliefs and actions. Children accustomed to looking for truth and falsity *prior* to entertaining universal judgments will be well served in avoiding stereotypical or prejudicial thinking. Such a rule, then, will expose overgeneralizations and expose them to be false.

I believe such a rule is to be found in *Harry Stottlemeier's Discovery*. In Chapter Twelve, the idea of contradiction is introduced. The definition appears simple enough: If two sentences contradict one another, they cannot both be true (not both be false); one will be true and the other false. Suppose my friend maintains that the sentence "All wood floats" is true, and I maintain that it is false. What must I do? I must name some wood that does not float. Since ebony does not float, I have established that "All wood floats" is false. By naming a counterexample, I have made my point to my friend; my contradiction is true.

Now, the assumption is that children rehearsed to the possibility of counterexamples are in a better position to resist the temptation of overgeneralization.

As we have seen, according to the sociological model the typical overgeneralization results from drawing implications from relative differences, that is, from perceptual differences. The assumption seems to be that groups do in fact exhibit common traits, but that the error consists in attributing the commonality to something genetic or innate. For the investigators, the propaedeutic for avoiding overgeneralizations is exposure to the social sciences. All well and good, but what about cases where the trait fails to appear or is unidentifiable, as in the Howard Beach and Bensonhurst incidents in New York City in the late 1980s? Aside from the fact that the victims were black, no further clue to their identity was available before the violence. Now, it could be argued that the perpetrators had long since overgeneralized according to the sociological model. However, if the perpetrators had never thought to *look* for counterexamples or had repeatedly ignored them, then the logic of the situation was likewise ignored. Or consider an addendum to the Bensonhurst violence: "If I wasn't a celebrity, I'd be just another nigger to them."[6] In view of the sociological model, Spike Lee is probably correct, the overgeneralization being something like "black people are naturally unambitious and lazy." Presumably, what appears to be an anomaly, namely, that a black motion-picture director will attract white fans in Brooklyn, would be accounted for not because Lee is a counterexample to the overgeneralization but because Lee is not black in the eyes of his fans. However, sensitivity to the logic of contradiction might very well convince fans that Lee *is* a counterexample precisely because he is black.

With a little practice and patience, children quickly grasp the rule of contradiction as being quite intuitive. True, there is some struggle with the relation between universal affirmative and negative sentences, "All" and "No" sentences, centered on why they do not contradict one another. Even returning to the definition that contradictory sentences cannot have the same truth value, and pointing out that, although as contraries "All" and "No" sentences cannot both be true, they certainly can both be false, often fails to persuade. A good deal of the problem may lie in the ease with which we jump to conclusions, a phenomenon referred to at the beginning of this chapter. In jumping to conclusions, we effectively endorse one contrary while precluding the other as being ipso facto false. In this way of thinking, "All" and "No" sentences cannot both be true, but neither can they both be false. Our thinking is a bit like either "All" or "No" but not both, the law of excluded middle notwithstanding, and especially when it comes to problems of prejudice, our hope is that children can marshal the thinking skills to reject both terms of the disjunction. Since it is the gray between contraries that more often than not makes up the real world, we want children to discover that the contraries more often than not are false. Moreover, we want them to see that the contraries are false because the world is full of counterexamples, and that a prudent way of life is one that seeks out such examples before fixation in overgeneralizations.

One further aspect of contraries, universal affirmative and negative, is that they seemingly have the emotive force of lawlike descriptions. They command our attention as to what to expect, exactly what is the case, as though the world must be filtered through their auspices before we take notice. To say that things are sometimes this and sometimes that fails to attract. For this reason, contraries can be incredibly dangerous when used to encapsulate in language the powerful emotions of prejudice. We have seen, though, that contraries do begin to lose their emotive force as we are constrained by counterexamples. A formidable argument, then, would be one that would defuse the emotive force of contraries by escalating the reasonableness of seeking out counterexamples.

Karl Popper proposes that natural laws and theories be conceived as prohibitions, and that rather than asserting that "something exists or is the case; they deny it."[7] The reason underlying this characterization is that laws and theories, in order to maintain their scientific status, must imply two nonempty subclasses, the class of statements consistent and the class of statements inconsistent with the law or theory. Rather than describing what is the case, Popper maintains, the law or theory prescribes the class of inconsistent statements.[8] Following this characterization of natural laws and theories, no disanalogy would arise in holding that prejudicial statements, universal affirmative or negative, are lawlike statements since they do imply the two subclasses. Prejudicial statements prohibit or proscribe counterexamples, statements with which they are inconsistent. Consequently, we would expect that a bigot would accede to the characterization of her or his position. However, to the extent the bigot disallows the class of inconsistent statements, denies that the class has membership, the less the position has lawlike status. We can see this by recalling that the sociological model of overgeneralization forces regression to question begging and redundancy—for example, Jews are like that because they are Jews. Nothing will serve as a counterexample.

In sharp contrast, the advantage of the rule of contradiction is that it *never* denies the membership of the subclass of inconsistent statements; rather, it provides the logical framework wherein perceptual inferences are continually monitored for their accuracy. Rather than allowing one to exclaim and conclude, as is likely to have been the case in Howard Beach and Bensonhurst, "There's a black—blacks are blacks," restraint would be in order, for the perceptual inference could not be properly assimilated to the tautology, since, according to the framework of contradiction, the class of inconsistent statements will always have possible membership. We can see that tenaciously held prejudices issue in nothing descriptive, nothing about the world insofar as they fail to allow for counterexamples; they merely mask their own inconsistencies. And to the extent they do allow for counterexamples, their emotive force is compromised. On the playground, racial and ethnic slurs betray the identical prejudice as at Howard Beach and Bensonhurst; they too mask inconsistencies, as children mimic their elders. They mark the beginning of unthinking overgeneralization. Inevitably name calling leads to inflamed passions and violence, and children so imbued are as much victims as are their targets. Therefore, it would make sense to foster in children the consciousness that name calling can never be so effective in the end as sensitivity to the sticks and stones of counterexamples.

COMMUNITIES OF INQUIRY AND PREJUDICE

When we turn to the possible impact of the school on prejudice, the main challenge is to uncover a pedagogical format to do the job. It seems unlikely that admonitions and exhortations will have much effect, especially with children already schooled in intolerance. In their study, Glock and his colleagues cautiously explore the possible role of schools in combating prejudice and admit that their work "has not produced a formula for action . . . has not even demonstrated that the schools have the capacity to do anything about prejudice" (*AP*, p. 174). The investigators do emphasize instruction, "appropriate didactic instruction to teach youngsters to be cognitively sophisticated about prejudice" (*AP*, p. 175). Moreover, they maintain that teachers must "have a sophisticated understanding of prejudice" and that teachers should "take a test to judge their comprehension" (*AP*, p. 179). Clearly, the investigators support an objectified approach to prejudice, whereby units and courses will be delivered by trained personnel; content will be something *there* to be learned. Knowledge about prejudice will be imparted to children by sophisticated teachers.

Whether such measures will succeed can be gauged, in part, by the effect of didactic teaching in general. At least with the customary disciplines, the objectification of content poses no special problems, and experience has shown that such instruction may or may not "take" with children. However, where the content is emotionally laden, the task could be much more difficult. The investigators admit as much, that they could have "grossly underestimated the emotive element in prejudice" (*AP*, p. 177). Also, we might question how knowledge *about* a discipline will translate into beliefs and actions consistent with that knowledge. We run the risk, in other words, of imparting knowledge that will yield satisfactory test scores without, however, any notion of its impact on prejudice.

Still, granting that this admittedly traditional approach can make inroads, we may nonetheless find that knowledge *about* prejudice can be complemented by internalized cognitive skills capable of being directed *at* prejudice wherever and however encountered. Remembering that the rule of contradiction deals with the process of deliberation *prior* to possible overgeneralization, we would appear to have the skill we need. Remembering too that the prominent feature of the rule is its capacity for counterexamples, we look to find a pedagogical forum wherein children's seeking out of counterexamples will be reinforced, a forum wherein habituation will lead to internalization. Such a forum is to be found in the community of inquiry. Here, children are encouraged to listen to and talk with their peers about issues of mutual interest and importance. Accordingly, the role of the teacher is that of facilitator of dialogue, one who asks follow-up questions, encourages children to address one another, summarizes, and points out differing opinions, all from the point of view of making the discussion child rather than teacher oriented. The community takes its lead from the children's position, their sense of interest or perplexity. In contrast to the instruction format described earlier, teachers do not manifest special competence (other than that of expert facilitators), nor do they divulge a given body of knowledge or insist on a specific agenda.

A central feature of the community is its capacity for self-correction. Though children are encouraged to take positions and defend them with the best possible reasons at their disposal, alternative views and reasons are likewise encouraged, and, in this manner, no particular position stands exempt from criticism. At any juncture in the discussion, children might reach consensus, but it soon becomes clear that consensus is not an aim in and of itself. As the same issues recur over time, new sights and angles, absent from previous discussions, emerge to compel the conversation in revitalized directions.

The kingpin of a community's capacity for self-correction is the counterexample, the engine driving discussion. Pointing out that the reasons given for a position are weak, that holding the position leads to absurd consequences, or that evidence is lacking, albeit powerful indictments, are still not so decisive as counterexamples, for counterexamples expose inconsistencies, and those no position can long survive. The logic of contradiction requires that a position exposed as being inconsistent be given up. We may attempt to prop up a position so exposed with ad hoc measures, but to the extent this is done, such measures have either changed the position, in which case we would be obliged to discover new counterexamples, or the position has been rendered so unwieldy as to be rejected for lack of parsimony. Think of a Ptolemaic universe replete with ever-proliferating epicycles, or, in the bleak history of prejudice, the utter hypocrisy of events in South Africa in propping up apartheid.

In the community of inquiry, children do think in terms of counterexamples, as though it were as natural as the use of language itself. Even very young children conscript their use, as here recorded in a fourth-grade exchange on the difference between humans and animals—"animals can only imitate, only do what they've been taught." To which a child counters with the observation that "maybe most of the time, but dogs for the blind have to make decisions on their own—you can't teach them everything." Imagine the ensuing discussion as the difference between humans and animals changes from one of kind to one of degree. In class after class, in much the same manner, we encounter how free and open discussion in the community allows counterexamples to flourish.

So much so, in fact, that one might think that the community institutional-ized counterexamples by subtle indoctrination. "Why this premium placed on exposing inconsistencies?" one might ask; "my only consistency *is* my incon-sistency." If we take the charge seriously, we might point out that consistency and exposure of inconsistency lie at the heart of what is meant by rationality, that rationality and the bare possibility of communication presuppose consis-tency. Of course, this argument would only be welcome to one who cherishes rationality, a further defense of which would take us far afield.

However, if we do not lose sight of our mission to find ways to combat prejudice, the matter can be settled by what we have already accomplished. Consider the alternative, a world in which counterexamples are systematically repressed, where doubts and proffered alternatives are answered by fiat. We have witnessed as much in the phenomenon of overgeneralization. In such a world all discussion would necessarily chronicle what persons believe and wish to opine; while interlocutors would be in short demand, prejudice rather than counterexamples would be allowed to flourish. In such a world, children would surely be repressed, overgeneralizations having the only currency, and indoc-trination would surely be the only manner of schooling. We have seen that counterexamples pose a great threat to prejudiced thinking by exposing incon-sistencies, and that the community of inquiry is by far the best forum wherein counterexamples are perceived and practiced. We would suspect, then, that children exposed sequentially through the grades to participation in such com-munities would have the best chance of combating prejudice whenever and however it occurs.

NOTES

1. Matthew Lipman, *Harry Stottlemeier's Discovery* (Montclair, N.J.: First Mountain Foundation, 1982), p. 21.

2. Ibid., p. 22.

3. Ibid.

4. Charles Y. Glock, Robert Wuthnow, Jane Allyn, and Metta Spencer, *Adolescent Prejudice* (New York: Harper and Row, 1975), p. 164. All further references to this work, abbreviated *AP*, will be included parenthetically in the text.

5. Lipman, *Harry Stottlemeier's Discovery*, p. 92.

6. Spike Lee, *Newsweek*, 11 September 1989. Lee was explaining his refusal to sign autographs for fans, most of them white, in Brooklyn, where a black teenager had been killed by a white mob.

7. Karl R. Popper, *The Logic of Scientific Discovery* (New York: Science Editions, 1961), p. 69.

8. Ibid., p. 86.

PART FIVE

Pedagogical Dimension

In "On the Art and Craft of Dialogue," Ronald F. Reed, after presenting a brief history of Philosophy for Children, offers four general characteristics of the process of inquiry: scholarly ignorance, free-floating curiosity, the presence of the problematic, and the employment of specific disciplines. He then provides a sort of checklist by means of which one might evaluate the mechanics of classroom conversation. The checklist serves, in effect, as a compendium of things that could go wrong when one attempts to inquire within a community.

Reed's argument in "Inventing a Classroom Conversation" springs from the four words of his title. He contends that conversation in the classroom must be invented and not discovered, and that as the participants change and new voices are heard from the nature of the invention will change. He argues on the basis of a need for coherence in the curriculum that one sort of conversation—a philosophical one—is appropriate. He attempts to show why conversation is suited to the classroom, and he suggests, arguing along Deweyan lines, that "conversation" might be a more telling way of describing Philosophy for Children discourse than, say, "dialogue."

The final chapter in this part takes the form of a letter from Ann Margaret Sharp to one of her former students. In "A Letter to a Novice Teacher: Teaching Harry Stottlemeier's Discovery," she discusses some of the salient features of Philosophy for Children pedagogy. She hopes for her former student the abilities to hear the philosophical dimensions of children's comments and to tease out the implications of those comments through appropriate follow-up questions. Sharp speaks of the nature of teacher talk and urges the letter's recipient to remember how that talk does and should change as the group matures. She reminds her student (and the reader) that teachers in Philosophy for Children act as kinds of thermostats. If, for example, a group has a habit of convergent thinking, the teacher has an obligation to encourage some facility in divergent thinking. In focusing on the dynamics of fostering philosophical communities of inquiry in the classroom, with its pedagogical, moral, and political implications, she, like many of the other authors, highlights the role of such classroom communities in bringing into existence significant educational reform throughout the world.

In the second part of the chapter, Sharp provides a set of questions that a teacher might pose that are meant to help her or him gauge the growth of the group as a community of inquiry. In closing, she goes beyond the typically mentioned cognitive and affective features of the community of inquiry to look at (and inquire into) its moral and political dimensions.

16

On The Art and Craft of Dialogue

Ronald F. Reed

■ ■ ■

THE TASK of this chapter is a fairly complex one. In the course of a few pages, I will attempt to explain this "thing" called "Philosophy for Children," paying special attention to assumptions, goals, strategies, and evidence regarding its success or failure. I will then try to relate discoveries made in the practice of Philosophy for Children to problems that may arise for art educators as they develop curricula designed to involve students in aesthetic inquiry.

Philosophy for Children, by most measures, is said to have begun around 1969 when Matthew Lipman, a professor of philosophy at Columbia University, became concerned with and attempted to do something about a number of problems in education.[1] Two of those problems, for purposes of simplicity, we might label the "cognitive" and the "affective" ones.[2] The first revolves around a claim that children (in 1969 and, perhaps, in 1989) did not think as well as they could *or* as well as they should *or* as well, say, as a democratic society would demand. In addition, Lipman and many other reformers of the late 1960s and early 1970s believed that the schools should be doing far more than they were to encourage the development of thinking skills.

The second problem (and here Lipman clearly echoes concerns that John Dewey expressed in "My Pedagogic Creed" and in the opening pages of *Democracy and Education*) relates to children's attitudes toward school and academics.[3] The problem that Lipman saw was that very young children seemed to be interested in and curious about making sense of their lives and learning how to deal with their experience. As they progressed through school, however, their native interest and curiosity, as well as their zest for inquiry, seemed to diminish dramatically. School, which should stimulate a child's curiosity, was frequently seen to be a place where that curiosity, the very fuel of inquiry, was killed. The better students might be forced to say, with Mark Twain, that they never let school get in the way of their education.

Lipman, as mentioned, was (and is) a professor of philosophy. Thus, it stood to reason that he would attempt to solve the two problems with the tools at his hands—philosophy and the skills of logic it demands. But there was more involved in the choice than simple convenience. Philosophy, historically, has dealt with at least three major subjects—the good, the true, and the beautiful. From those three categories, it is not very hard to derive most of the main questions that have preoccupied philosophers for millennia and, not so coincidentally, the sorts of "why" questions with which very young children tend to overwhelm their parents and grandparents. Stated simply, Lipman noticed a significant similarity between the activity of philosophers and the activity of children. He set about trying to use that similarity to speak to educational concerns.

In addition, although the learning of philosophy does not make one a better physicist or musician or historian, what philosophy does tend to do is to concentrate on raising procedural issues (most notably logical and criteriological ones). Such issues are generic to the other disciplines, but they are often overlooked in the pursuit of the substantive issues of those disciplines.[4] This concentration on the legitimacy of the questioning of procedure, this turning of a discipline back upon itself, this sort of self-reflection, is precisely the kind of movement one makes in the attempt to encourage thinking, thinking well, and critical thinking in young children. Thus, Lipman thought that philosophy would be an excellent tool to use in dealing with the cognitive problem.

Still, it was, and in many cases remains, a part of the educational credo that although it might be logically possible that young children could handle philosophical questions in a respectable fashion, what might be called the "actual" possibility (or the probability or the real chance) that they could do so was insignificant. Packed into this credo was the belief that children learn best and most thoroughly when they start with the simple and progress to the complex—this despite the fact that infants learn some exceedingly complex concepts, "Mommy" and "Daddy" for examples, and learn how to manipulate those concepts to their own advantage with very little formal training.

Thus, the task at hand was no small one. It involved introducing an alien subject—a subject whose teaching demanded a sort of expertise, one that, in many ways, was outside the scope of the ordinary schoolteacher—into an already overburdened curriculum and within an environment that was not particularly conducive to successfully completing the task. Now, if there is one single stroke of genius in Philosophy for Children, it revolves around three assumptions:

1. children were capable of dealing with and interested in the traditional problems of philosophy, but
2. what kept them away from developing their capacity and interest was the forbidding terminology of philosophy, and

3. that it would be possible to present the traditional problems of philosophy to children in such a way that these questions would be divested of their forbidding terminology.

Harry Stottlemeier's Discovery is, in effect, a testing of these assumptions.

From 1970 onward, this book, a novel that introduces students, typically fifth- or sixth-graders, to the traditional problems of philosophy (personal identity, truth, induction, the mind-body problem, and so on) and to the beginnings of formal logic, along with the six other novels that grew to form the corpus of the Philosophy for Children curriculum, has been subjected to a great deal of scrutiny. Results of tests conducted by Lipman (1970), Haas (1975), Shipman (1978), Karras (1979), Cummings (1979), Higa (1980), Cinquino (1981), Burnes (1981), Yeazell (1981), Reed and Henderson (1985), Schleifer, Lubuis, and Caron (1987), Jackson and Deutsch (1987), Allen (1988), and Camhy and Iberer (1988)[5] show that when a group of students is exposed to Philosophy for Children regularly[6] that group will demonstrate a statistically significant improvement from pre- to posttest on standardized reasoning, mathematics, and reading tests over a control group.

There is reason to believe, then, that Philosophy for Children is effective in dealing with the cognitive problem. While very little work has been done on studying children's attitudes toward academics, this may say as much about our educational concerns in the 1980s as it does about anything. In any event, it is fairly safe to say that between a quarter and a half million children have participated in Philosophy for Children programs,[7] that there are now twenty or so Philosophy for Children centers around the world, and that, with the inclusion of Philosophy for Children as a recommended program in the federally sponsored National Diffusion Network, the program is fairly healthy.

So far, Philosophy for Children has been described through its history, its goals, its curriculum, and the testing that has been done on it. Still, the curious reader might have two rather fundamental questions. What is the practice of Philosophy for Children like? (Stated another way, How is teaching Philosophy for Children different from teaching other subjects?) What is it about this approach that might prove transferable to art education?

The description of a typical Philosophy for Children classroom experience has a disarming simplicity that belies the complexity of what is described. A teacher trained in Philosophy for Children leads the session.[8] Children read, typically, a paragraph each, out loud, until they finish a chapter of one of the novels.[9] The teacher then solicits "leading ideas" (things that the students found interesting in the chapter) from the group. Those ideas are listed on the blackboard and form the agenda for discussion. When enough issues have been raised, the class begins discussion and inquiry, with an eye toward moving from the specific to the general. A typical example comes in the third chapter of *Harry Stottlemeier's Discovery*, where a discussion of a specific incidence of unfairness leads to an inquiry into the nature of "fair." [10] As the discussion progresses, the teacher's task is to facilitate the discussion and encourage inquiry. The teacher has at his or her disposal the training received, a series of teacher's manuals, and this living, breathing thing called the classroom discussion.

This, of course, is precisely the place where things begin to become problematic and where one becomes aware of the enormous complexity of what is called, almost flippantly, an inquiry model or a discussion model or a Socratic model of education. [11] It is not sufficient—and there is ample historical evidence to support the claim that it is not—to tell teachers that they should inquire with children, that they should have open discussions with them, or that they should emulate the character of Socrates. Practitioners demand, with good reason, that the details of this shared inquiry be made more explicit. Otherwise, the teacher is in the position of the man in a James Thurber cartoon. Leaning against his car, owner's manual in hand, desiring to change a spark plug, he discovers that the task can be achieved in a "simple" two-step procedure: remove engine; change spark plug. That first step, like the suggestion to inquire, is a big one. The next section of this chapter will sketch some of the details of the inquiry, or dialogical, process.

INQUIRY

If one looks at the Socratic definition of wisdom, given in the *Apology*, [12] and at the successful practice of Philosophy for Children, one finds a perhaps not-so-surprising convergence. Socrates, very conscious of his own ignorance after hearing that the Oracle at Delphi had proclaimed him the wisest of persons, tried to disprove the Oracle's pronouncement. Socrates went to those with a reputation for wisdom and discovered, in effect, that the reputations were undeserved. These "learned" people thought that they knew far more than they really did; Socrates, on the other hand, was aware of his ignorance and limitations and, to that extent, was wiser than those with greater reputations. Human wisdom lies in not claiming that one knows more than one really knows. Stated another way, it involves the recognition of one's ignorance. [13]

What is essential, then, to the process of inquiry is what Alfred North Whitehead termed "scholarly ignorance." [14] If the traditional classroom praises the accumulation of information, the community of inquiry must prize its own ignorance. The very recognition that there is something we do not know, that there is something important to be gained by the process, is what gives the community its existence.

But ignorance, scholarly or not, is not sufficient. Along with it must go at least three more factors. First, and as a sort of backdrop to the inquiry process itself, there must be a kind of free-floating curiosity, a desire, sometimes earnest (and sometimes playfully earnest and sometimes earnestly playful) to, simply, understand more, to figure things out. If the world is viewed as closed and settled, if nothing is seen as curious or novel, then, as practice in Philosophy for Children shows over and over again, the process of inquiry will have little reason to be.

Second, and as a sort of addendum to the backdrop of curiosity, something, some idea or some cluster of concepts, must be experienced as problematic. If curiosity is not to be diffuse, it must, ultimately, center around the resolution of a problem. One sees this sort of focusing in the classroom practice of Philosophy for Children. The process is not neat and certainly is not linear, but, when things go well, a focusing of attention does take place. For example, the community may begin by trying to figure out the nature of a specific discovery in the first chapter of *Harry Stottlemeier's Discovery*. The conversation tends to center on the mechanics of the discovery (in this case, the logical move of conversion). At some point, when the group learns all it can or all it wants to learn, the problem shifts, say, to the nature of discovery. And then, a new set of problems arises. What happens, over and over, is that the specifically problematic gives impetus and direction to the conversation.

The last element in this incomplete list has something to do with expertise.[15] When one inquires, especially when one does so in an academic environment, one does so within the context of a specific discipline or, if one is involved in an interdisciplinary program, within the contexts of a number of different fields. Disciplines, at least in part, are made up of a series of routine, standardized moves. Stated another way, each discipline has its own techniques and, in order to inquire within it, one must know what its techniques are and have achieved a certain facility in their use. Thus, while the community inquires, it must busy itself with the task of learning how to use the disciplined tools of inquiry.[16]

So far, this section has been concerned with some very general characteristics of the process of inquiry: scholarly ignorance, free-floating curiosity, the presence of the problematic, and the employment of specific disciplines. These must be characteristics of the teacher. She or he must possess, if one can be allowed a bit of poetry, the gift of scholarly ignorance. She or he must be curious and must have the ability to recognize the problematic. She or he must be an expert in some discipline(s). The demands that inquiry makes on the teacher are, to say the least, daunting. Alas, there is also what is sometimes disparagingly called the "mechanics of discussion." The teacher is charged with seeing that the classroom dialogue contributes to the inquiry process. The topics that follow, derived from practice in Philosophy for Children, form a checklist that might be used as a guide through the thickets of classroom conversation. In effect, it is a compendium of things that can go wrong when one attempts to inquire within a community.

Extent and type of direction. The classic statement of what might be termed underdirection occurs in Neil Postman and Charles Weingartner's *Teaching as a Subversive Activity.*[17] There, the authors make it explicit that the teacher's task, almost in toto, is to ask a few interesting questions and then step back and let the conversation build according to its own dynamic. The problem that teachers encountered when they used that "methodology" was that it did not work frequently enough to justify its use.[18] Simply put, there is nothing magical about classroom dialogue. It demands monitoring and nurturing.

On the other hand, dialogue cannot be mandated. Just as one cannot command love, one cannot dictate that a conversation take place. The conversation depends upon the wit, intelligence, sense of fair play, and cooperation of its participants. One may be able to force a child to stay on certain tasks, but conversation does not seem to be one of them. The teacher who is running a classroom discussion might view herself or himself as an apprentice conductor of an orchestra of skilled musicians.[19] As conductor, she or he leads, but that leading is always based upon cues received from the members of the orchestra.

The nature of teacher talk. In the ideal community of inquiry, each member, including the teacher, would have an equal opportunity to speak.[20] Unfortunately, we are, typically, far from the ideal. Teachers, given their traditional roles as director, enforcer, dispenser of praise and punishment, and so on, have to be quite careful about how they enter the classroom discussion. Teachers tend to err in two basic ways. They either fall into a trap of wordiness, trying to explain and clarify everything that is said, or they maintain an almost sphinx-like silence, contenting themselves with asking only the barest of psychological questions—What do *you* think about that? or How do *you* feel about that? Keep in mind that, when inquiry works in groups, it does so as individual members actively participate. If one member dominates the group or, conversely, if one member refuses to participate, the inquiring community becomes less effective.

The difficulty of translation. When people communicate with one another, translation takes place all the time. *S* has experience *p* and *S* wants to communicate *p* to *T*. *S* must, somehow, translate that experience into verbal symbols that "capture" it and that I can understand.[21] *T*, in turn, may want to communicate her understanding of *p* to some other person. The obvious thing about communicating ideas, concepts, and experience is that they are not like "bricks."[22] They cannot be handed from one person to the next. Translation is an exceedingly complex procedure that demands the deft touch of, if not the artist, then the skilled artisan. The trick is to capture this fluid thing called a meaning and deliver it, as intact as possible, to one's listener.

Feelings and discourse. When philosophers and artists and other professionals get together and inquire, there is a presumption, justified or not, that everyone can take care of himself or herself. It is permissible to disagree strongly with another person's position because, it is assumed, the other person will not view the attack as personal. While that assumption may be justified for persons with a certain amount of expertise and a good deal of character armor, it is certainly not justified when dealing with persons who are new to the rough-and-tumble of discussions. Discussions tend to expose the feelings of participants. Someone—and if the community has not evolved enough to do it, then it should be the teacher—must accept the responsibility of ensuring that when children talk they run a minimal risk of sustaining psychological injury.

The teacher as filter. Classroom conversations tend to arise from a discussion of some "text." In Philosophy for Children, it is a novel. The text, however, could be a work of art, a literary or scientific theory, a historical explanation, and so on. What the text does is to provide the discussants with a common and public starting point. It also acts as a sort of principle of coherence for the conversation. If one gets too far from the text, one may, in effect, lose one's way, and the conversation may become so diffuse that individual participants go off on their own tangents. What was a dialogue turns into a series of monologues. On the other hand, if one forces the discussants to stick with simple textual analysis, if one precludes the development of issues that arise from the text or from a discussion of it, the conversation may very well lose the zest and vitality, the feeling of openness, that makes it so appealing.

The abuse of the controversial. Controversy can be abused in two ways. One may be so afraid of it—and in many parts of this country teachers have ample reason for such fear—that one checks or hinders a conversation as it inches near the controversial. The problem, then, is that inquiry constantly runs against contrived barriers, and inquirers are placed in a position where they begin to doubt that they will ever have the freedom that inquiry demands. If one is to inquire, one has to be prepared to follow that inquiry wherever it may lead.

The suggestion is not that one should aim for the controversial, but that there are times when it cannot and should not be avoided. Conversely, there are times, especially in terms of methodology, when the controversial could and should be avoided. What controversy does is to electrify conversations. It wakes the participants, pulling them out of the lethargy of the quotidian. Occasionally, it may be necessary to set off some sparks. It is just as necessary, however, to learn that inquiry is frequently prosaic, is not always exciting, and that one has to push through the most ordinary of thickets without the artificial stimulation of controversy.

Interest as a starting point. When children are exposed to a text, their interests must provide the starting point if they are to inquire. As Dewey suggests in "My Pedagogic Creed," to ignore the child's interest is to leave education dry and sterile.[23] This is not to say (and Dewey does not say) that one wallows in the child's interest. Education is a process of change, of transforming the given, but what has to be remembered is that the given is the child's specific interest(s).

Pedagogical reasons for avoiding indoctrination. When people are busy at a task, when their attention is focused on, say, inquiry, it is relatively easy for the unscrupulous person to slip in a hidden agenda—to somehow force belief. There are myriad ethical reasons for finding this sort of deception repugnant, but just as important may be pedagogical considerations. When one inquires, one "shines a light" on things in an endeavor to figure out what makes them what they are. Indoctrination is done "in the dark." It sidesteps the reasoning process that is inquiry and, hence, devalues the very process one is trying to encourage.

The clock. The school day, our school life, is timed. Inquiry, alas, does not always fit into neat timetables. Still, the intelligent practitioner has to have a sense of the clock. This does not mean that every lesson will achieve what educators call "closure." Again, real inquiry does not work like that. What it does mean, however, is that the teacher will be working toward a kind of coherence, where members leave class being able to say what they have accomplished and what remains to be done.

In addition to these general observations about time, there are two time-related factors that deserve specific attention.

The first is the overuse of personal anecdotes. When we inquire together, it is almost impossible not to argue from personal experience, to relate bits and pieces of our histories. There is nothing wrong with using anecdotes to facilitate the process of inquiry. The problem, however, is that all too frequently inquiry tends to degenerate into a mere recitation of personal history. A good rule of thumb might be to eliminate all anecdotal reports unless there is a compelling reason to share them.[24]

The second is the fear of silence. If one paid strict attention to dialogue, one might discover that there are as many silences as there are kinds of talk. Space limitations preclude the attention this topic warrants, and so I can make only the barest utterances. Conversation consists of words and the space between them—the silences. Efficiency and time effectiveness, by themselves, demand that practitioners cultivate all parts of the conversation.

The use and misuse of humor. Philosophy for Children by its very nature engenders a sense of humor. There is something odd, something not just a little funny, about grown persons in end-century New Jersey or Texas or Madrid or Taiwan dealing with problems that stumped Plato and Aristotle and Augustine and Descartes. There is something even odder and funnier about very young children performing the same activity *and* doing it well, with zest and vitality. If one does not see the humor, and if one does not bring a sense of playfulness to the serious business of inquiry, one may not be paying sufficient attention to what one is doing.

On the other hand, humor can be misused. It has the ability to defuse and deflect attention. If we are having a serious conversation about racism or sexism, that conversation can be derailed by the clever remark. The joke releases pressure. The problem, however, is that sometimes, when pressure is released, the conversation may lose its driving force. It is better, then, not to joke.

There is far more that could and should be said. In particular, what could stand a good deal more discussion is the relationship of the teacher's function as expert and dispenser of information (the traditional role) to the teacher's function as questioner and scholar (the not-so-traditional role). But, again, space limitations preclude delving into that area. What is left, then, are a few comments relating the preceding thoughts to the practice of art education.

Discipline-based art education is an ambitious business. One thinks about the magnitude (and the necessity) of relating aesthetics, art history, art criticism, and studio art to the practice of teaching art. It does not take great insight to know that the art teacher must have a thorough knowledge of those disciplines. She or he must have the sort of knowledge and expertise that comes from immersion in those fields.

In a similar way, inquiry is not something that can be just attached to the scholastic endeavor. It must permeate it, as well as the training and education of the art teacher.[25] Lists and essays (like this one) can be helpful devices; they can point the way. As Dewey said in *Democracy and Education*, however, the reason that inquiry does not take hold in education is that we "tell" about inquiry, rather than inquire.[26] If one is serious about using inquiry and dialogue in the classroom, one must see to it that teachers and prospective teachers are, themselves, taught by methods of inquiry and dialogue. When schools of education begin to realize that teachers, at their best, are Socratic—curious and blessedly ignorant sorts of persons—and when schools of education begin to realize that the good teacher is the good scholar, then they will take inquiry and dialogue seriously, and we will see significant progress in education.

NOTES

1. The history here is greatly oversimplified. More complete versions exist in Matthew Lipman, Ann Margaret Sharp, and Frederick S. Oscanyan, *Philosophy in the Classroom*, 2d ed. (Philadelphia: Temple University Press, 1980), and in Matthew Lipman, *Philosophy Goes to School* (Philadelphia: Temple University Press, 1988).

2. If current thinking in the field of critical thinking is correct, we may, in fact, have only one problem here. See, for example, Harvey Siegel, *Educating Reason: Rationality, Critical Thinking, and Education* (New York: Routledge, 1988).

3. John Dewey, "My Pedagogic Creed," in *The Philosophy of John Dewey*, ed. John J. McDermott (Chicago: University of Chicago Press, 1981), pp. 442–54; and John Dewey, *Democracy and Education* (1897; reprint, New York: Free Press, 1966), pp. 6–9.

4. I owe this distinction to one made by Professor Lipman in the course of a classroom discussion in February 1989.

5. The test results are reported in two IAPC publications, "Philosophy for Children: Where Are We Now?" and "Philosophy for Children: Where Are We Now?—Supplement No. 2." Both publications may be obtained from IAPC, Montclair State College, Upper Montclair, NJ 07043.

6. The notion of the regular varies with location and age group. In general, it means two or three forty-five-minute classes per week for at least twenty weeks.

7. By "participated," I mean regular attendance (see preceding note).

8. The extent and duration of training varies. At Texas Wesleyan University, training consists of at least six graduate hours (ninety hours). IAPC offers a series of other training options.

9. The important point is that the reading can be done aloud. The reading serves as a bridge from a typically private activity, thinking, to a typically public activity, talking.

10. Matthew Lipman, *Harry Stottlemeier's Discovery* (Upper Montclair, N.J.: First Mountain Foundation, 1985), pp. 9–14.

11. Throughout this chapter, I use "discussion models," "inquiry models," and "Socratic models" synonymously.

12. Plato, *Socrates' Defense* (Apology), in *The Collected Dialogues of Plato*, ed. Edith Hamilton and Huntington Cairns (Princeton, N.J.: Princeton University Press, 1961), pp. 7–9.

13. Ibid., p. 9.

14. A. N. Whitehead, *The Aims of Education* (1929; reprint, New York: Free Press, 1976), p. 37.

15. I have not always seen the need for this characteristic. My vision, if it is clearer, may be due to reading John P. Portelli, "On Reed and Discussing Philosophy with Children," in *Philosophy of Education: Introductory Readings*, ed. William Hare and John P. Portelli (Calgary, Canada: Detselig Enterprises, 1988), pp. 227–33.

16. One might argue that the only way to learn is through use. I come very close to presenting a variant of this argument in the final paragraphs of this chapter.

17. Neil Postman and Charles Weingartner, *Teaching as a Subversive Activity* (New York: Free Press, 1969).

18. Indeed, John Dewey suggested that this sort of procedure involved the denial of a methodology. See Dewey, *Democracy and Education*, p. 57.

19. By the time most children get to school, they are fairly skilled inquirers. Most teachers, however, are somewhat unfamiliar with orchestrating the inquiry process.

The orchestra analogy is a fairly popular one in Philosophy for Children. One teacher, after a particularly difficult class, suggested that it was like being an apprentice conductor trying to lead a group of skilled musicians while they tuned up.

20. For amplification of "teacher talk," see Ronald F. Reed, "Discussing Philosophy with Children: Aims and Methods," *Teaching Philosophy* 8, no. 3 (July 1985): 229–35, and Ronald F. Reed, *Talking with Children* (Denver, Colo.: Arden Press, 1983).

21. The "must" should be taken loosely. There are, of course, symbols other than verbal ones.

22. Dewey, *Democracy and Education*, p. 4.

23. Dewey, "My Pedagogic Creed," p. 452.

24. A compelling reason, by the way, could have something to do with the age of the child. When one works with first-graders, one realizes that an attempt to eliminate the telling of all anecdotes is an effective way of stopping inquiry.

25. For an explicit and thorough development of how inquiry might permeate a community, see Ann Margaret Sharp, "What Is a Community of Inquiry?" *Journal of Moral Education* 16, no. 1 (1985): 22–30.

26. Dewey, *Democracy and Education*, p. 38.

17

Inventing a Classroom Conversation

Ronald F. Reed

■ ■ ■

MY TITLE points to four pivotal questions, or families of questions, that determine, in part, the scope of this chapter and that, I suggest, could and should form a basis for educational reform. Taking the questions as they spring from the four words of the title—

Why invent, and not, say, discover, a classroom conversation? Are the patterns of classroom conversation social constructs, or are they "packed" historically, if not theoretically, into the nature of effective classroom conversation? For example, when we tell the new teacher to imitate the example of Socrates, do we assume that such imitation is based on a discovery by the new teacher as to what Socrates' methodology *is*?

Why, if invention is what we are about, invent one classroom conversation? Why not invent as many conversations as there are classrooms? Stated another way, why not invent at least as many conversations as there are disciplines?

What is the importance of conversation in the classroom? In a time when the need for educational reform appears to be a priority, why should emphasis be placed on how children talk among themselves and with adults?

Finally, why conversation at all and not, say, dialogue or lecturing or suggestive questioning or drill and recitation? Why, in fact, spend time on a "methodology" that of necessity is as amorphous as it is unwieldy?

The rest of this chapter will be divided into four parts corresponding roughly to the four families of questions just posed.

Rosalyn Sherman Lessing was not the first to notice that there is a problem with the admonition to teach Socratically, but she is one of the clearest critics of that admonition.[1] Simply put, a negative definition of Socratic teaching, where it is defined as "not lecturing," will be of little pedagogical use to the prospective teacher. In a similar vein, to suggest that one exhausts the definition of "Socratic teaching" by means of a stipulation that the Socratic teacher asks questions is to ignore that Socrates asked many different sorts of questions for many different sorts of reasons. If one is to be in a position to imitate Socrates' behavior, especially as it relates to questioning, one must first have a feel for the variety of contexts in which those questions were posed.

To become sensitive to those contexts is to learn, quickly and forcefully, that there is more than one "Socrates" to imitate. The callow youth one meets in the *Parmenides* asks questions that cause Socrates a good deal of discomfort, not to mention throwing suspicion on the entire Theory of the Forms.[2] On the other hand, the mature Socrates we encounter in the *Meno* uses questions to lead the slave boy to a series of "correct" answers that, not coincidentally, lends support to a Platonic doctrine of the recollection of knowledge.[3]

The problem, then, is that discovery in Plato will differ from dialogue to dialogue and that if we are to choose among the discoveries, if we are to figure out which one to imitate, we must have some criteria in place to make that choice. Presumably, those criteria will be related to the educative worth of the conversation. If that is the case, however, the use of Socrates as a model will be merely heuristic, and we could be as well served by simply listing those criteria. The same, of course, might be said of any existing models that are recommended—that is, in order to recommend them, we must have some criteria in mind.

Recent scholarship, especially in feminist philosophy and in Philosophy for Children, suggests that previous models and the criteria used to evaluate them will be of marginal help in constructing the conversations to take place in contemporary classes. These models and criteria were basically exclusionary— significant portions of the population were either precluded or hindered from participating fully in the conversation. As Gilligan, Martin, Sharp, and others have eloquently pointed out, the conversation in which, say, women and children, have equal access with men is a historical curiosity.[4] That exchange is being "born," and the criteria for evaluation are not just emerging from the interplay of different "voices" in it but are, in fact, being invented by that interplay.

As for the second family of questions, John McPeck's influential work, *Critical Thinking and Education*, caught many people in the relatively amorphous field of thinking skills by surprise.[5] McPeck undercut the ground of the thinking-skills movement in at least two ways. First, by suggesting that thinking *always* occurs in the disciplines, he made many thinking-skills programs redundant. Second, by suggesting that thinking occurs *only* in the disciplines, he precluded the existence of thinking-skills programs that are not discipline related.

The field, as fields tend to do, has responded to many of McPeck's claims, but he still presents, as it were, a sort of logical puzzle of coherence. The puzzle might be stated like this: If thinking is always discipline related, and if the curriculum (on the grounds of coherence) "demands" that the disciplines talk with one another, then either the demand cannot be satisfied and, hence, the curriculum by its nature is incoherent, *or* one must assume that there is a sort of discipline of the disciplines in which that talk can take place.

It is the latter way of dealing with the puzzle that is most helpful for the purposes of this chapter. If conversations are important educationally, then students must have a way of "moving" from one conversation to another in such a way that they can see the connections among them. There must be, in effect, a conversation of the conversation in the same way that there is a discipline of the disciplines. Stated another way, if students are to begin to learn from and to use the educational conversations in which they are engaged, they must have some way of analyzing and evaluating the worth of those conversations, and if conversation is a good tool for such analysis and evaluation, what is needed is a conversation that focuses on such analysis and evaluation. For want of a better term, let us label such a conversation a "philosophical" one. The claim then is that, for reasons of coherence, one needs to create a conversation that will, somehow, reflect upon myriad conversations that occur in the classroom.

The third family of questions relates directly to classroom practice. What is the importance of conversation in the classroom? In a time when the need for educational reform appears to be a priority, why should we emphasize how children talk among themselves and with adults?

At first blush, the questions would appear to demand some kind of statistical sorting out among competing educational claims. Regardless, however, of the educational payoffs, we do have certain reasons to believe that conversations might have something to recommend them that other techniques do not. First of all, conversations provide an ideal place to discover interest. One can, of course, force a person to talk, but conversation seems to depend for its very life on the interest and sense of involvement of the participants. Thus, in order to discover interest, one typically needs look, merely, at this very public thing called "conversation." If Dewey is right in his claim that interest provides the starting point of education, one has ample reason to believe that conversation is, at the least, a valuable educational tool.

Second, conversations are, in a sense, freely chosen. They are functions of desires to talk about this and not that, to talk with these people and not some others. One can mandate that a person come to a conversation, that a person refrain from making noise during the conversation, that a person talk during a conversation, even that a person appear to take part in a conversation. What one cannot do is mandate psychological states of affairs. Just as it is wrong-headed (i.e., it misunderstands the activity) to command love, where love is understood as involving a psychological state of affairs, it seems a mistake to attempt to command participation in a conversation. At best, one can invite participation, recognizing that the person's interests and desires will have an impact on whether the invitation is viewed as desirable. Thus, to invite to a conversation is to recognize implicitly that the person invited has the freedom to accept or reject the invitation.

The conversation, then, is a function of desire and reflects the freedom of the individual to participate or to refrain from participating. In regard to the former, if we assume (and this would seem to be a relatively trivial assumption) that, *ceteris paribus,* a subject that is related to existing desires would be more easily learned than one that is not so connected, then conversation would have something to recommend it over many of the other activities in the typical classroom. Insofar as the latter goes, one might argue along progressive lines that in times of educational practice when issues of student freedom seem to be largely ignored a method that stresses such freedom warrants serious consideration.

Third, since a primary concern of educators, critics of American schooling, educational reformers, and others revolves around a claim that children do not know what they should or, stated another way, do not remember what they once knew, there is something about the amorphous, nonlinear quality of conversations that is especially appealing. In a conversation, things are not just introduced, incorporated, and then dropped. A conversation is decidedly not like a thesis. Conversations thrive on redundancy and repetition. An idea is introduced and as it were, tried on by different speakers. If drill and repetition are legitimate mnemonic instruments, then a conversation can be seen as a place par excellence where reflective mnemonic instruments are used. The constant passing around of ideas, which is endemic to a conversation, entails, if we are to accept Dewey's disanalogy between the handing of bricks from one person to another and the sharing of ideas among persons, constant reflection on those ideas.[6] There is, then, good reason to believe that if the conversation touches on what Bloom or Hirsch would label the great tradition,[7] participants would not only remember those ideas but also have a fairly good start on understanding them and their implications.

Finally, as feminist critics have pointed out, people tend to define themselves by and in the conversations of which they are a part.[8] If the schools are to have an educative impact on students, if they are to contribute to the definition of the child and her or his community, there is something about the nature of conversation that lends itself to this task.

The fourth family of questions—Why conversation at all, and not, say, dialogue or lecturing or suggestive questioning or drill and recitation? Why, in fact, spend time on a "methodology" that, of necessity, is as amorphous as it is unwieldy?—provides a bridge to the premise of a correction of educational reform that was mentioned at the beginning of this chapter.

My previous discussion has involved an attempt to show that conversation has something to recommend it to the attention of educators, that conversation can be viewed as an important educative tool. As I attempt to deal with the fourth family of questions, I will argue that conversation is not *just* one tool among many (educative) tools. Conversation may be seen as providing the context in which those other tools lose their discreteness and arbitrary quality and take on a relationship with their "fellows" that, in turn, facilitates their own educative qualities. The conversation has a kind of logical priority over other educative tools.

Scholars in Philosophy for Children, in their attempts to distinguish what they do from what other educational-reform movements attempt to do, may have devoted the most time to focusing on the nature of conversation. From the primary work of Matthew Lipman, Ann Margaret Sharp, and Frederick S. Oscanyan that appears in the opening pages of the teacher's manual that accompanies *Harry Stottlemeier's Discovery*[9] to the more recent publications of Lipman, Sharp, Weinstein, Pritchard, Silver, and Reed,[10] practitioners of Philosophy for Children have gone a long way toward distinguishing the talk with children that they consider philosophical from other kinds of talk. Along the way, with feminist and minority-group philosophers, they have, not so coincidentally, begun to erect the scaffolding of classroom conversation.

There is neither time nor necessity to follow those scholars into the details of their work. A look at a few of their findings might prove sufficient to support a claim that conversations have a logical priority over the other educational tools mentioned in this chapter.

The first thing that becomes clear is that conversation has the flexibility to incorporate the other tools, whereas when conversation "enters" into the other tools it drastically changes their nature. Thus, in the course of a conversation, lecturing and telling can take place without altering it. Questions, both suggestive and nonsuggestive, are posed without necessarily changing the nature of the conversation. Dialogue—the focused investigation of a specific topic or family of topics—does take place without changing the nature of the conversation. Indeed, drill and recitation can easily be incorporated into the conversation without changing its character. All of the tools mentioned may, indeed should, have an impact on the course of the conversation, but there is no reason that they must change its nature.

On the other hand, when one introduces conversation into the other tools, one seems to alter their characters. Speaking metaphorically, conversation seems to kill them, while the other tools seem to be essential to the health of conversation. For example, when one allows conversation in the dialogue, when one allows the speakers to follow their interests as opposed to staying on the task that is the dialogue, one effectively derails it.

If it turns out that there are many ways that teachers should and must talk with their children in the classroom, a method, such as conversation, that enabled the other approaches should be preferred over one that was, in effect, in opposition to them.

Another reason that conversation seems to take priority is that it allows for and can incorporate two (typically) competing models of the teacher-student relationship: the model of expert–acolyte, where the teacher dispenses knowledge to the children, and the model of community of inquiry, where the teacher and the students are viewed as partners engaged in the solution or dissolution of some shared problem. Since there are times in the classroom when simple telling is called for, when drill and recitation are both helpful and necessary, when a premium is placed on teacher expertise, a method, like conversation, which allows for that should be prized. In a similar sense, since there are times when questioning and the more or less free-form pursuit of interests is appropriate, when the scholarly ignorance that is the hallmark of communities of inquiry is essential, a method like conversation commends itself over other methods by virtue of its very versatility.

Another thing suggesting the priority of conversation is its flexibility and the way that characteristic is related to one of the psychological commonplaces encountered in the classroom—students' inability to stay "on task." Rather than force children to stay on task as, say, a dialogue might, conversation is flexible enough to follow the students' interests and uses those interests to determine tasks. The challenge that Dewey posed for education in "My Pedagogic Creed,"[11] identifying interests and transforming them, might best be fulfilled through the conversation.

The last item in this incomplete list of reasons supporting the primacy of conversation over other educational methods is the way in which conversation, even more than its close relative, dialogue, demands active involvement. In a dialogue, for example, participants can depend on the skilled interlocutor to keep the discussion on course—they can play a passive role. Conversations, on the other hand, depend on the active and continual involvement of the participants. Conversations do not happen to participants in the way that, say, the *Meno* "happens" to the slave boy. If philosophers from Augustine through Dewey to, most recently, Jane Roland Martin are right in their claims that education is active, that it must be claimed and not received,[12] then conversation, the most active of the tools mentioned here, seems to provide the most fruitful context in which education could occur.

NOTES

1. Rosalyn Sherman Lessing, "Is It Possible to Teach Socratically?" in *Philosophy of Education: Introductory Readings*, ed. William Hare and John P. Portelli (Calgary, Canada: Detselig Enterprises, 1988), pp. 243–59.

2. Plato, *Parmenides*, in *Plato: Collected Dialogues*, ed. Edith Hamilton and Huntington Cairns (New York: Pantheon Books, 1964), pp. 920–57.

3. Plato, *Meno*, in ibid., pp. 353–84.

4. Carol Gilligan, *In a Different Voice: Psychological Theory and Women's Development* (Cambridge, Mass.: Harvard University Press, 1981); Jane Roland Martin, *Reclaiming a Conversation: The Ideal of the Educated Woman* (New Haven, Conn.: Yale University Press, 1985); and Ann Margaret Sharp, "Women and Children and the Evolution of Philosophy," *Analytic Teaching* 10, no. 1 (1989): 46–52.

5. John McPeck, *Critical Thinking and Education* (New York: St. Martin's Press, 1981).

6. John Dewey, *Democracy and Education* (1917; reprint, New York: Macmillan, 1966), pp. 4–6.

7. Allan Bloom, *The Closing of the American Mind* (New York: Simon and Schuster, 1987); and E. D. Hirsch, *Cultural Literacy* (Boston: Houghton Mifflin, 1987).

8. Martin, *Reclaiming a Conversation.*

9. Matthew Lipman, Ann Margaret Sharp, and Frederick S. Oscanyan, *Philosophical Inquiry* (New York: University Press of America, 1984), pp. i–ii.

10. Matthew Lipman, *Philosophy Goes to School* (Philadelphia: Temple University Press, 1988); Ann Margaret Sharp, "What Is a Community of Inquiry?" *Analytic Teaching* 8, no. 1 (1987): 13–18; Mark Weinstein, "Extending Philosophy for Children into the Standard Curriculum," *Analytic Teaching* 8, no. 2 (1988): 19–31; Michael Pritchard, "Reciprocity Revisited," *Analytic Teaching* 9, no. 2 (1989): 54–62; Ruth Silver, "Giving Grades in Philosophy for Children's Classes," *Analytic Teaching* 9, no. 2 (1988): 3–10; and Ronald F. Reed, "Discussing Philosophy with Children: Aims and Methods," *Teaching Philosophy* 8, no. 3 (1985): 229–34.

11. John Dewey, "My Pedagogic Creed," in *The Philosophy of John Dewey*, ed. John J. McDermott (Chicago: University of Chicago Press, 1981), pp. 442–53.

12. St. Augustine, "Concerning the Teacher," in *Foundations of Education in America*, ed. James Noll and Sam P. Kelly (New York: Harper and Row, 1988), pp. 52–57; Dewey, *Democracy and Education*; and Martin, *Reclaiming a Conversation.*

18

A Letter to a Novice Teacher: Teaching Harry Stottlemeier's Discovery

Ann Margaret Sharp

■ ■ ■

My dear friend,

It was good to hear that you have completed your training in *Harry Stottle-meier's Discovery* and will begin teaching it next semester. I only hope that you have experienced what it is to participate in a community of inquiry and will be able to create such a community in your classroom very soon.

Yes, you are right. I have taught *Harry* for many years to elementary students, college students, and teachers. There have been times, to be honest, when I have thought that if I heard the first chapter of *Harry* read one more time I would bang my head against the wall. But then, I would recall the surge of excitement when the reading ends and the teacher asks the group for questions, or things in the chapter they found of interest, or puzzles they discovered in their own reading, or observations they would like to make about the characters and their thinking. It's as if, at this point, a new world opens up and another chapter commences on the interpretation of the novel.

Harry Stottlemeier's Discovery is a world unto itself, always set in juxtaposition to the world you, as a teacher, enter with the particular group that has assembled. It's a rich world full of much philosophy that has been reconstructed so as to make it accessible to children and laypeople. In a sense, it hints at philosophy as a whole: philosophical reasoning (formal and informal logic, relational logic, hypothetical reasoning, the good-reasons approach) together with the concepts drawn from the various subdisciplines of philosophy itself. There are chapters on epistemology, philosophy of education, social and political philosophy, philosophy of religion, art, and science, and philosophy of mind. An ethical dimension runs through each chapter. The characters model various philosophical styles of thinking. There is Mr. Portos's didacticism, and perhaps dogmatism, and Mrs. Portos's questioning

165

and openness to alternative positions. There is Mr. Spence's love of inquiry, Tony's analyticity, Lisa's dialectical thinking, and Harry's experimentalism. And who can forget Mr. Partridge's conventional and devious thinking?

The characters in *Harry* not only portray philosophical styles of thinking but often take philosophical positions drawn from the history of philosophy. One can spot the views of Plato, Aristotle, Augustine, Thomas, Spinoza, Leibniz, Kant, Descartes, Marx, and Dewey—just to mention a few. To the extent that the students in your class grapple with the different characters' positions, they are grappling with the ideas that have come down to us through the great philosophers, and they enter into the conversation of humankind. Unlike what happens in traditional philosophy courses, however, they enter as *active* participants who are trying to understand the alternative positions while being encouraged to develop views of their own.

The philosophy that you have studied will stand you in good stead as you go through the seventeen chapters of *Harry* with your students. It is not that this study of philosophy will give you answers that you should want to pass along to the pupils. But it ought to have prepared you to *hear* the philosophical dimension of what your students say and enable you to ask appropriate follow-up questions so that they might be able to develop their own positions as best they can. This modeling of follow-up questions is very important in teaching *Harry*—it might be your most important role. These questions that probe for assumptions, clarification, counterinstances, alternative perspectives, consequences, and appropriate contexts—these are the questions that your students must internalize and, in a short time, put to each other. You can view these questions as your students' tools to be used collaboratively in finding the best reasons possible to support their own views.

I hope your study of philosophy will also serve you well in another way. I hope it will help you to understand the structure of many of the discussion plans in the *Harry* manual. These discussion plans have been designed to help children and adults form for themselves concepts that are essentially controversial and philosophical, but in a way that considers alternative positions that have been offered by past philosophers. I'm referring to the central concepts that you and your students ought to explore in doing *Harry*: truth, knowledge, friendship, mind, meaning, education, freedom, rights, art, the good, human nature, language, science, and the community of inquiry.

I wish you good hearing for another reason. You should be able to hear the philosophical dimension of what is said and be alert for the omission of philosophical reasoning in the classroom dialogues. Your hearing should enable you to detect what your students are lacking. At times you might detect their need for practice in finding assumptions or in drawing inferences. At other times, you might detect their need for giving counterinstances or for asking appropriate questions. And at still other times they might need to become sensitive to bad analogies or faulty informal reasoning. Take the time to give them practice when you hear they need it.

Watch your talking. It is understandable that in the beginning you will be doing more talking and the pattern of discourse will be primarily teacher–student, with you asking the questions or giving counterinstances or suggesting alternative ways of looking at things. But in a short time this pattern should change. Students should be asking the appropriate follow-up questions of each other, with your role becoming more participatory. At this point, you should speak no more than any other member of the conversation. And when you do decide to talk, ask yourself, "What pedagogical purpose will my remark serve?" It's not your role to retell the history of philosophy, but there may be times when a point of information or clarification can move the dialogue along. In the beginning, you might want to record the classroom dialogues and use a Flander's Analysis Instrument to decipher for yourself who exactly is doing the most talking. It's easy to misjudge. There have been times when I thought I did very little talking only to discover that I talked more frequently and longer than anyone else in the group. And this was well into the semester when it was not necessary.

Each group is very different, and it's your job to know your group well. Some reason well and can detect reasoning mistakes immediately. Others do not. Some have a feel for ideas and the dialectic of opposing ideas. Others do not. Some are very comfortable with divergent thinking. They love to explore concepts and are willing to entertain alternative positions. Others are only comfortable with convergent thinking. They love to explore the logic in *Harry* and do the exercises in the manual. But, as their teacher, you have an obligation to give them practice in both divergent and convergent thinking. Thus, it is going to be important for you to strike a balance between two aspects of the course, reasoning and concept formation. On occasion the students might resist, but with time and trust they will experience satisfaction from both enterprises.

Of all the programs in Philosophy for Children, *Harry Stottlemeier's Discovery* is the one that models the community of inquiry in such a way that children are encouraged to inquire collaboratively and at the same time think for themselves. We have a saying at IAPC that you should be pedagogically strong but philosophically self-effacing. I have often thought, when I hear it said, that it means very little until one has had years of experience teaching *Harry*. But one thing I can say is that, in the beginning, it is up to you to monitor the logical procedures for the students until they can do it for themselves. At the same time, when it comes to substantive philosophical issues your view is only one among many. Toward the beginning of the course, I would refrain from giving any views. When you think your students are strong enough to conduct a rigorous discussion without you, at that point you might want to submit your own views for their scrutiny. This is a matter of professional judgment. I have had classes where I never felt the students were ready to treat my views as just one more position to be taken into account. As a result, I have had to discipline myself to confine my remarks to procedural comments. At times this is hard, especially when your favorite issue is on the table. It becomes a little easier if you ask yourself what you want to accomplish. I would think you want your students to object to weak reasoning, accept the responsibility for making their contributions within the context of others' remarks, follow the inquiry where it leads, respect the perspective of others, and collaboratively engage in self-correction. Further, I would think you would like them to be able to take pride in the accomplishments of the group, as well as their own. In short, you want to give them practice in the art of making good judgments about matters of importance.

I would advise you and your students to take stock every two weeks to evaluate the group's progress in becoming a community of inquiry. Initially, you can ask yourself a variety of questions that fall into three categories: cognitive, social, and, for want of a better word, psychosocial. Eventually, the group should be able to do this with or without you. With regard to the cognitive category, ask yourself after the first month:

1. Are the students asking philosophical questions?
2. What is the quality of their follow-up questions to each other?
3. Are the students making good inferences?
4. Are the students giving good reasons for their views?
5. Do they probe for assumptions?
6. Can they detect contradictions?
7. Can they recognize bad analogical reasoning?
8. Can they detect fallacious reasoning?
9. Do they ask for criteria?
10. Can they standardize well?
11. Do they manifest a concern for logical criteria?

If the answer to all of these questions in four weeks is yes, I would be very surprised. So don't be too hard on yourself or your students. Some of these skills take time to develop. For example, knowing how to ask appropriate questions and appropriate follow-up questions at the right time is a very complex skill that assumes you have mastered a feel for philosophical issues and many of the single-step logical skills introduced in *Harry*.

The community of inquiry is not just a cognitive enterprise. It is also a social enterprise that can take on great meaning for children and adults if guided well in its formative stages. Some of the social and psychological questions you and the group can ask yourselves every once in a while are:

1. Who is doing the talking? Do the same people seem to talk all the time? Do some people take too long to say what they have to say?

2. Do the students seem to care for one another?
3. Do the students seem able to correct each other with sensitivity?
4. Do students listen to one another and build on one another's ideas?
5. Do students consciously mute themselves at times in order to follow the inquiry where it leads?
6. Do students help each other find the best reasons for their opinions even if they don't agree with the position?
7. Are students developing a certain philosophical humility?
8. Are students becoming more tentative in their knowledge claims?
9. Are students more willing to revise their positions in light of the dialogue?
10. Do students seem to trust you and each other?
11. Is a group solidarity beginning to form?

We often forget that communities of inquiry are made up of people, some of whom are extroverts, some introverts, some of whom are trusting, some mistrusting. This puts a burden on you to establish an atmosphere of trust as soon as possible. The students must see you as someone who

1. doesn't think he knows it all,
2. really loves ideas,
3. respects them as persons,
4. takes what they have to say seriously, and
5. demands logical rigor of them.

If you manifest these traits, I think they will come to trust you and each other, at least enough to try on ideas openly and submit them to inquiry. As you can imagine, this will be harder for some than for others and will require sensitivity on your part. To the extent that some students hold their ideas very rigidly and take them very seriously, they will experience a sense of risk when they voice their views and subject them to public scrutiny. These persons are going to need support until they become more confident.

Communities can progress toward the ideal, but they can be impeded also. There are certain signs that should warn you that something is wrong. If some participants (and this includes you) are engaging in long monologues at the expense of others sharing their views, you know something is wrong. (I've often told my students that if you talk for more than one minute, you've probably talked too long.) If a student puts down another student, you should feel free to overtly stop the behavior. Correcting one another's reasoning is one thing, and giving counterinstances and voicing alternative views is another. But making fun of a student's view or calling one another names is destructive. In general, the breakdown of the community occurs not when views are corrected but when persons are hurt. This happens when one person exploits another, that is, uses the relations that have been formed for some purpose other than communal inquiry, pursuit of meaning, and furthering the growth of each member of the class.

This is not to say that there should not be a certain tension in the group. Although such tension may produce conflict, it is not itself conflict. When violin strings have just the right tension, they can be used to produce the most beautiful music. Similarly, when a certain creative tension is manifested in the expression of divergent views, the group has the potential for inquiry and growth, and each participant has the potential for developing her or his own ideas. Such tension is painful for teachers, I know. You might be tempted to get rid of it. But this would come at a very dear price.

Finally, I remind you that the community of inquiry has a moral and political dimension that you must be aware of at all times. If we assume that the purpose of education is not only to transmit a body of knowledge and some intellectual skills but to equip children with the dispositions they need to create new knowledge and make better judgments in their daily lives, then the traditional classroom approach of "telling" is not appropriate when teaching *Harry*, even when it comes to moral and political issues. Further, if we assume that the purpose of education is the forming of persons—persons of responsibility and integrity, capable of making good judgments—then the dialogue becomes the important instrument and the community of inquiry becomes a means and an end, satisfying in itself, while at the same time cultivating the traits essential for a morally discriminating person.

In becoming members of a community of inquiry, your students will have the opportunity to develop the virtues of courage, perseverance, and self-esteem. It takes courage to submit one's views to public inquiry. It takes perseverance to struggle continually for understanding. In the community of inquiry, students experience an intellectual and affective complementarity. One student questions and the other answers. One student puts forth a hypothesis or a position and another offers a counterinstance or an alternative position. The counterinstance or alternative view often issues in still a third position. Students and teacher find themselves working on a team in which there is a division of labor. Yes, one aim of yours is to make sure students internalize the procedures of inquiry so that they can inquire when they are away from the group. But another aim that is equally important is to help students inquire well together. Thus, you might say that in one sense you are encouraging similarity (mastery of tools of logic and inquiry), but in another very important sense you are encouraging uniqueness. You are urging people to think for themselves within the context of the community.

The division of labor that they experience when working together teaches the group the value of individual differences. The student who speaks out and criticizes the community's procedures is, as John Stuart Mill pointed out, a positive contributor to its health. The student who comes up with what appears to the others as a very strange position gives rise to inquiry that might issue in an even more extraordinary and original position. When the other students see the individual speaking out, this in turn helps them to become courageous and submit their ideas for scrutiny. Thus, the community of inquiry is not only rational and rule governed, not only consensus guided. It also supports intellectual independence. This means that you have to be on your guard to protect the individual who shares his views no matter how different. Peer pressure can be very subtle in a community of inquiry. Further, it can be just as destructive to adults' intellectual autonomy as to that of children. On the other hand, a community that practices intellectual tolerance can foster the growth of courage, competence, and self-esteem.

One can look at the community of inquiry as a means of personal and moral transformation that inevitably leads to a shift in meanings and values that affects the lives of all participants. One of the most striking characteristics of a community of inquiry is that, over time, its members change for the better. They often find themselves capable of saying such things as:

> I find I am no longer pressured into accepting views that I suspect are harmful.
> I can tolerate ambiguity more.
> I am no longer in need of pretending what I feel or what I think.
> My taste in many things is changing.
> I'm beginning to experiment with patterns of behavior that make more sense in my daily life.
> What other people say can make a difference in what I finally think.
> I find myself listening more.
> I'm beginning to understand how very little I really know.
> I find myself holding my own views far more tentatively.
> I think I'm becoming more careful in how I think about things. I don't admire sloppy thinking.

One can explain such claims as a slow, progressive release from subjectivism, intellectual and social conformity, and preoccupation with the self into finding the world and other people more and more meaningful. As time goes on, students may discover the moral guidelines they want to live by and the moral virtues they want to exemplify in their daily lives. In a real sense, they can come to discover and create themselves as they inquire together about philosophical concepts. They create and discover the persons they think they ought to be.

I'm sure that I'm not the first to tell you that teaching *Harry* using the community-of-inquiry model is, itself, a political enterprise. In a very practical and concrete way you are forming persons who will be committed to open inquiry, tolerance, pluralism, and democracy. To the extent that people have had the experience of shared dialogue, then they can have shared understanding, shared ideals, shared meanings. Such experiences are a precondition for the communal reflection and action essential for the existence of a strong democracy. Thus, you can view yourself as preparing the next generation dispositionally, cognitively, and socially to engage in the necessary dialogue and evaluation processes that are vital to the existence of a democratic society. To convert classrooms into communities of inquiry moves us beyond arguments and theories into the realm of concrete actions aimed at changing the world for the better.

I don't mean to overwhelm you. I'm just trying to help you think about the complexity and richness of teaching *Harry Stottlemeier's Discovery*. And remember what I said earlier: Teaching the novel is like opening up the world for yourself and for your students. It's an elementary-school discipline that should be as full of wonder and meaning for you as for them. I hope that you will learn as much from your pupils as they will learn from you. They can help you become a better philosopher. After seventeen years, I can still say that I find the course vital and meaningful for me in my own struggle to make sense of my world. The dialogues in the classroom should prompt you to read books you've never heard of and to reread books that you thought you understood, only to find out in speaking your ideas with the students that you didn't.

My wish for you is that teaching *Harry* will give you a great deal of satisfaction. Not only should it be rigorous, it should be fun. You should be able to enjoy doing philosophy with your students. In a short time, you should be able to perceive that you are making a significant difference in their lives— that you are really helping them grow and become the persons they can be. Further, you'll come to discover that you have been instrumental in helping them realize just how much they can do when they inquire together.

All the very best to you,

Ann

(Ann Margaret Sharp)

EPILOGUE

19

A Critical Look at Harry Stottlemeier's Discovery

Frederick S. Oscanyan

■ ■ ■

SINCE ITS RECENT introduction as an elementary-school philosophy text, Professor Matthew Lipman's *Harry Stottlemeier's Discovery* has enjoyed a string of successes.[1] First employed in an experimental class in Montclair, New Jersey, in 1970, it is now being used in Newark, New Haven, Omaha, San Antonio, Milwaukee, Pasadena, and Cleveland, and it is moving overseas in Danish, French, and Spanish translations. Its use is associated with astounding increases in reading scores, as well as strong improvements in logic and verbal abilities.[2] It has helped spawn the Institute for the Advancement of Philosophy for Children[3] and has encouraged the founding of a National Forum for Philosophical Reasoning in the Schools.[4] With all this in its favor, it is surely important to examine its philosophic credentials.

Lipman's work constitutes a direct challenge to long-established presumptions about the character of an introduction to philosophy. It is not organized in standard introductory format: It is neither "problem" nor "history" oriented. There is no use or mention of any technical philosophical term anywhere in the book; the word "philosophy" itself appears only on the cover and title page, unobtrusively, in small print. It is not taught by professional philosophers but instead by regular elementary-school teachers, many of whom have had little training in philosophy save for a workshop in teaching *HSD*. And, most important, it defends no recognized philosophical thesis, nor does it display well-developed arguments that articulate a new one. In place of all this, *HSD* is instead composed of a variety of conversations between children, and between children and adults, which focus on topics of concern to the children. It has thus been aptly described by a critic as "just a story about a bunch of kids." A superficial glance at *HSD* and its uses can thus lead one to wonder whether the book is any more—or less—philosophical than, say, *Treasure Island*, or the old

Hardy Boys series, or even *The Bobbsey Twins*. But a more careful examination of *HSD* can radically modify, and perhaps even eliminate, such suspicions.

HSD is constructed of a series of dialogues between children. Though adults often make contributions, the book consistently retains this child-centered perspective. As to its overt structure, while it is divided into seventeen short chapters, the dialogues are its core. They are composed of a variety of themes, some overlapping, some confined to particular discussions. These include such diverse concerns as what the nature of the mind is, whether the pledge to the flag should be mandatory, how to distinguish between differences in degree and kind, how persons differ from things, what shapes we see in clouds, who threw a rock at Harry Stottlemeier, how reasons differ from causes, and what the varieties of thinking are. Entwined with these strands is a main theme that appears in various guises in every chapter: the development of effective ways to think about thinking.

The basic purpose of the book is to provide its ten- to twelve-year-old readers with a means for attending to their own thoughts and to ways that their thoughts and reflections can function in their lives. This is approached through a discovery of rule-governed thinking and by illustrations of a variety of nondeductive types of thought. The logical rules are not simply stated for the reader to learn; instead, the book provides illustrations of rules and of search techniques so that its readers can come to identify such rules on their own. This is most important—the book is designed to encourage its readers to pay careful attention to their own thoughts and ideas, rather than to acquire significant reflections by constantly trying to think someone else's thoughts, as is the case with even the most up-to-date grade-school texts. Together with the discovery that certain kinds of thinking are rule governed, readers are also made aware of such contrasting modes of thought as imagining, dreaming, and pretending, in which such logical rules play little or no part. Through coming to appreciate and enjoy this broad variety of kinds of thinking, the readers can then realize that while their thinking often has logical form, and occasionally fails to when it should, much of it does not and need not.

Given this outline of the work, we can begin to see how it can be assessed in a critical philosophical fashion. For one thing, we can examine the logical model used in the treatment of the rules, and for another examine the search techniques employed in teasing out these rules. Yet another approach can investigate the contrasts between differing styles of thought, and, finally, we can consider the whole enterprise in the light of well-known educational ideals. In the remainder of this chapter, I will address the first three of these approaches. I think it is clear that we cannot expect to make much headway comparing the purposes of *HSD* with broader aims of education until we have a much more definite view of what it is about, and so of what purposes it in fact serves.

A close look at *HSD* shows that it employs two distinct logical models.

One, exhibited through a progressive discovery of rules explicitly stated, is that of a deductive syllogistic system. The other consists of a kind of "good reasons" approach. In place of abstract rules and specified varieties of inference patterns, this emphasizes the *seeking* of reasons for opinions, actions, and beliefs, together with the *assessment* of the reasons given.[5] The latter does not usually take the form of an investigation of the formal structure of inferences, but instead often depends upon an intuitive sense of what can count as a good argument. As a result, in place of the syllogistic rules of the first model, this second logical model yields a string of exemplary arguments that do have certain family resemblances but do not conform to any fixed deductive patterns.

By contrasting these two logical models, I do not mean to imply that the first of them applies only when the children talk about thinking, while the second is confined to their actual arguments. In two prominent cases, the discovery of a syllogistic rule is followed by its successful application to a matter of direct concern to the children, where both these applications are recognized to be in argument form. The contrast between the models is more clearly connected to a common ambiguity in what is meant by "rule-governed thinking" than to any solid difference between actual states of affairs.

In the case of the first, deductive model, to say that it is a model of rule-governed thinking is to say that the rules of which it is composed are structural, putting specific constraints on the kinds of inferences permitted in terms of the internal structure of the sentences involved. For example, one of the first explicit rules in *HSD* is a rule of simple conversion: "If a true sentence begins with the word 'no,' then its reverse is also true. But if it begins with the word 'all,' then its reverse is false" (p. 4). In contrast, the second, good-reasons model is a model of rule-governed thinking in that it involves normative rules, rules that put general constraints on the sorts of reasons that can be put forth in support of a conclusion. For example, when one of the children supports an opinion by reference to what her father says, this is challenged by questioning whether her father is an authority on the matter under dispute: "I'm afraid that that won't do. You should only use someone else's opinion as a reason for your own view if that other person is a recognized authority on the subject in question" (p. 49). The criterion here does not apply to the internal structure of the reason in any way, but instead appraises such reasons when they are appeals to authority, permitting a certain kind of appeal, disallowing others. Such criteria can of course be deductive—syllogistic rules of inference may be used as norms in appraising purportedly deductive arguments. But there are other types of criteria of appraisal, such as those appropriate to inductive arguments, to arguments from analogy, to arguments justifying beliefs or actions, to arguments from authority, and so on.

Unfortunately, while the good-reasons approach provides much of the logical substance to *HSD*, it is never explicitly recognized as such in the book. Thus, all talk about logical rules, or rules of thinking, is confined to the developing syllogistic. As a consequence, only the rules of deductive logic are treated in terms of explicit searches, and we can only talk sensibly of search techniques in relation to this one model.

The first rule mentioned is discovered by accident, tried out on some examples, then modified. The source of this rule is two sentences that happen to illustrate it, but the other rules are acquired in a variety of ways, including seeing an analogy, asking help from other members of a class (including the teacher), consulting a teacher directly, thinking out logical alternatives, shared inquiry between two children, something learned from a cousin who teaches high-school math, and generalizing from instances. Rules are modified in some cases by discovery of counterinstances (in a style rather like hypothetico-deductive reasoning), in others by a teacher who combines a plurality of rules into one general rule. Most stated rules are subsequently illustrated by examples, but there is no specific technique advocated for testing them; in some cases they are treated as generalizations to be tested against examples, in others they are simply accepted, for example, as when coming from an authority. These search procedures thus raise the interesting question of whether the components of the syllogistic model can be justifiably regarded as rules only by reference to criteria of appraisal of the good-reasons approach.

HSD flirts with an extensional interpretation of its syllogistic logic. An Euler diagram is used to illustrate why simple conversions of sentences beginning with "all" are invalid (p. 14), and syllogisms in Barbara are said to be valid because the word "are" "really means 'belong to the class of'" (p. 40). But *HSD* comes closest to questioning the adequacy of its rules not by piecemeal interpretations in a metalanguage but through questioning the point to discovering such rules in the first place. This theme first appears in Chapter Two, echoes in subsequent chapters, and reaches a crescendo in the final (seventeenth) chapter. While the argument there is entwined in the dramatic context of the discussion, in essence its claim is that we should try to see things from other people's points of view, that some people think in patterns that conform to the rules, hence that in order to see things as they do, we need to get to know the rules. The key to shared access to these rules is then said to be that they "work with the way we talk" (p. 95).

Now clearly, if this is an argument at all, it is of the good-reasons variety. The main premise, that "we should try to see things from other people's points of view," constitutes a rich metaphor that ranges in interpretation from literally seeing physical objects from a variety of physical perspectives to developing an empathic understanding of the thoughts and feelings of other persons. But it is just this ambiguity that prevents using the premise in any deductive sense for deriving the conclusion. As a metaphor, talk about seeing things from the viewpoints of others does supply a reason for studying syllogistic—insofar as syllogistic rules do apply to the ways we talk, they provide criteria for assessing discussions that can lead to understanding the views of others, although whether this is a good reason is left to the reader of *HSD*. The primary justification for the explicit logical theme of *HSD* thus depends upon the second unarticulated model of logic—one is reminded of C. I. Lewis's comment about the arguments provided by certain symbolic logicians supporting their analysis of belief sentences: "The logic they use is better than the logic they recommend."[6]

Among the main themes of *HSD*, sharply reiterated in the arguments of the closing chapter, is the view that only some people typically think in patterns conforming to syllogistic rules and that such rules are appropriate to only certain types of thinking. *HSD* presents, in explicit contrast, a broad variety of other sorts. This plurality of styles of thinking is exhibited in two crisscrossing ways. First, each of the twenty individual children in the book displays his or her own predominant style of thought. Second, each child eventually uses more than this one style. Thus, while one type dominates for each child, what is characteristic of one is also exhibited—less often, though occasionally—by others. The result is a complex matrix of types of thinking, such that for certain strands the developing syllogistic is appropriate, for others obviously not so, while the rest provide a gray area to which good-reasons logic applies. This is all sufficiently complicated and close to the philosophic core of *HSD* to warrant more detailed attention.

A survey of *HSD* shows that there are no less than eighty-six different kinds of mental acts attributed to the children in the book. These range from being suddenly aware that one is being looked at to sharing a special insight with a friend, from wondering whether one's grandfather will keep a promise to buy a football to constructing a rule of deductive inference. Those most commonly displayed (used by the same child in at least five different situations) include thinking something to oneself, thinking about oneself, remembering, being uncertain, drawing an inference, consciously expressing an opinion, devising an example for a proposed rule, trying to figure something out, wondering (whether, why, how, what), and making a decision.

Among the major characters, certain kinds of mental acts, especially logical ones, recur. These predispositions to think in certain ways constitute differing styles of thinking; one such style is deductive, others encompass variants of the good-reasons approach. Those that predominate are wondering (Harry Stottlemeier), thinking deductively (Tony Melillo), intuitive or hunchlike thinking (Lisa Terry), seeking and enjoying explanations (Fran Wood), being sensitive to the feelings of others (Anne Torgerson), and thinking independently (Mickey Minkowski). While this is only a partial list of the types of mental acts and associated styles of thinking illustrated in *HSD*, one can readily see that they constitute a broad network. Both mental acts and styles of thinking are uniformly attributed to individuals; of literally hundreds of references to mental acts, only four attribute a mental act to children as a group.[7] This concreteness and specificity strongly contributes to the reader's awareness of the plurality of styles indicated.

The diversity in styles of thinking is further illustrated by occasional overlaps. For example, one character, Lisa Terry, characteristically reaches conclusions by means of hunches and sudden insights, while Harry's inferences are generally discursive, yet both make snap judgments that turn out to be faulty. They differ again in that Lisa promptly expresses hers, while Harry's remains implicit until he is eventually led to revise it in the face of new evidence. Another example: Harry shares with Anne an ability to understand other people well, yet for Harry this depends largely upon verbal clues, while Anne's are visual. Thus, while Lisa and Harry do differ, they are similar in some respects, and so too for Harry and Anne. The lack of any overt contrast between Lisa and Anne shows that the matrix of kinds of thinking is not fully articulated, thus leaving room for the reader to add in his or her own ideas on similarities and differences between the characters and their thinking styles.

The main connection between the matrix of styles of thinking and the syllogistic rules lies in the successive dramatic settings of the conversations of which *HSD* is composed. Here too there is a large number of instances: A few examples will have to serve as illustrations.

In the first part of Chapter Sixteen, two main patterns of the hypothetical syllogism, *modus ponens* and *modus tollens,* together with the associated fallacies of affirming the consequent and denying the antecedent, are illustrated. Meanwhile, it is announced that one student (Jane Starr) has accused another (Sandy Mendoza) of stealing a briefcase containing a wallet. Through Jane's subsequent responses to questions, together with his own testimony, Harry establishes that although the briefcase was recovered well outside the room, Jane still had it there at 2 P.M., and that Sandy Mendoza had not left the room between 2 and 2:45, when Jane first noticed it to be missing. Harry then argues, using *modus tollens:* "Now, if Sandy had taken the briefcase, it would still be here in the room. But it wasn't found in the room. Therefore, Sandy didn't take the briefcase." Lisa then remarks that she believes another student, Mickey Minkowski, took the briefcase. This idea is described as a hunch, and she tries to justify it by claiming that hiding the briefcase where it was found is "just the sort of thing Mickey would do." Tony Melillo next shows this to be structurally fallacious: "If it was Mickey who took the briefcase, then he would have to have hidden it behind the water fountain. Second part true: *The briefcase was hidden behind the water fountain.* But what follows? Nothing. We already agreed that just because the second part is true, you can't prove that the first part is also true." Now Sandy drags Mickey onto the scene, insisting that Mickey admit to having taken and hidden the briefcase.

Here we see not only some handy illustrations of syllogistic principles, but a juxtaposition of discursive thinking with intuitive thought. When the children discussing hypothetical syllogisms first learn that Jane has accused Sandy, they are told that Sandy denied taking the briefcase, that although he admitted to having teased her earlier, making her believe that he was going to take it, he had not actually done so. Jane's accusation is thus similar to Lisa's accusation of Mickey, and we have the following pattern: Jane's hunch (incorrect) versus Harry's *modus tollens* (sound); Lisa's hunch (correct) versus Tony's fallacy of affirming the consequent (valid, but not materially helpful). The episode closes with a hint of the good-reasons approach. Lisa admits that her idea was just a feeling, a kind of hunch, and a teacher replies: "Yes, Lisa, you made a shrewd guess. And as it happened, you were right. But if you'd been wrong, another innocent person, like Sandy, would have suffered. You weren't actually wrong to have tried guessing who might have done it. But guessing isn't a substitute for careful investigation. What it all amounts to is that I don't like reckless accusations." An accusation, of course, may well be supported by reasons other than deductive premises; Jane had some reason to suspect Sandy, and Lisa's hunch had indirect inductive support.

Another example can be drawn from Chapters Two and Three. Tony Melillo shows himself to be unhappy, and in response to Harry's query remarks that his father always talks as if he (Tony) will become an engineer as is the father, and that when Tony suggests that he might do something else when he grows up, his father gets angry. Harry asks Tony why his father believes that he will make a good engineer, and Tony replies: "Because I always get good grades in math. He says to me, 'All engineers are good in math, and you're good in math, so figure it out for yourself.'" Harry realizes that concluding from this that Tony is to be an engineer violates a previously discovered rule of simple conversion: "Your father said, 'all engineers are good in math,' right? But that's one of those sentences which can't be turned around. So it doesn't follow that all people who are good in math are engineers." Later, in Chapter Three, Tony has a conversation with his father. Tony points out that from the sentence "all engineers are good in math" alone, it does not follow that he should be an engineer, even though he is good in math. Challenged to explain this, Tony momentarily forgets Harry's account, is confused and afraid, but then recalls the rule. When his father questions the rule, Tony admits that he cannot explain why it works. His father then draws an Euler diagram for the sentence "all engineers are people who are good in math." As a result, Tony concludes that "that's the reason we can't turn sentences with 'all' around. . . . Because you can put a small group of people or things into a larger group, but you can't put a larger group into a smaller group" (p. 14).

This use and justification of a rule of immediate inference at first seems rather straightforward, but a closer examination shows a wider, less simple context than first appears. In one sense, Tony's thinking obviously improves.

He learns to spot a fallacy and, in the process, successfully overcomes some fears and confusions. But from a broader perspective, this improvement has its limitations. Tony is happy with the extensional explanation for the rule of simple conversion and does not question this new metarule. His advance in his thinking is thus confined to replacing a confusing and uncomfortably disordered situation with a pleasing, rule-governed one—he shows no sensitivity to potential limits of rule-governed thought. For example, insofar as his confusions and discomforts stem from his father's pressures on him to become an engineer, he has not yet met this source of difficulties; if anything, he has resolved one point of confusion in a style no doubt quite similar to his father's own, and in that sense is now all the more like him than before. Tony's discomfort when confronted with suggestions that he should grow up to be like his father thus remain untouched by this rule of inference, and the two contrasting modes of thought remain at odds—semiarticulate though highly developed feelings versus syllogistically rule-governed discursive thoughts.

There are many more examples. Twenty-two rules are cited in the book, eighteen of which are standard rules of syllogistic logic. And a related set of analyses using the good-reasons model would reveal a truly immense number of comparisons and contrasts between verbal thinking that is structured by syllogistic principles, verbal thinking that can be judged by one or another set of standards of the good-reasons model, and the many sorts of mental acts and related styles of thinking, both verbal and nonverbal, that compose neither deductions nor arguments.

I have tried to show that *Harry Stottlemeier's Discovery* is a philosophically respectable work that deals primarily with uses of reasons and arguments, placed in entertaining and instructive dramatic settings. In so doing, it attributes a broad variety of mental acts to the children that are its main characters, acts that are often—but not always—logical, in at least one of two senses. Many of these mental acts are under the conscious or semiconscious control of the children—they do not mechanically infer, they figure things out; they are not made to think, they consciously wonder and think things to themselves, getting ideas that they actively keep or else choose to put out of their minds. Such mentalistic talk, primarily expressed in an active vocabulary, provides images of children who think—and especially think things out—for themselves. This image of children is, I believe, the special philosophical merit of *Harry Stottlemeier's Discovery*, and it is through this image that one can begin to fruitfully evaluate the educational significance of the work as a whole.

NOTES

Acknowledgment.
This essay was originally presented as a paper at the Eastern Division Meeting of the American Philosophical Association, December 1975. I am indebted to Professors Nancy Maull and Thomas Morawetz for suggested revisions. I alone am responsible for the results, but they deserve credit for some very good suggestions.

1. Revised edition, published by the Institute for the Advancement of Philosophy for Children, Montclair State College, Upper Montclair, New Jersey, 1974. I will employ *HSD* for subsequent references to the book.
2. See Matthew Lipman, "Philosophy for Children," *Metaphilosophy* 7, no. 1 (January 1976).
3. At Montclair State College, Upper Montclair, New Jersey.
4. At Washburn University of Topeka, Topeka, Kansas.
5. See C. L. Hamblin, *Fallacies* (London: Methuen, 1970), chapter 7: "The Concept of Argument," and S. E. Toulmin, *The Uses of Argument* (Cambridge: Cambridge University Press, 1964). See also D. W. Pole, "The Concept of Reason," and Gilbert Ryle, "A Rational Animal," in *Education and the Development of Reason*, ed. R. F. Dearden, P. H. Hirst, and R. S. Peters (London: Routledge and Kegan Paul, 1972).
6. From Professor Robert Gahringer, to whom this gem of a remark was originally made.
7. Namely, as a class (in school). See *HSD*, pp. 38, 49, and 81 (two references).

20

A *Second Look at* Harry

Frederick S. Oscanyan

■ ■ ■

HARRY HAS HARDLY changed since 1975. There have been some minor stylistic improvements, and a few passages have been rewritten, most notably the neat application of Harry's discovery toward the end of Chapter One and the discussion with Mr. Portos about differences between animals and human beings in Chapter Seven. But on the whole the book is the same now as earlier. Its educational context, however, is almost unrecognizably different. In 1975, no other novel yet existed; *Lisa* was still just a gleam in Mat Lipman's eye. Since then, although the National Forum for Philosophical Reasoning in the Schools died in infancy, the Institute for the Advancement of Philosophy for Children has flourished, and many additional materials have been written. There are now translations into several languages, well-established graduate programs (as well as regional and foreign centers), and implementations in thousands of schools.

For all these changes, *Harry* remains at the center of Philosophy for Children. It is typically the first piece read by teachers new to the program, a mainstay of seminars and workshops, and the first book translated into yet another language. While no doubt accorded this honor in part because of age and reputation, it also deserves a special place because of its vividly clear images of actively thoughtful children. That was the main theme of my first critical look at *Harry Stottlemeier's Discovery*, and it is a theme that deserves reconsideration.

In his *Second Meditation*, having established to his satisfaction that he exists, Descartes asks what he is, and after considerable reflection responds as follows: "What then am I? A thinking thing. What is that? It is a thing that doubts, understands, asserts, denies, wants to know, wishes not to be deceived, . . . a being that imagines, that perceives, that feels, that desires."[1] Setting aside the mysteries of Cartesian philosophy, these characteristics describe, in part, what it is to be a person. And, taking into account differing styles and patterns of thinking, they also apply to each character in *Harry*.

Views akin to Descartes's concept of a thinking being are common in philosophy. Similar concepts can be found in the studies of John Locke and Sidney Shoemaker, the dramas of Plato's dialogues, the theologies of Saint Thomas Aquinas and Paul Tillich, and the skepticism of Montaigne. In ancient times such concepts were associated with having a soul; more recently, they are understood as self- or personhood. That *Harry* uses ideas drawn from the philosophical tradition is no surprise; Philosophy for Children is largely built upon such ideas. *Harry*'s enduring contribution to education is that it teaches us how to look at children as persons without denying that they are children.

Lipman's depiction of the child as a special kind of person not only sharply contrasts with familiar sentimental descriptions of children as happy innocents but it also differs from legal concepts of childhood. Earlier legal accounts described children as property, and concepts of personhood simply did not apply; they were legally protected as—and insofar as—all property was protected.[2] More recent legal views of children have pictured them as incomplete adults, and such concepts also differ significantly from the characters in *Harry Stottlemeier's Discovery*.

Thinking of children as imperfect adults invites justifications of their protection that rely on arguments from paternalism. Such paternalistic arguments rest on claims that children need overall protection because of their lack of knowledge, lack of experience, lack of self-control in the pursuit of long-term versus immediate and short-term interests, lack of emotional development, and lack of cognitive development.[3] Any such lack may purportedly be traced to the sheer absence of the trait in question to the presence of some other factor, a pleasure principle, for example, or inborn wickedness, or being at earlier stages of development. Following the legal tradition of identifying adult individuals as persons, these paternalistic ways of thinking imply that since children lack one or more of the adult capacities they are not truly persons. This whole approach does not fit in well with Lipman's fictional children; although the characters in *Harry* are occasionally in need of adult protection, the main theme of the book concerns not their inabilities but their active pursuit of shared independence.

Among contemporary authors who have sought alternatives to broadly paternalistic views of children, Natalie Abrams calls for a new understanding of childhood based on a concept of dignity.[4] Founding that idea on a legal concept of free and informed consent, Abrams argues that dignity applies to children when they are able to make autonomous decisions in cases that will have no bearing on their welfare. She also suggests that decision making in harmless situations can enable children to develop the autonomy necessary to protect their own interests as adults.[5] For Abrams, the dignity of a child hinges on the degree to which he or she functions like an adult in making autonomous decisions, although children and adults differ in that the latter are sufficiently knowledgable and independent to be able to handle decisions that affect their own well-being. Abrams thus implies that insofar as children are capable of self-determination, albeit in matters independent of their own welfare, they are to be respected as persons.

Abrams's views more closely approximate Lipman's than does paternalism broadly conceived, because the characters in *Harry* display the decision-making abilities that Abrams requires in order that children be accorded personal respect. Harry's decision in Chapter Two to ask Mr. Spence for help with a question that troubles him is one example; there are several others. Nevertheless, Abrams's theory does not fully capture the concept of childhood that Lipman's characters best represent. They are most vivid as unique individuals not because of their abilities to make decisions but in their efforts to make sense of their own ideas and to understand each other's thoughts. Such intellectual independence is not the same as practical self-determination, a point perhaps difficult to grasp, since from a more mature perspective they may easily seem as one. But autonomy as Abrams understands it is confined to making practical decisions, and that differs from independence of thought and self-directed inquiry.

Lipman's children illuminate that special respect deserved by living girls and boys. His characters lend dignity to children's ideas and opinions, most especially their efforts to understand and be understood, by teaching us to see in such concerns intellectual self-determination—not just the promise of it, not only a struggle to attain it, but actually deciding for oneself what to think about and committing oneself to thinking it through. Harry, Lisa, Tony, Fran, Suki, and the rest deserve respect, not for being adult nor to the extent that they act like adults, but because they think on their own.

Lipman's concept of childhood in *Harry* is built upon the idea that children deserve respect because of their doubts as well as their understandings, their desires to know and wishes not to be made fools of, their abilities to perceive, to imagine, to be aware. For all the success of Philosophy for Children, this remains as yet a largely unrealized ideal. So long as that is the case, so long as we do not treat children as that special class of persons who have dignity precisely because of their autonomy of thought, *Harry* will stand as a reminder and an encouragement to us all.

NOTES

1. René Descartes, *Oeuvres de Descartes*, ed. Charles Adam and Paul Tannery, vol. 7, *Meditationes de prima philosophia* (Paris: Vrin, 1973), pp. 28–29. My translation.
2. For a more extended discussion, see Robert A. Horowitz, "Children's Rights:

A Look Backward and a Glance Ahead," in *Legal Rights of Children*, ed. Robert A. Horowitz and Howard A. Davidson (Colorado Springs, Colo.: McGraw-Hill, 1984), pp. 1–6.

3. Laurence D. Houlgate, "Children, Paternalism, and Rights to Liberty," in *Having Children*, ed. Onora O'Neill and William Ruddick (New York: Oxford University Press, 1979), pp. 266–78.

4. Natalie Abrams, "Problems in Defining Child Abuse and Neglect," in *Having Children*, ed. O'Neill and Ruddick, pp. 156–64.

5. Ibid., pp. 160–61. I am indebted to Vanessa Lynn Armstrong for improving my understanding of Abrams's argument here.

Sources and References for
Harry Stottlemeier's Discovery

Matthew Lipman

A NOTE ON SOURCES AND REFERENCES

This sequential bibliography matches Harry Stottlemeier's Discovery *page by page and virtually line by line. It contains both sources and references.*

By sources, *I mean works that I can remember having had an influence on the writing of a particular passage.*

By references, *I mean works that were not influential in the composition of a passage but that the reader might profitably consult if interested in further exploration of the themes under investigation.*

The sources are pinpointed specifically. They therefore do not represent the broader influences that causally affected the writing of the whole book.

The references are sketchy, at best. Vast areas of scholarship have not been cited, even where these would have been relevant and helpful, because of overriding considerations of space and time.

Nevertheless, I have frequently attempted, with the assistance of Ann Margaret Sharp, to provide an additional commentary that would give the reader further guidance (above and beyond what the instructional manual, Philosophical Inquiry, *offers) in unpacking the passages in question to find out what lies behind them and what they point to. In no way should this commentary be considered an "official interpretation" of the text. It resembles instead a kind of tourist's guide to aspects of the work that might all too readily be overlooked.*

I hope that future teacher–scholars who revisit the Stottlemeier text every year with their classes will find in this bibliography an invitation to mine the rich ores that underlie every philosophical concept.

—Matthew Lipman

Teachers and scholars working with Harry Stottlemeier's Discovery *will find that the bibliographical material facilitates study in accordance with their areas of interest rather than in accordance with historical or other criteria. In this regard, the sources and references commentary functions analogously to the instructional manual: Both are keyed to the sequence of themes in the novel and are to be used as those themes arise either in classroom discussion or independent research. In this sense, the bibliography represents a kind of concordance to the novel, enlightening the practitioner with regard to relevant scholarship in the same way that the instructional manual enlightens him or her with regard to relevant activities and exercises. These sources and references are keyed to the 1982 edition.*

Since Harry Stottlemeier's Discovery *is already widely used in other cultures, we expect that these sources and references, in translation, will need to be adapted for the purposes of the scholars in those cultures. Here, we would suggest that the materials that were obviously sources for the author be preserved, while remaining references, which are largely to works in Anglo-American literature, be replaced with works on the same themes in the literature of the culture for which the translation is being made. In this way, practitioners in every culture would have available to them the references in their own culture that would make* Harry Stottlemeier's Discovery *almost as meaningful to them as if it were an indigenous product.*

   The cultural diversity that would result from the production of many different bibliographies would nevertheless be held together by the unity of the novel and by the universality of its characters. Harry Stottlemeier's Discovery *should be a vehicle that will help children, regardless of their language, come to see how much they have in common. The bibliography can also be a vehicle that will enable practitioners, regardless of their cultural differences, to see the universality of the philosophical themes that run through their various traditions.*

CHAPTER ONE

Page, Line	Theme	References and Comments
1:1–2	the opening sentence as a counter-factual	There is a sense in which the form of the opening sentence (in effect, "If Harry hadn't fallen asleep, then it probably wouldn't have happened") foreshadows the speculative character of the book. The sentence is a counterfactual conditional, the logical status of which has fascinated many philosophers in recent years. Perhaps the most astute and intricate treatment is that of David Lewis, in his book *Counterfactuals*, but it is much too technical for general use. One can look at *Logic: A Comprehensive Introduction* by Samuel D. Guttenplan and Martin Tamny, pp. 345–46, or at Nelson Goodman, *Fact, Fiction, and Forecast*.
1:5–8	movement of planets	For a discussion of the motion of the planets, see Marx Wartofsky, "The Primary Experience of Motion," in his *Conceptual Foundations of Modern Science*.
1:9–11	mental acts	There are at least three mental acts in these three lines and many more in the chapter and in the whole book. (In fact, Frederick Oscanyan counted more than seventy.) While there is considerable literature on mental acts, ranging from Wittgenstein to Peter Geach, there does not seem to be an authoritative single work. On the other hand, it is a rare issue of a contemporary philosophy journal that fails to contain a single article on some particular mental act such as deciding, believing, assuming, etc.
1:12–15	dog star	Spinoza remarks somewhere in his *Ethics* that some people are ridiculous enough to think there must be a connection between a dog and a dog star, just because they have the name in common. While Harry's joke is far-fetched, it remains true, as William James pointed out in *The Principles of Psychology*, that finding resemblances among objects that are only remotely alike is one of the most important aspects of creative thinking. It is precisely this ability that is essential in formulating syllogisms, since the middle term is the feature that links unlike classes together.
1:16	a sense of humor	John Poulos's book *Humor and Mathematics* includes a chapter on the (alleged) humor to be found in the reversal of relationships. See also Francis Sparshott's *Looking for Philosophy*, as well as Jordan Brown, *Humor and Problem Solving*.

192

1:21–24	things that go around the sun	For an astute comparison of the differences between the geocentric theory of Aristotle and the heliocentric theory of Galileo, see Kurt Lewin, "The Conflict between Aristotelian and Galilean Modes of Thought in Contemporary Psychology," *Journal of General Psychology*, (1931): 141–77.
1:28	puzzlement	Puzzlement corresponds to the initial stage of inquiry as described by both Peirce and Dewey, except that for Dewey it is a "felt difficulty," which is less cognitive and more organic than the word "puzzlement" suggests. See Peirce, "The Fixation of Belief," in *Collected Papers*, and Dewey, *How We Think*.
1:28	How had he gone wrong?	This is a critical point in Harry's reflection, because he is assuming here that he went wrong and that his mistake must be corrected. He is assuming that his own inquiry is a self-corrective process, and self-correctiveness is what Peirce claims to be the central characteristic of inquiry. See Peirce, *Collected Papers*. There are two points here that need attention, Harry's error and what he chooses to do about it. The role of error in inquiry has been given much attention since Peirce. For example, Josiah Royce discusses what he calls the "possibility of error" as presupposing the notion of truth. (See his *Spirit of Modern Philosophy*, p. 378.) Elsewhere, in dealing with the notion of truth, Royce argues that if there were no truth, there would be no error. But there is error. Therefore, there is truth. This argument was developed further by Henry Perkinson in *The Possibility of Error*, in which he sees error as central to education. Perkinson, however, derives his orientation primarily from Popper's theory of falsification, in which he argues that verifying a theory is much less significant than proving it wrong. There are important similarities between Popper's theory of falsifiability and Peirce's fallibilism, although Popper denies that they are the same. When Harry asks himself "How did I go wrong?" he is raising a question of *method*. Most of us don't do this. If we find ourselves on the wrong road, we proceed to look for the right one. We don't ask ourselves how we went wrong and proceed to focus on the breakdown of our method.

2:1–2	the thing
	with the tail
		On page 1, lines 18–20, Harry is guilty of the following invalid reasoning:
		    All planets revolve about the sun.
		    <u>The thing with the tail revolves about the sun.</u>
		    The thing with the tail is a planet.
		This is something like saying, "All boys are children,"

"Mary is a child," "Therefore, Mary is a boy." Harry
learns that, as a matter of fact, the thing with the tail
is a comet, not a planet. But he accuses his reasoning
of having let him down. And he is right. He did make a
logical mistake. This is a key point in the chapter: that
Harry grasps the notion of logical reasoning. He does
not explore the *factual* differences between comets and
planets.

2:6   A sentence   Here Harry discovers the principle of conversion—some
           can't be   sentences stay true when reversed, and some do not.
           reversed.   Aristotle uses this principle as the cornerstone of clas-
                             sical logic, and introduces it at the very beginning of his
                             Prior Analytics (bk. 1, part 2.) For more on conversion,
                             see M. R. Cohen and E. Nagel, *Introduction to Logic and
                             Scientific Method*, pp. 58–59.

2:7   true   This is the first indication that Harry assumes the original
                             statement to have been true. For some discussion of the
                             notion of truth, see Cohen and Nagel, *Introduction to
                             Logic and Scientific Method*, pp. 58–59.
                             For further discussion, see John Dewey, *Essays in Ex-
                             perimental Logic*, pp. 211–41 (where Dewey develops his
                             notion of truth as *warranted assertibility*), and A. J. Ayer,
                             Language, Truth, and Logic. See also Bertrand Russell,
                             Human Knowledge: Its Scope and Limits. One should
                             also look at the exercise on truth in *Philosophical Inquiry*
                             (the instructional manual to accompany *Harry Stottle-
                             meier's Discovery*.) There one can see the influence of a
                             line of development from Frege through the later Witt-
                             genstein to Dummett and finally to Habermas. "Speakers
                             and hearers understand the meaning of a sentence when
                             they know under what conditions it is true." See Jürgen
                             Habermas, *The Theory of Communicative Action*, vol. 1.
                             For more recent works, see D. M. Armstrong, *Belief,
                             Truth, and Knowledge*; Michael Dummett, *Truth and
                             Other Enigmas*; Hilary Putnam, *Reason, Truth, and His-
                             tory*; Anthony Quinton, *The Nature of Things*; Nicholas
                             Rescher, *The Coherence Theory of Truth*; Richard Rorty,
                             Philosophy and the Mirror of Nature; C. I. Lewis, *An
                             Analysis of Knowledge and Valuation*; and Ludwig Witt-
                             genstein, *On Certainty*.

2:12   trying it out   Harry decides to engage in a thought experiment by test-
                             ing his hypothesis ("A sentence can't be reversed") with
                             a few examples. For more on the notion that thinking is
                             experimental, see John Dewey, *Essays in Experimental
                             Logic*, pp. 13–18, 94–95, 176–78, and 242–44.

2:12   a few ex-   Harry's hypothesis of the irreversibility of sentences
           amples   can be tested through exemplification, and examples are
                             examples of concepts. For more on concept formation,

see Rom Harré, "The Formal Analysis of Concepts," in H. J. Klausmeier and C. W. Harris, *Analyses of Concept Learning*. See also J. L. Austin, *Sense and Sensibilia*.

2:17   didn't follow   Harry is bringing to consciousness here what is implicit in children's use of language: Given a particular sentence, certain other sentences follow from it and others do not. Children do not formulate the notion of valid reasoning as such, but they seem to understand that if one has a true statement and claims to derive a second (false) statement from it, then the second statement can't possibly "follow from" the first. This is what it means to say that reasoning *preserves the truth* of the premises: In valid reasoning, if the premises are true, it is absolutely certain that the conclusion must be true.

When Harry says that "the reverse didn't follow," he means that the second sentence is not logically implied by, or cannot be inferred from, the first sentence.

2:19   discovery   This is an infinitely rich topic. For a start, one might look at Norwood Russell Hanson, *Patterns of Discovery*; Thomas Kuhn, *The Structure of Scientific Revolutions*; R. G. Collingwood, *Essay on Philosophical Method*; and D. MacKinnon, "Idealism and Realism," in *Proceedings of the Aristotelian Society* (1976–77).

2:19–20   one value of a rule for thinking   The value of the discovery, for Harry, seems to lie in its capacity to prevent embarrassment. In other words, the rule would not so much be a key to unlock the mysteries of thinking as a safety net to prevent embarrassing lapses.

2:19–20   the social context of inquiry   Charles Peirce argues repeatedly for recognition that scientific inquiry is a social process taking place in a community of inquirers. See his *Collected Papers*.

Harry has discovered a rule and is delighted because it has a use: It will help him to avoid embarrassing mistakes. This suggests that he senses how logic and language, if improperly used, can distort our understanding of facts. A very young child may think that all errors arise from misinformation. An older child may realize that some errors stem from misinformation and some from faulty reasoning or the careless use of language.

The reader of Wittgenstein might even conclude that we make most of our mistakes about the world because of the "bewitchment of language." Children might be encouraged to identify the social, interpersonal, and emotional strands that run through this chapter, such as Harry's embarrassment, his ridicule by other members of the class, and his resentment and gratitude toward Lisa. Another assignment might be to pick out character traits, whether they are explicitly identified or not (e.g., Harry's

persistence, Mr. Bradley's patience and absence of
humor, Lisa's cooperativeness, and Mrs. Stottlemeier's
pleasantness).

3:3–4	a sentence with two kinds of things	Harry seems to know already that the kind of sentence he is looking for is one whose subject and predicate are both nouns or noun phrases. What he may not realize is that the examples he offers Lisa are of two different kinds: the first kind, composed of dogs and cats, consists of nonoverlapping classes. The second kind consists of overlapping classes.

Where overlapping classes are involved, the statement expressing their relationship can begin with *all,* as
in "All astronauts are people." Where nonoverlapping
classes are concerned, however, *all* cannot be used, and
one would have to turn to such a quantifier as *no,* as in
"No dogs are cats." Thus, by giving an illustration involving nonoverlapping classes, Harry prepares the way for
Lisa's counterinstance "No eagles are lions."

3:9–10	analogy	These lines use an analogy between the way Harry pounces on a sentence and the way a cat pounces on a ball of string. But there are two kinds of pouncing: one intellectual and the other physical. They are alike only analogically.
3:14–15	working	Harry seems to realize, when he says, "It worked before . . ." that the criterion for accepting or rejecting a rule of logic is not whether it corresponds to anything in the world, but whether it works, i.e., whether it permits inquiry to proceed, rather than remain blocked. In thus resorting to the criterion of success, Harry reveals a certain pragmatism. (For more on the notion that truth is what works, see William James, *Pragmatism.*)
3:16	stupid sentence	Harry here has another striking insight—that the form of a sentence can be independent of its content. A rule applies equally to brilliant and stupid sentences (as a civil law applies equally to brilliant and stupid people.) Just the same, many people are distracted by the contents of their thought to a point where they cannot draw valid inferences. Psychologists of reasoning call these distractions "atmosphere effects." See Peter Wason and Philip Johnson-Laird, *The Psychology of Reasoning.*
3:17	resentment	Harry's flash of resentment may just be momentary and superficial. There is a deeper variety that Nietzsche calls *ressentiment,* the suppressed hatred that conformists feel for anyone who is "different." (See his *Genealogy of Morals* and *Beyond Good and Evil.*) It is also treated by Max Scheler in *The Nature of Sympathy.*
3:18	rules	Wittgenstein presents a fascinating exploration of rules

in *Foundation of the Principles of Mathematics*. See also Jean Piaget, *The Moral Judgment of the Child*, ch. 1, "The Rules of the Game."

3:20	failed	Harry is very sensitive to failure. It is interesting to note the sorts of things such people think they fail at. For example, Michael Oakeshott, in his essay "On Being Conservative" (in *Rationalism in Politics*), makes fun of romantics like Shelley who must always behave in ways that are fresh and new and for whom "to contract a habit is to have somehow failed."
3:23	tried it out	See page 2, line 12.
3:28	distinction	A sentence beginning with *no* expresses a distinction— the verbal and logical formulation of a perceived difference. For the psychology involved in the perception of differences, see William James, *The Principles of Psychology*, ch. 13, "Discrimination and Comparison." For a more philosophical treatment, see Robert Sokolowski, "Making Distinctions," *Review of Metaphysics* 32, no. 4 (June 1979): 639–76.
3:29	difference	Lisa's sentence behaves differently from Harry's. How can we explain this? Presumably by another difference. The hypothesis here is that the difference between "all" and "no" is the cause of some sentences being convertible and others not. (More generally, this illustrates the pragmatic principle that every difference makes a difference and that, conversely, every difference is to be explained by a difference.) See William James, *The Will to Believe*; see also Nelson Goodman, *Languages of Art*, pp. 99–112.
4:6–8	theory	In this rudimentary effort at theory construction, Harry attempts to put together the various insights he and Lisa have had and to formulate a more comprehensive theory of conversion. He sees now that Lisa's objection did not invalidate his original position but supplemented it by providing a special case of the general principle he had in mind.
4:16	Mrs. Bates	The model for Mrs. Olson is the garrulous but harmless gossip Miss Bates, whom Emma insults in Jane Austen's novel *Emma*.
4:20	Mrs. Bates is like them	Harry's mother's question involves a judgment of similarity. This contrasts, of course, with judgments of difference. For more on judgments of similarity, see William James, *The Principles of Psychology*, ch. 13, "Discrimination and Comparison," and ch. 14, "Association." The "*click*" or "Aha!" experience is a favorite of Gestalt psychologists attempting to explain the insight that occurs when all the parts of the puzzle fall into place and we see

the situation whole for the first time. See Kurt Koffka, *Principles of Gestalt Psychology*, and Wolfgang Köhler, *Gestalt Psychology*.

4:22–24	application	See *Philosophical Inquiry*, "The Process of Inquiry," p. 4, and John Dewey, *How We Think*.
4:25–26	double messages	This involves Harry's mother's comment and expression. What she says to Harry is a "put down," but the look on her face reveals that she is pleased. For more on this general ambivalence, sometimes called "double binds," see Harry Stack Sullivan, *Conceptions of Modern Psychiatry*, and R. D. Laing, *The Politics of Experience*, *Knots*, and *Self and Others*.
4:29	happy time	The chapter begins with Harry embarrassed and ends with him happy. It also begins with him puzzled and ends with the successful application of a hypothesis. This suggests that there are two major currents in the chapter, the affective and the cognitive. The problem is to arrive at a resolution that combines the two currents into one. This is pointed out because it is so common to think of inquiry as a purely cognitive enterprise and to neglect the affective and social side of it completely. But not all theorists of the inquiry practice are so one-sided. See, for example, Abraham Kaplan, *The Conduct of Inquiry*; John Dewey, *Logic: The Theory of Inquiry*; and George Santayana, *Reason and Science*.

CHAPTER TWO

Page, Line	*Theme*	*References and Comments*
5:13	what good is it?	See G. E. Moore, *Principia Ethica*, pp. 6–17, 82–84, and 146–50; C. I. Lewis, *Analysis of Knowledge and Valuation*, pp. 397–403; and C. L. Stevenson, *Ethics and Language*, pp. 20–23 and 153–56. See also Spinoza, *Improvement of the Understanding*, and Dewey, *Theory of the Moral Life*.
5:15	all	See the article "All" in *The Encyclopedia of Philosophy*. See also Zeno Vendler, *Linguistics and Philosophy*.
6:2	a "for instance"	This is another way of saying "for example." Exemplification is treated in Edwina L. Rissland, "The Structure of Knowledge in Complex Domains," in Susan Chipman, Judith Segal, and Robert Glazer, eds., *Thinking and Learning Skills*, vol. 2.

6:8	Harry's analogy between language and math	See Peter Wason and Philip Johnson-Laird, *The Psychology of Reasoning.*
6:15	Mr. Spence as teacher	The model for Mr. Spence was Sidney Poitier's character in the film *To Sir, with Love.* For an analysis of good teaching, see Dewey, *Democracy and Education*, chs. 13 and 14.
6:22	every	See Fred Sommers, "Some, Every, Most, Just One," in *The Logic of Natural Languages*, pp. 369–71. The treatment of standardization that was generally followed in the writing of *Harry Stottlemeier's Discovery* can be found in Monroe Beardsley, *Practical Logic.* Beardsley had a good ear for spoken and written language, such as one would expect to find in a former English teacher. He also had a lively awareness of contemporary logical developments (in Frege and Wittgenstein, for example) and a realization of the need for simplicity and clarity in formulating rules of standardization.
7:4	"A"	Neither Harry nor Mr. Spence notices that "a" is ambiguous in certain contexts and can mean either "all" or "a particular individual," as in "A member of this class has been chewing gum."
7:12	no modifier	Children may question Mr. Spence's judgment here. It is true that logicians accept the rule that, where there is no modifier, it can be supposed that "all" was intended. But this is not necessarily the case, and if the sentence should be an empirical generalization, such as "cars are expensive," it might be argued that the quantifier "some" would be better than "all."
7:13–15	Timmy's "if–then"	Timmy's move is bold—it connects the class logic that Harry has been working out with the propositional logic that will not appear in the book until Chapter Thirteen. For a brief treatment of the "if–then" proposition and a discussion of entailment, see Gary Iseminger, *An Introduction to Deductive Logic*, pp. 19–21, and Irving Copi and James Gould, *Readings on Logic.* From the point of view of modern logic, the conditional form of the universal (if p, then q) is preferable to the categorical form because, as Cohen and Nagel argue, "universal propositions in science always function as *hypotheses*, not as statements of fact asserting the existence of individuals" page 43, in Cohen and Nagel, *An Introduction to Logic and Scientific Method.* Most contemporary logicians would reject any claim that "all" and "if–then" have the same meaning.

8:5   Harry's   Harry wonders why Tony's father thinks he will make
               question,   a good engineer. As Tony interprets this (lines 6–7), it
               "Why?"   is a question of his father's criterion for being a good
                                engineer—"getting good grades in math." Presumably,
                                Mr. Melillo invited Tony to reason:
                                    All engineers are good in math.
                                    You are good in math.
                                    Therefore, you're an engineer.
                                But this suggests that Tony will make a good engineer be-
                                cause he already is one. His father's syllogism is anything
                                but convincing.

8:9–10   "it's not   When Harry says "it's not right," "it" refers to the reason-
               right"   ing. But Tony thinks Harry means the way Mr. Melillo is
                                pressuring Tony to be an engineer. The "it" is ambiguous.

8:11–16   application of   Harry doesn't analyze Mr. Melillo's syllogism and point
               Harry's rule   out that the conclusion fails to suggest what Tony's father
                                thinks it does. Instead, Harry isolates the major premise
                                and applies his conversion rule to it. This is all he knows,
                                but it works.

8:17–19   all/only   Tony recognizes here that "all," a principle of inclusion,
                                should not be confused with "only," a principle of ex-
                                clusion. Had Mr. Melillo been able to show that "only
                                engineers are good in math," then it would likely follow
                                that, given Tony's mathematical expertise, he should
                                consider becoming an engineer. According to Harry's
                                rule, the relationship between an "all" statement and its
                                converse is that (except for identity statements) their
                                truth-values are the reverse of one another. Now, an "all"
                                and an "only" statement are equivalent to an "all" state-
                                ment and its converse. Consequently, if one is true, the
                                other is false except in the case of identity statements. If
                                a syllogism is sound when it contains a premise beginning
                                with "only," it is unlikely to be so when that same premise
                                is converted and begins with "all."

CHAPTER THREE

Page, Line   *Theme*   *References and Comments*

9:8   can thoughts   In his account of hysteria, Freud develops the radical
               cause ill-   theory that hysteria is the result of repressed memories
               ness?   of traumatic experiences. See "The Origin and Develop-
                                ment of Psychoanalysis," in John Rickman, ed., *A General
                                Selection from the Works of S. Freud.*

9:13–16	Sandy's names	It is not surprising for a collie to be named "Sandy." Collies are from Scotland, and the name Sandy is a favorite of the Scots. The name "Romeo," we can infer, comes from the dog's having so much erotic affection that he jumps up on people. "Haggis McBagpipe" also has Scotch associations but is derived from Al Capp's comic strip, *Li'l Abner.*
9:25–10:6	having thoughts and thinking	Aristotle (in book 1 of the *Nicomachean Ethics*) speaks about the rational part of man's being as twofold, a state or an activity. "The life of activity is a truer form of man's rationality," he concludes.
10:9–10	figuring things out	Here it would be worthwhile considering the approach to thinking of Jerome Bruner in *Beyond the Information Given* and *A Study of Thinking*. Note also, on line 10, "go[ing] beyond what you already know." F. C. Bartlett, in his classic work, *Remembering*, defines thinking as "filling in the gaps."
10:13	thoughts as bubbles in the soda	Fran first thinks of thoughts as effervescent. Kant, in the latter part of the *Critique of Judgment*, says that the way champagne bubbles from a just-opened bottle is remarkable, but it would be even more remarkable if we could figure out a way to put the champagne back inside.
10:16	the mind as a cave	The immediate association is with Plato's cave in *The Republic*. But a more precise reference would be Richard Wilbur's poem "The Mind," which is reprinted in *Philosophical Inquiry* (ch. 17).
10:18	thought as a bird	See Richard Wilbur's poem "The Writer," in *Writing: How and Why*, p. 118. In the poem, a thought is depicted as an escaping bird that finds its freedom.
10:20	the mind is like a world of its own	If each mind is like a world of its own, are they all independent or are they somehow interrelated? Leibniz claims that each mind is a separate world, or microcosm, but that they are all orchestrated and form a single macrocosm. See his *Principles of Nature and of Grace*, as well as his *Monadology*.
10:20	the mind as a room	This is a common analogy. Erik Erikson has discussed it in *Childhood and Society*.
10:23	thoughts we don't want to think about	See Freud's essay "Repression," in John Rickman, ed., *A General Selection from the Works of S. Freud*.
10:24	the reality of thoughts	Some have argued that Locke's conception of the mind and the thoughts it contains is analogous to Newton's conception of the world and the atoms it contains. Locke's notion of thoughts in the mind is the counterpart of Newton's notion that particles of matter exist in space.

10:29	thought as a copy or imitation	The copy theory has a long history. For Plato, our ideas are copies or replications of the Forms (see *The Republic*, the *Parmenides*, and *The Seventh Letter*). For Locke, our knowledge consists of copies of things in the external world; hence his epistemology is known as a Copy, or Representational, theory of knowledge. More precisely, Locke thinks that ideas of primary qualities like shape and figure are resemblances or copies, but this is not true of secondary qualities like taste and color. See his *Essay Concerning Human Understanding*, bk. 2, ch. 8.
11:1–2	thoughts as noncopies	Locke has already admitted this regarding secondary qualities. Berkeley subsequently denied that any of our ideas are copies: His theory of knowledge is presentational rather than re-presentational. What Lisa says in lines 4–10 is an instance of one aspect of Berkeley's reasoning. He argues that surely pain is only in the mind and not a copy of the pain in a fire. But, of course, he claims that fire is as much in the mind as the pain (*Treatise Concerning Principles of Human Knowledge*, sec. 41).
11:11	feelings	See Richard Wollheim, *The Thread of Life*, pp. 62–96, and Hannah Arendt, *The Life of the Mind*, vol. 2, *Thinking*. (Other authors whose works might be consulted are Max Scheler, Susanne Langer, and Jean-Paul Sartre.)
11:24	Mrs. Halsey's reprimand	Mrs. Halsey apparently jumped to the conclusion that Fran had initiated the interchange with the boys. Her comment to Fran can be seen as an example of "jumping to conclusions." Her jumping is an intellectual one that precedes Fran's physical jumping. This appears to be the "fallacy of false cause."
11:26–28	the leaping	We all know situations in which verbal protests are either prohibited or are thought to be of no avail, with the consequence that individuals may resort to symbolic acts of expression, such as burning draft cards. It is conceivable that this is the case with Fran's symbolic act.
12:1–9	the dream	See Freud's *Interpretation of Dreams* and *On Dreams*. For the semiphilosophical dreams of a child, one could consult *Alice in Wonderland* and *Through the Looking-Glass* by Lewis Carroll. Lisa's feline menagerie is no stranger than the cook's baby that keeps turning into a pig.
12:14	make-believe	See Jerome Bruner, "On Teaching Thinking: An Afterthought," in Chipman, Segal, and Glaser, eds., *Thinking and Learning Skills*, vol. 2. Bruner deals with the importance of play in the cognitive growth of the child, but unfortunately he makes little reference to the intellectual aspects of play or to cognitive play, of which philosophy could serve as an example.

12:15	imagination	Do Harry's rules apply in imagination? For an argument that logical rules do apply in dreams and imagination, see G. K. Chesterton, "The Ethics of Elfland," *Thinking*, vol. 1, no. 2: 13–20.
		On imagination itself, see Mary Warnock, *Imagination*, as well as the four books by Gaston Bachelard on the literary imagination: *Water and Dreams, Air and Thought, Earth and the Reveries of Repose,* and *Psychoanalysis of Fire.* See also Jeremy Bentham, *Chrestomathia,* and S. T. Coleridge—either *A Preliminary Treatise on Method* or *The Friend.* Also see John Dewey, *A Common Faith,* where he considers the role of imagination in the construction of ideals, and *Art as Experience,* pp. 267–69.
12:17–25	practice in inferential reasoning	This paragraph provides an opportunity to give students practice in inferential reasoning by having them cite the statements that, when reversed, give rise to the possible worlds cited here. Thus, they should be able to identify such forms as "All ten-year-olds are people" and "All onions are vegetables."
12:22	dreaming	Cf. Heraclitus, *The Fragments.* The *recent* book on Heraclitus by Charles Kahn can be especially valuable. Descartes's *Meditations* is also useful. See the essay by O. K. Bousma, "Am I Not Now Dreaming?"
12:27	mathematics	See Wittgenstein, *Remarks on the Foundations of Mathematics.*
12:28	grammar	Wittgenstein apparently feels that the conventions that govern the use of language rest, in turn, upon implicit agreements among ourselves to use language only in certain ways. There is, in other words, a kind of linguistic social contract that is the basis of community. Investigation of these implicit conventions is what Wittgenstein calls "philosophical grammar." See his *Philosophical Grammar.*
13:1–4	Tony's theory of language	Tony's conception of language is a mechanical one and does not seem to involve an understanding of the intangible programming that enables the parts of the alarm clock to function in an organized fashion, to say nothing of the intangible programming of language.
13:11–16	Tony's reasoning	Tony's syllogism in lines 11–12 is quite sound. In lines 14–16, however, he apparently suspects that his father has done something invalid by switching the verb from "are" to "should be." But then, in lines 21–22, he loses this train of thought and claims that the invalidity of his father's reasoning rests on its violation of the principle of conversion.

13:29	Mr. Melillo's disposition to inquire	Mr. Melillo says that he doesn't know but he is willing to find out. It might be useful to alert students to look for similar instances of inquiry dispositions, i.e., passages in which the characters announce themselves or show themselves ready, willing, and able to inquire. Cf. John Passmore, "On Teaching to Be Critical," in R. F. Dearden et al., eds., *Education and the Development of Reason*.
14:1–12	Diagrams	For an authoritative, reliable exposition of the history of logic, see William and Martha Kneale, *Development of Logic* (Oxford, 1962), pp. 349ff. (Euler diagrams) and 420ff (Venn diagrams). The facility that the characters in *Harry* have for illustrating their views is quite remarkable. Most of us have nowhere near such facility. In the case of logic, the capacity to cite good examples is all the more valuable and all the more difficult because the slightest variation can make the difference between validity and invalidity. Children are uninhibited example givers. What we must teach them is not to suppress their tendencies to offer examples but to be more responsible in doing so.

CHAPTER FOUR

Page, Line	*Theme*	*References and Sources*
15:1–2	reality of thoughts	The idealistic tradition generally affirms the reality of thoughts, with positions ranging from thoughts being real but different from things to thoughts being real *and* being things. (The latter is Berkeley's position in *A Treatise Concerning the Principles of Human Knowledge*.) See also Bernard Bosanquet, *The Distinction between Mind and Its Objects*. For approaches that affirm the unreality of thoughts, one would have to turn to such materialists as Hobbes, Holbach, LaMettrie, Diderot, Lenin, and Santayana. Again, there is a wide range of differences among these various treatments.
15:5–7	circum-scribing a thought	Suki's remark comes from a comment made by a two-year-old and reported by Meyer Shapiro in the course of a lecture on the phenomenology of mental experience.
15:9–12	are thoughts even more real than things	Although no source can be cited for this remark of Harry's, it is worth referring here to an interesting discussion of this paragraph by Pierre Cohen-Bacrie as part of a detailed analysis of *Harry Stottlemeier's Discovery* that appeared in the *Bulletin de la Société de Philosophie de Québec* 12, no. 1 (January 1986): 72–73. The entire "dossier," pp. 64–106, is a very valuable critique.

15:14	there's nothing to do	Why do people get bored? Among the countless answers, these stand out: the contention of Marx and Engels, in the Communist *Manifesto*, that boredom is the symptom of the worker's alienation from the products of his own labor; and Dewey's suggestion, in *Human Nature and Conduct*, that laziness and boredom are the consequences of the psychological tension induced, among people in industrialized countries, by the schism between theory and practice. One can find many references to the theme of ennui in the poetry of Baudelaire, Rimbaud, and Mallarmé.
15:26–27	ambiguity	Any textbook dealing with logic, and particularly informal logic, contains some consideration of ambiguity. Here are two examples. Howard Kahane's *Logic and Contemporary Rhetoric* contains several discussions of ambiguity. One of particular interest, because it deals with elementary-school textbooks, is his treatment of "Dick and Jane Ambiguity," pp. 214–15. Or, see Trudy Govier, *A Practical Study of Arguments*, 2d ed., pp. 44–46 and 146–49.
16:10–12	vagueness	A fine discussion of vagueness is to be found in John Hospers, *An Introduction to Philosophical Analysis*, 2d ed., pp. 67–77. See also William P. Alston, *Philosophy of Language*, pp. 90–105.
16:19–26	thinking and understanding	Harry's essay suggests the primacy of *understanding* as an educational objective. This is a very traditional notion. For Harry, evidently, thinking is a means to understanding. What is peculiar in his formulation is that the means is more interesting than the end. (See Dewey, *Theory of Valuation*. One can find in almost any of Dewey's works a rejection of Aristotle's notion that ends are higher than means. Means for Dewey have their own immediacy and value. They are consummatory as well as instrumental. See, for example, his *Experience and Nature*, pp. 114–16.)
17:1–5	thinking about thinking	That philosophy is thinking about thinking is a theme that goes back at least to Plato's *Theaetetus* and is found again in book 12 of Aristotle's *Metaphysics*, where God is portrayed as engaged in the highest kind of contemplation, which is thinking about thinking. Among modern philosophers, there are the Hegelians, Heidegger in particular, and there are the analysts, among whom Wittgenstein and Ryle stand out. Both groups have made thinking central, although during the analytic movement it was hard to tell where the analysis of thinking began. Today, we see these as two fairly distinct enterprises—for example, in logical treatments of linguistic inference as contrasted with rhetorical treatments of argument.

17:4–5	self-under-standing	The notion that philosophy involves self-understanding descends from Socrates, especially his emphasis in the *Apology* upon the examined life. He, in turn, might have been indebted to the popular wisdom embodied in the inscription on the temple of the Delphic Oracle: Know Thyself. Gilbert Ryle's essay "Thinking and Self-Teaching" (*Thinking* 1, nos. 3–4) contains interesting insights into the relationship between thinking about thinking and self-understanding.
17:11–13	basic sentences and simple language	It is not so long ago that I. A. Richards advocated the construction of a simple language in his book *Basic English*. We should also remember that the Vienna Circle in the 1920s stood for the creation of an ideal language, as opposed to everyday language. See Rudolf Carnap, *The Syntax of Logical Language*, as well as Richard Rorty, *The Linguistic Turn*.
17:23–29	all and some	Harry's problem with quantification is a familiar one to logicians. Among those who have dealt with it are Peter Strawson in his *Introduction to Logical Theory*, Fred Sommers in *The Logic of Natural Language*, and W. V. Quine in such works as *Elementary Logic* and "Logic as a Source of Syntactical Insights" in *The Ways of Paradox*.
19:5	Dale's mistake	Dale's comment is characteristic of literal-minded students who find it difficult to make counterfactual assumptions or to treat examples as merely examples.
19:14–19	the four logical propositions	One of the most reliable modern treatments of propositions is in Cohen and Nagel, *An Introduction to Logic and Scientific Method* (ch. 2, "An Analysis of Propositions").
19:26–27	"there's no fact"	This theme is a variant of Kant's remark that "the two most important things in the world are the starry skies above us, and the moral law within us." Both make a claim as to the equivalence of mind and nature. The comment does lend itself to a dualistic interpretation, as opposed to the naturalistic unity of mind and nature that one finds in Spinoza and Dewey.
20:1–5	jumping to conclusions	Harry is a bit superstitious in Chapter Two and quite uncritical in Chapter Four. On the basis of very little evidence, he has the thought that Tony threw the stone. In this, he undoubtedly jumps to a conclusion, or commits "the fallacy of hasty generalization," where one generalizes from too few cases. See W. W. Fearnside and W. B. Holther, *Fallacy: The Counterfeit of Argument*, pp. 13–14.

CHAPTER FIVE

Page, Line	Theme	References and Sources
21:1	continuity between thinkers	The last paragraph of Chapter Four begins with the same word, "grown-ups," as the first paragraph of Chapter Five. Virginia Woolf uses this device to show the continuity between what individual minds are thinking. See her *Mrs. Dalloway* or *To the Lighthouse*. Sartre employs a similar technique in his novel *Les Chemins de la liberté*.
21:3–7	jobs and role distance	Whether people can say or do things they don't mean when they are in a given job depends on how much they distance themselves from their jobs or roles. Erving Goffman discusses the problem of role distance in *Encounters* and in *The Presentation of Self in Everyday Life*. In the latter, he takes up the question of performances and analyzes their effect on one's belief in the part one is playing.
21:8–9	disagreeing and not knowing why	Plato likes to distinguish between holding a correct opinion without knowing one's reasons for holding it and knowing the reasons why one holds such an opinion. See *The Republic*, bk. 7, 532–34.
21:10–11	Is Harry sexist?	Harry offers some candies to Maria "almost as an afterthought." It is as if Maria weren't initially present. Whether this is a case of sexism or merely "selective inattention" is open for question.
21:13–24	moving from one to all	The thinking moves from one course (history) not being good, to Harry's "some courses are good and some aren't," to "None of the courses are any good. They are all bad." Mark moves from one particular history course to all courses, whether observed or not. This is the fallacy of hasty generalization, in which an isolated or exceptional case is used as the basis for a general conclusion that is unwarranted. In his discussion of this fallacy in *With Good Reason*, S. Morris Engel offers a comparable example: "I had a bad time with my former husband. From that experience, I've learned that all men are no good." Maria points out Mark's fallacy in lines 23 and 24.
21:25	Mark's remark	Mark says, "It doesn't *mean* it. They just *are*." Maria seems to have accused Mark of a fallacy of inference. His reply is that he is not *inferring* that they are all bad. He is *stating* that they are bad *as a matter of fact*. He's denying that it is a fallacy. The obvious response to what he is saying is that he has not observed all courses. Perhaps what Mark is insinuating is that courses in school are a *natural kind* and all have the same essential characteris-

tic—being boring. In other words, if you have seen one, you have seen them all.

21:26–27	Maria's inference	Maria infers that if some courses are not interesting, there must be others that *are* interesting. Under ordinary circumstances, this would be an invalid inference. In a situation in which each instance has been identified and enumerated, however, it may be possible for "some *x* are not" to imply "some *x* are *y*." For example, if a teacher has finished grading all the examinations and is asked if everyone passed, she may reply, "Some didn't." It would be legitimate to infer, in this case, that "some did." But if she hadn't yet graded all the papers, the inference would be invalid.
22:2–3	Mark's standing on his head	Are there physical correlates of cognitive experiences? For example, does standing on one's head have anything to do with turning sentences around? Mark Johnson, in *The Body and the Mind*, holds that there are many "schemata" (a term he takes from Kant) in which particular bodily behaviors function so as to connect percepts and concepts. In the Talmudic tradition, there is a dialectical move of turning one's opponent's argument upside down. In fact, this is what Karl Marx says he did to Fichte's dialectic: He stood it on its *Spitze*.
22:4–20	induction	For a highly influential version of induction, see David Hume, *An Enquiry Concerning Human Understanding*, sec. 4, part 2, and sec. 5, part 1. Karl Popper has provided a helpful commentary in his article "Hume's Explanation of Inductive Inference," in Alexander Sesonske and N. Fleming, eds., *Human Understanding: Studies in the Philosophy of David Hume*. See also the article by P. F. Strawson, "The Justification of Induction," in the same volume. And see Cohen and Nagel, *An Introduction to Logic and Scientific Method*, pp. 279–86.
22:20	jumping to conclusions	Jumping to conclusions is another example of hasty generalization. In psychological literature, it is generally referred to as *stereotyping*. See D. L. Hamilton, ed., *Cognitive Processes in Stereotyping and Intergroup Behavior*.
22:29	part–whole reasoning	Mark says that "*all* the classes in this school are awful. It's an awful school." Students might wonder if this is valid part–whole reasoning.
23:8–9	authoritarianism	Mark accuses the schools of being authoritarian. See Theodor Adorno et al., *The Authoritarian Personality*.
23:13–15	"they'll *call* it good, no matter what they do"	The source of this is the cynical remark by Thrasymachus in *The Republic*, bk. 1, 336b–347e. See also Nietzsche (*The Genealogy of Morals* and *Beyond Good and Evil*), who develops a theory in which instinctive behavior is

concealed by calling it its opposite. Nietzsche's theory postulates two moralities, one of the leaders and the other of the followers. Whatever the strong do is called good. One can also look in Freud's writings for his theory of *reaction-formation*. He suggests that one masks one's aggressive or libidinal instincts by converting them into their opposites; see *The Ego and the Id*.

23:16–22	Maria's speech	In Plato's *Republic* (bk. 1), Thrasymachus argues that we entrust specialized tasks to experts rather than to laymen and that these experts are infallible in what they do (since one would cease to be an expert at the moment of making a mistake.) Socrates does not wholly disagree with him, but tries to show that the expert or professional acts not from self-interest but in the interest of his client (336b–347e). Maria, analogously, argues that grown-ups rather than children must run the schools because they possess the necessary expertise that children do not. The difference between Thrasymachus and Socrates is that although both are antidemocratic, Thrasymachus is prepared to condone powerful self-interested authority, whereas Socrates argues for an enlightened elitism in which the rulers would take their professionalism seriously and act in behalf of the people they serve. Maria evidently accepts Socrates' position.
23:23–25	Mark's reply	Mark says, "things wouldn't be any worse than they are now." He rejects the authoritarianism of Thrasymachus and the enlightened elitism of Socrates, suggesting that things couldn't be worse if the people were to rule themselves, or if the children were to run the schools. See Locke and Jefferson in political theory and A. S. Neill, *Summerhill*, in education. (Of course there is a difference between Locke and Jefferson, who favored representative democracy, and the idea of children directly assuming authority in running the schools.)
23:26–29	Harry's position	Harry seems to side with Maria and Socrates rather than with Mark, whose proposal seems too drastic for him. Harry argues, like Socrates in the passage just cited, that the real issue is whether or not those in power know what they are doing. Of course, Socrates would go further than this and demand that they act for the people and not for themselves.
24:1–5	knowing what they're doing as understanding	With regard to people who understand not only children but why we are in school in the first place, see Sylvia Ashton-Warner, *Teacher*. With regard to the concept of understanding, see Stephen Toulmin, *Knowledge and Understanding*.
24:8	education as learning answers	For someone who is very close to this position, see E. D. Hirsch, Jr., *Cultural Literacy*. Hirsch is an example of an educator who thinks that certain contents must

be learned by all schoolchildren. In general, however,
the position that one goes to school to learn answers is
seldom formulated theoretically and defended. Nevertheless, it is a prime maxim of traditional educational
practice.

24:9–10   education   In *How We Think*, Dewey argues that there is a continuity
              as learning   between problem solving in everyday life and problem
              how to solve   solving in scientific inquiry. He goes so far as to depict a
              problems   series of stages through which inquiry proceeds in each
case. Dewey's formulation of the stages of problem solv-
ing has been interpreted by innumerable educators as a
paradigm for education. In recent years the process of
problem solving has been systematized and presented as
an essential characteristic of education. See, for example,
John R. Hayes, *The Complete Problem Solver*, 2d ed., and
Arthur Whimby and Jack Lockhead, *Problem-Solving and
Comprehension*, 3d ed.

24:12–13   education   See Paulo Freire, *Pedagogy of the Oppressed*, and Maurice
              as asking   Merleau-Ponty, "Philosophy as Interrogation," in *Themes
              questions   from the Lectures*, pp. 99–113. See also Felix Cohen,
"What Is a Question?" *Thinking* 4, nos. 3–4, and
Arthur C. Graesser and John B. Black, *The Psychology of
Questions*. Robin Collingwood has also written about the
relationship of questions to answers in his *Autobiography*.

24:14–15   education as   See Robert Glaser, "Education and Thinking," *American
              learning how   Psychologist* (February 1984), and Dewey, "Education as
              to think   Thinking," ch. 12 of *Democracy and Education*. Also see
John Stuart Mill, "Inaugural Address at St. Andrews";
Alfred North Whitehead, *The Aims of Education*; Jean-
Jacques Rousseau, *Émile*; John Henry Newman, *The
Idea of a University*; and Richard and Maria Edgeworth,
Practical Education, 3 vols. (1802).

24:15–16   education   Kant uses the phrase "thinking for oneself" in his *Logic*,
              as learning   and in his essay "On Enlightenment" he discusses intel-
              to think for   lectual autonomy in the sense that it is shameful to have
              oneself   other people do our thinking for us. There is also a dis-
cussion of thinking for oneself as autonomy in Paul Hirst,
"Education and Diversity of Belief," in M. C. Felderhof,
ed., *Religious Education in a Pluralist Society* (1985).
One of the main aims of Philosophy for Children is to
help children think for themselves, as discussed in Lipman, Sharp, and Oscanyan, *Philosophy in the Classroom*,
2d ed., pp. 82–84 and 203–4. Also see Philip C. Guin,
"Thinking for Oneself," in this book.

24:20–25:7   making   See John Wilson, "Making Subjects Interesting," *Jour-
              school inter-   nal of Philosophy of Education* 21, no. 2 (1987): 215–22.
              esting   See also T. S. Champlain, "Doing Something for Its Own
Sake," *Philosophy* 62 (1987); Michael Oakeshott, "Edu-

		cation: The Engagement and Its Frustration," in R. F. Dearden, P. H. Hirst, and R. S. Peters, eds., *Education and the Development of Reason*; and John Dewey, *Experience and Education* and *Democracy and Education* (chs. 10 and 15).
25:16–20	the cloud	Cf. Wittgenstein's notion of "seeing as" in *Philosophical Investigations*. The whole theory of Rorschach analysis, in which the patient's associations with visual forms are analyzed, is most insightfully discussed by Ernst Kris in *Psychoanalytic Explorations in Art* and by Ernest Schachtel in *Metamorphosis*. One of the first things translators quite properly do with this section is to substitute the contours of their own country for North America. Otherwise, the imperialistic connotations of this passage becomes overwhelming. See Rudolf Arnheim, *Visual Thinking*, and E. H. Gombrich, *Meditations on a Hobby Horse*.
25:23	our idea	The notion of idea as perception is richly developed in Locke's *Essay Concerning Human Understanding*. Harry recognizes an analogy between Mark's experience of the cloud and Mrs. Halsey's analysis of his essay. The analogy is something like: The cloud we see as North America is to our understanding of the universe as the actual cloud is to the actual universe.
26:4–6	the wonderful	See Aristotle, *Metaphysics* (bk. 1), "Philosophy begins in wonder," and G. K. Chesterton, "The Ethics of Elfland," reprinted in *Thinking* 1, no. 2.
26:5–6	the wonder of the everyday	See Wittgenstein, "A Lecture on Ethics," reprinted in *Discovering Philosophy*; Ninian Smart, *Philosophers and Religious Truth*; and George Santayana, *Scepticism and Animal Faith*. See also Santayana, "Ultimate Religion," which appears in *Obiter Scripta*. This is a main theme in Dewey's *Art as Experience*.
26:7	getting excited by one's own ideas	In *The Birth of Tragedy*, Nietzsche analyzes mental activity into Apollonian intellect and Dionysian ecstatic reverie. He talks of how these two come together in Socrates.

CHAPTER SIX

Page, Line	*Theme*	*References and Sources*
27:3–6	*The Sorcerer's Apprentice*	This tone poem by Paul Dukas is familiar to children through the Disney movie *Fantasia*. Perhaps there is an analogy: The sorcerer's apprentice has unleashed the

powers of nature through magic—Harry's key is logic.
(Marx and Engels, in the Communist *Manifesto*, cite the
fairy tale of the sorcerer's apprentice as an image for
capitalism.)

27:7–8	being haunted by a tune	This calls to mind lines in an Irving Berlin song: "A pretty girl is like a melody / that haunts you night and day."
27:13–16	being haunted by the dead	Several works by Edgar Allan Poe are on this theme, e.g., "Ulalume." Freud discusses the role of dreams in grieving in "Mourning and Melancholia." He considers the fear of death in children in *Beyond the Pleasure Principle*.
27:19–22	causes of dreams	Dreams are the survival of strong impressions, according to Jill. This theory is strictly an empirical one. Hume distinguishes impressions (the more lively perceptions when we see, feel, hear, love, hate, desire, or will) from thoughts or ideas (the less lively perceptions): "All our ideas or more feeble perceptions are copies of our impressions or more lively ones" (*Enquiry Concerning Human Understanding*, sec. 2, "Of the Origin of Ideas"). Presumably Hume thinks that dreams are the echoes of strong impressions made on our senses.
27:22–25	Laura's causal explanation of thought	Laura's argument that thoughts in the mind are caused by things outside the mind is reminiscent of Locke's explanation that most of our ideas come from the material world outside us. Bodies' primary qualities produce in us such simple ideas as solidity, extension, figure, motion, rest, and number. See Locke's *Essay Concerning Human Understanding* (bk. 2, chs. 1 and 8).
27:26–27	imaginary things	Such ideas are produced, Locke says, by the mind's reflection upon its own ideas. Our senses supply our minds with the materials of thinking, and our fancy, or imagination, reconstructs these materials endlessly through the process called reflection. Ibid.
28:2–4	believing and believing in	Philosophers generally distinguish between believing and believing in by claiming that to believe is to believe *that* some proposition is true, whether it be true in fact or not. On the other hand, to believe in may mean that certain things exist or that certain things *ought* to exist. Thus, a person can believe *that* a day is twenty-four hours long and believe *in* angels and children's rights.
28:3–4	Laura's skepticism about elves and monsters	Even though we don't invent elves and monsters ourselves, Laura says, other people do and cause us to think about them.

28:5–6	what is in and not in the mind	Many philosophers have ridiculed the notion that the mind has an "inside" and an "outside." See, for example, Whitehead's fallacy of misplaced concreteness and fallacy of specific location in his *Process and Reality*. See also Gilbert Ryle's *Concept of Mind*. The point is of critical importance if one is to understand the difference between Locke and Berkeley. Locke takes it for granted that there is an independent material world outside the mind, although he admits that he cannot demonstrate its existence. Berkeley argues that Locke cannot do so because its independent existence is an absurdity. Things either exist in the mind or nowhere.
28:8–9	knowing one has a mind	In the second of his *Meditations on First Philosophy*, Descartes tries the thought experiment of assuming that nothing exists. If now he is persuaded that he does not exist, he must exist, since he is persuaded. If he supposes that a diabolical being is trying to deceive him about his existence, he still must exist, inasmuch as he is deceived. Thus, he says in this Ontological Argument, he must exist if he thinks. "I am, therefore, only a thinking thing, that is, a mind, understanding or reason. . . . I am, however, a real thing and really existing."
28:8–9	knowing one has a body	In Meditation 6, Descartes asserts that he knows he has a body because he has a clear and distinct idea of himself as a physical body. Another claim that the body is known intuitively and with certainty is to be found in G. E. Moore, "A Defense of Common Sense," in *Philosophical Papers*. In his lectures, Moore would hold out his hands and profess himself absolutely certain of their existence.
28:14–15	the mind is the brain	This is today a very popular interpretation of the mind. See D. M. Armstrong, *A Materialist Theory of Mind*, and also W. V. Quine, "Mind vs. Body," in *Quiddities*, pp. 132–34, in which he says that he is not *denying* consciousness but merely explaining mental states and events as bodily ones. "Mental events are physical, but mentalistic language classifies them in ways incommensurable with the classification expressable in physiological language."
28:15	only things you can see or touch are real	This is standard empiricism of the Locke, Berkeley, and Hume variety continuing into twentieth-century positivism. See A. J. Ayer, *Language, Truth, and Logic*.
28:16–24	mind as behavior (Laura)	We often attribute this position to Gilbert Ryle in *The Concept of Mind*, forgetting that the behavioristic interpretation of mind had earlier been explored extensively by George Herbert Mead in *Mind, Self, and Society* and by John Dewey in *Experience and Nature*.

28:25–27	denial of identity of mind and brain (Fran)	See James Cornman, *Materialism and Sensations*.
28:28	the mind is something electrical in the brain	That thoughts are electrical is a version of classic materialism, which, as in Holbach and LaMettrie, was mechanical and reductivistic. The electricity theory is more dynamic, conceiving the mind as energy. For some suggestive impressions of this approach, see James L. Christian, *Philosophy: An Introduction to the Art of Wondering*, pp. 191–203.
29:7	mind is thin smoky stuff (Mrs. Portos)	Such pre-Socratic philosophers as Democritus held this view. See W. K. C. Guthrie, *The Greek Philosophers*.
29:20–25	the mind as language (Mrs. Portos)	Since Mead conceived of mind as linguistic behavior, or linguistic communication, his theory in *Mind, Self, and Society* can be cited in this category as well as in the category of behaviorism.
29:26–29	Fran's theory: thoughts are traces of things in our memories	This may be an echo of Plato's theory of knowledge as recollection, in which everything one learns is something one had already known. See the *Meno*.
30:10	minds as what people have and animals don't have (Laura)	Descartes, in his *Meditations on First Philosophy*, argues that animals are simply machines and do not have minds. Some of the recent work of sociobiologists holds that the order of intelligence among animals is so different from human intelligence that the two are incommensurable. See, for example, the writings of Thomas Sebeok.
30:13–16	any animal has a mind to the extent that it has a culture	In his new (1929) preface to *Experience and Nature*, Dewey seems to come close to identifying mind and culture. He elaborates on this in the new first chapter of that book, "Experience and Philosophical Method." Hegel preceded Dewey in identifying mind and culture, particularly in *The Phenomenology of Spirit*.

A close examination of what Mr. Portos actually says shows that he has not explicitly identified mind and culture. He has made two assertions: We believe man has a mind because he is an animal with a culture, and any animal has a mind *to the extent that* it has a culture. This latter merely indicates that mind and culture always go together: It does not assert their identity. Of course, what Mr. Portos says does not *exclude* the possibility that mind is culture, either.

While Mr. Portos's comments demand careful attention, the inquiry should not leave students with the impression that this position is a favored one.

30:17–21	sounding like a book	Jacques Derrida has tried to show that Plato's opposition to writing, as put forth in the *Phaedrus*, expresses, in part, his fear that people will no longer have to remember what they said, nor will they need to engage in face-to-face conversation. Writing is therefore a threat to community. See Christopher Norris, *Derrida*, pp. 28–45.

CHAPTER SEVEN

Page, Line	*Theme*	*References and Sources*
31:18–20	Mr. Portos's views	Mr. Portos seems to be arguing in opposition to people like Thomas Sebeok. Sebeok has been critical of the claim made by such students of animal behavior as Jane Goodall that animals like gorillas and chimpanzees have an intelligence much closer to humans than anyone had realized.
31:18–32:10	differences of degree and of kind	See Robin G. Collingwood's chapter "Degree and Kind" in *Essay on Philosophical Method*. See too the transcript of children discussing this issue in *Thinking* 1, no. 1. Much of the traditional controversy over degree and kind was formulated in other terms, such as the contrast between quantity and quality—a difference of quantity being a difference of degree, a difference of quality being a difference of kind. For Marxists following Lenin, differences of quantity became differences of quality. See Lenin's *Essays in Empirio-Criticism*.
32:11	culture	See Edward Tylor, *Primitive Culture*, vol. 1, pp. 1–6. See also Clyde Kluckhohn, "The Study of Culture," in Lerner and Lasswell, eds., *The Policy Sciences*.
32:22–33:5	evolutionary developments	In this passage we can distinguish a foreground and a background conception. The foreground conception is the distinction between humans and other animals. Humans can survive despite environmental changes because they have the capacity to make inventions by which to protect themselves. Animals cannot make such inventions, but they can adapt their bodies to changes in the environment, as the whale changed from a land to a sea creature. The language of this portrait of events is teleological and purposive. According to Darwin, however (and this is the background conception to the passage), the evolution of species is not teleological at all. Those species that are

internally diversified are likely to have some varieties
that can survive under changing circumstances. And it is
this mechanism that makes for evolutionary change. See
Charles Darwin, *The Origin of Species*, ch. 15.

For a lively exposition of the difference between
the evolution of tools and the evolution of organs, see
David R. Olson, *The Social Foundations of Language and
Thought*, pp. 2–3. Olsen brings in some very pertinent
comments by Jerome Bruner, Peter Medawar, Samuel
Butler, and Karl Popper. The passage in *Harry Stottlemeier's Discovery* was largely derived from its treatment
by A. L. Kroeber in *The Nature of Culture*, pp. 23–30.

33:7 and 14	the alleged rigidity of animal behavior	With more information about human communication with animals and with consequent reestimation of animal intelligence, we can expect increasingly frequent documentation of cases in which animals invent, or engage in innovative, behavior.
33:15–20	the thoughts of mankind	See Hegel's notion of objective mind in his introductions to *The Philosophy of History* and *The Philosophy of Fine Art*. Just before Hegel, Edmund Burke had said something similar in *Reflections on the Revolution in France*, speaking of human traditions as embodying "the wisdom of mankind."
34:2–18	the logic of relationships	Modern logic of relations comes from Augustus De Morgan, Charles Peirce, and Bertrand Russell. See Stephan Korner, "On the Logic of Relations," in *Proceedings of the Aristotelian Society* (1976–77): 149–64. For a clear introductory discussion of symmetrical and transitive relationships, see Philip Wheelwright, *Valid Thinking*. Dewey takes the position (in *Logic*, pp. 307–9) that Aristotelian logic, which recognizes only the subject-predicate form, is thoroughly inadequate. To him, all particular propositions are relational, and all propositions about relations of kinds, even though they lack subject-predicate form, are relational. Dewey is much more comfortable with propositions of the form "A is greater than B" and "If A, then B," or "All A are B."

CHAPTER EIGHT

Page, Line	*Theme*	*References and Sources*
35–37	mental acts	The literature on mental acts in the past half century is enormous. (P. T. Geach's book *Mental Acts* is not particularly helpful.) Students are encouraged to consult back

issues of *Mind, American Philosophical Quarterly, Journal of Philosophy*, and *Philosophy and Phenomenological Research* dealing with specific mental acts, as well as *The Encyclopedia of Philosophy*. J. L. Austin often provides the model philosophical analysis of a mental act, as in his *Philosophical Papers*. He also, in *How to Do Things with Words*, provides a useful typology. Another typology is to be found in the meticulous study by Zeno Vendler, especially his *Res Cogito*. Another useful work is "On the Nature of the Psychological," by Roderick M. Chisholm, in *Philosophical Studies* 43 (1983): 155–64. Gilbert Ryle's late essays on thinking contain many excellent references to specific mental acts, but he does not comment extensively on any particular act.

35–35	phenomenology of thinking	The major work here is Hegel's difficult *Phenomenology of Spirit*. Much more readable are Charles Peirce, "Phenomenology," in *Selected Papers*; William James, "The Stream of Conscious Thought," ch. 9 in *The Principles of Psychology*; James Joyce, last monologue of Molly Bloom in *Ulysses*; Marcel Proust, *Swann's Way*; and Virginia Woolf, *Mrs. Dalloway*. See also Eugene O'Neill, especially *Desire under the Elms*.
35:7–8	trying to remember	See F. C. Bartlett's *Remembering*, which develops the important notion of memory schemas. See also A. D. Baddeley, *The Psychology of Memory*.
35:9	wondering	Wondering and philosophizing have been seen as intimately connected ever since Aristotle pointed out the association in Book 1 of the *Metaphysics*. Several books in celebration of wonder have been written by Sam Keen. Lewis Carroll in *Alice in Wonderland* has a nice sense of what wonder involves.
		Of course, we are dealing here with a vast family that includes wondering how, wondering why, wondering at, wondering that, wondering whether, etc.
35:11	decision making	See Arthur Whimby and Jack Lockhead, *Problem-Solving and Comprehension*; H. Raiffa, *Decision Analysis*; and A. Tversky and D. Kahneman, "The Framing of Decisions and the Psychology of Choice," in *Science* (1981).
35:13	figuring out	J. S. Bruner et al., *A Study of Thinking*, and J. S. Bruner et al., *Studies in Cognitive Growth*.
35:22	considering advantages and disadvantages	See Jonathan Baron, *Rationality and Intelligence*. For consequentialist thinking, see Jeremy Bentham, *Principles of Morals and Legislation*. For an antiutilitarian response, see Samuel Scheffler, *Against Consequentialism*.
35:23–24	aesthetic reasoning	An excellent example would be John Wilson, "Education and Aesthetic Appreciation," in Lipman and Sharp,

eds., *Growing Up with Philosophy*, pp. 300–310. See also
R. W. Hepburn, "Aesthetic Appreciation of Nature," and
Paul Valéry, "Man and the Seashell," both reprinted in
Lipman, ed., *Contemporary Aesthetics*.

35:26–28	ethical reasoning	See Gilbert Harman, *The Nature of Morality*; John Dewey, *The Theory of the Moral Life*; Kurt Baier, *The Moral Point of View*; J.-P. Sartre, *Existentialism*; Maurice Mandelbaum, *The Phenomenology of Moral Experience*; and James Rachels, *Moral Problems*.
36:9–12	metaphysical optimism	See Voltaire's *Candide* (particularly the character of Dr. Pangloss), as well as the pompous philosophical puppets in *Monsieur, Monsieur* by Jean Tardieu. There is a version of this optimism in Leibniz's claim that "this is the best of all possible worlds" and in Augustine's optimistic treatment of the nature of evil. But in neither philosopher is the overall picture a particularly sunny one.
36:9–12	perfection	In Spinoza, reality and perfection are one and the same, and both are identical with infinity. Thus, in Spinoza, only the finite is less than real and therefore less than perfect. In Plato, the Forms are perfect, and the various embodiments are imperfect.
36:13	persuasion	Starting with Aristotle's *Rhetoric*, there has been a continuous line of scholarly inquiry into the nature of persuasion. For a typical contemporary and popular approach, see Nicholas Capaldi, *The Art of Deception*. For a more scholarly treatment, consult any of the works of Chaim Perelman, particularly *The New Rhetoric*.
36:17	remembered	See John Bransford, *Human Cognition: Learning, Understanding, and Remembering*, and A. L. Brown, "Knowing When, Where, and How to Remember: A Problem of Metacognition," in R. Glaser, ed., *Advances in Instructional Psychology*.
36:19	puzzling	See Esther Markman, "Realizing That You Don't Understand," *Child Development* (1977), and "Realizing That You Don't Understand: Elementary School Children's Awareness of Inconsistencies," *Child Development* (1979).
36:21	deciding	A. Newell and H. A. Simon, *Human Problem Solving*; W. A. Wickelgren, *How to Solve Problems: Elements of a Theory of Problems and Problem-Solving*. See also M. F. Rubenstein, *Patterns of Problem-Solving*, and H. A. Simon, "Problem-Solving and Education," in D. T. Tuma and F. Reif, eds., *Problem Solving and Education: Issues in Teaching and Research*.
36:26	Randy's cave	Randy's fantasy about exploring the cave is, in a sense, emblematic of philosophical speculation itself, starting with the cave in Plato's *Republic*. Plato's cave is filled with

prisoners. Randy's cave opens into an "enormous room."
(e. e. cummings wrote a novel about his experiences in
World War I, particularly those in a prison camp, called
The Enormous Room.)

36:28	trying not to think	A classic technique of meditation, especially in Zen Buddhism, is the purging of the mind of all distractions and of all content. Whether we can think so as to induce a state of not thinking, and whether we can think without thinking of something, are perplexing questions.
37:1–2	doing the wrong thing with the right means	When we read the first sentence on page 37, it sounds as if Mickey decides hitting Laura would be morally wrong. When we read the second sentence, we see that hitting her is all right, but hitting her with a wadded-up ball of paper would be wrong.
37:3–5	Can the colors of nature be ugly?	Anne raises the question of whether we can judge nature's colors to be poorly chosen. Her position is precisely the opposite of that of Jill Portos, who thinks that nature's colors are perfect as they are and would be equally perfect if they were different.
37:6–7	coming to a conclusion	Jane Starr comes to a conclusion but she doesn't show us how she proceeds. She gives us no criteria for judging what is a "bad family."
37:11–14	how nice the world would be	The twins Mark and Maria seem to have somewhat similar thoughts. Both are thinking counterfactually of what the world would be like under certain different circumstances.
37:15–17	Fran's questioning	Fran's first question seems to be one of legitimacy or constitutionality. The second question moves ahead to imply that there might be barriers of custom and prejudice despite the lack of legal barriers. Her questions also reflect her incredulity that what has never happened before could occur now.
37:18–20	Sandy's naïveté	Sandy seems to think that the only obstacle to his buying a racing car is getting enough money to buy a lottery ticket. He seems not to doubt that if he had such a ticket, he'd win.
37:21	planning	Karl Pribram has approached the problem of planning in *Plans and the Structure of Behavior.* Also, Michael Bratman has proposed that intentions be considered as partial plans in his *Intention, Plans, and Practical Reason.*
37:23	Laura's reasoning	There is no internal evidence, at least so far in the book, that Tony is always looking at Laura, although she presents it as a fact that he seemed to be doing so. One can legitimately wonder if Laura is not projecting her own behavior on Tony.

37:27	putting a thought out of one's mind	This mental act involves shifting one's attention so as to cease thinking about one thing and start thinking about another. It is not clear just how one does this.
37:27	concentrating	Presumably, to concentrate is to attend to something very directly and intently without having other things "at the back of one's mind." Children are said to have a short attention span (which might be questioned); even if it is so, this doesn't mean that they don't concentrate well during that span of time. What is more, their attention may be recurrent rather than sustained.
38–40	symmetry and transi-tivity	Aristotle alludes only rarely to a logic of relationships. He moves directly from conversion to the categorical syllogism. Harry, however, needs intervening steps. Aristotle concentrates on the verb "are" and constructs a syllogism, such as "Barbara," which is so familiar and clear that we hardly notice how it involves transitivity. It seems merely to involve class membership. Harry uses a quite different strategy. He and his classmates begin by identifying a broad array of relational propositions, some of which they recognize as transitive. Harry starts to wonder (middle of p. 40) if "are" stands for a carryover relationship. His reasoning may be less direct, but he seems to take for granted that transitivity is what makes a syllogism possible.
40:23	The verb "are"	Does "are" mean "belong to the class of"? This is what Harry concludes, but it is not obvious that he is correct. This topic has been dealt with elsewhere in the curricu-lum (e.g., *Suki*, Chapter Three, episode 4, and *Elfie*, Chapter Eight, episode 2). Three alternative interpreta-tions are provided in the *Elfie* episode: 1. "Are" means "belongs to the class of." 2. "Are" means "belongs to" in the sense that the predicate is a property of the subject (thus, when we say "lemons are yellow," we mean that "yel-low" belongs to "the lemon," i.e., is a trait of, or property of, the lemon). 3. One can see the subject as an *example* of the predi-cate in the sense that lemons are examples of yellow things. For more on the meaning of "are," and on predication generally, see Edward E. Smith and Douglas L. Medin, *Categories and Concepts* (Cambridge, Mass.: Harvard University Press, 1981), particularly the discussion of predication as exemplification, pp. 143–61. Also see Fred Sommers, "Predicability," in Max Black, ed., *Philosophy in America*.
41:1–11	Harry's four-part fallacy	It would be too much to expect Harry to discover the syllogism *and* to get it right the first time. The syllogism he works out is a four-term fallacy. Valid syllogisms can

have only three terms, and Harry's has more than three:
The (Shetland Islands) are (a part of Scotland).
(Scotland) is (a part of Great Britain).
This shows that, although transitivity was an important
clue for Harry that led him in turn to discover the syllogism, it doesn't follow that all cases of transitivity can
be validly formulated as syllogisms. That Harry makes
this particular mistake (a mistake in terms of Aristotelian
logic) suggests that he is confusing the logic of relations
(to which transitivity belongs) with the subject–predicate
logic to which the syllogism belongs.

41:14	Do we "figure out" a third sentence?	Harry concludes that, given two carryover sentences, we can "figure out" a third. Some critics have argued that the conclusion of a categorical syllogism is not really figured out, because it is already contained in the premises and so must be known in advance. Others have held that people do not really think this way very often, that we are much more likely to begin with the conclusion and figure out the premises we had been assuming than to start with the premises and figure out the conclusion.
41:15–16	Do people really think this way often?	Harry asks himself this question but really doesn't answer it. Had he not been distracted, he might have wondered whether people engaged in inquiry really think very often in terms of classes or whether they are more likely to think conditionally, such as "If x, then y," or relationally, as in "X is related to y."
41:20	thinking about how to think correctly	When Harry thinks this, what does he believe is involved in thinking correctly? So far, he hasn't given us much of a clue. Does he think that it is a matter of following rules, as he seems to have thought in Chapter One, or does he think it is a matter of developing a skill? In this regard, Wittgenstein spends a great deal of time trying to figure out how, when we think, we might be said to be following rules, and then seems to conclude, in *On Certainty*, that good thinking is not rule governed, but skillful, thinking. This raises the question, formulated so explicitly by Kant, of whether goodness is a matter of obeying the rules solely for the sake of the rules or a matter of acting "as duty requires but not because duty requires." That is, do we learn the rules of thinking in order to obey them or so that we can develop skills of thinking that will enable us to think "*as* the rules require, but not *because* the rules require?"
41:20	What good is good thinking?	By "good thinking" here, Harry seems to mean reasoning, and he seems to be saying that reasoning is a subject or discipline like any other. He does not make more grandiose claims for it, such as that reasoning is a generic skill that is presupposed by all the disciplines. In some ways, he is reasoning by analogy. Presumably, we know

that adding, subtracting, and speaking correctly are good.
And so, by analogy, ought we to know that thinking correctly is good. His argument rests on the strength of the
analogy, and he doesn't explore it any further. How would
Hume have reacted to this analogical argument? In the
Dialogues Concerning Natural Religion, he does everything possible to destroy the credibility of the analogical
argument as popularly employed, and then concedes that
we don't have much alternative to it, so we had better
learn how to use it prudently. Harry is raising a question
about the practical value of good thinking, and this question has agitated people from Aristotle (with his concern
for practical judgment and practical wisdom in the *Nicomachean Ethics*) down to present-day advocates of critical
thinking.

42:4–11	Why did Bill throw the stone?	Tony says that Bill has been acting "kind of crazy" since his father was killed in the war. Does this explain his throwing the stone at Harry? Would it help to have a more precise characterization of Bill's state of mind? This is where we come to the logic of emotions, as discussed by such Renaissance writers as La Rochefoucauld and Hobbes and by such modern ones as Robert Solomon (in *The Emotions*).

For example, would it be more accurate to call Bill
resentful, envious, or *jealous* of Harry? Students could try
to define these terms behaviorally. (Paul Lazarsfeld, the
sociologist, used to say in his lectures that the difference
between envy and jealousy is that if he saw a man with a
pretty girl, he would be envious, but if it were *his* girl, he
would be jealous.)

42:17	I think he should know	Why does Mark think that Harry should know? On when it is appropriate to tell one person about the actions of another, especially when it involves them personally or professionally, see Maurice Mandelbaum, *The Phenomenology of Moral Experience*. Mandelbaum has an interesting illustration, on pages 76–79, of the right of a person to know the truth.

CHAPTER NINE

Page, Line	*Theme*	*References and Comments*
43:1–3	Dale's despair	Such themes as depression and despair are treated philosophically by Robert C. Solomon in *The Passions: Myth and Nature of Human Emotion*. See, in particular, the treatment of despair (pp. 298–300) and the section "Emo-

tions as Judgments" (pp. 185–91). Solomon argues that such emotions as anger or shame involve moral judgments and appeal to moral standards. They are therefore normative.

43:17–18	parental authority	Many books on children's rights deal with the question of the nature and scope of parental authority. An example would be William Aiken and Hugh LaFollette, *Whose Child: Children's Rights, Parental Authority, and State Power.*
43:21–22	Dale's reasons	Under questioning from Mr. Partridge, Dale engages in a series of appeals. The first is to his parents' authority. Then he explains that his parents, in turn, invoke the authority of their religion and that their religion invokes the authority of the Bible. He does not introduce the notion of revelation as the justification of the Bible's authority. It is good to remember that each time Mr. Partridge pushes him, Dale has no trouble in defending his actions by means of justifying reasons. See Alasdair MacIntyre, *Whose Rationality Which Justice?*
43:28	symbol	Two philosophical treatments of the nature of symbols are Ernst Cassirer, *Philosophy of Symbolic Forms* (3 vols.), and Mircea Eliade, *The Sacred and the Profane.*
44:1 and 2	"standing for," or representation	Peirce deals with the problem of how some things can stand for or represent other things in his semiotic treatment of indices and icons; see his *Collected Papers.* For another important treatment, see Nelson Goodman, *Languages of Art.*
44:4–6	worship	Philosophers have treated the notion of worship in various ways. For a sampling, see Rudolf Otto, *The Idea of the Holy*; Bertrand Russell, *A Free Man's Worship*; Alfred North Whitehead, *Religion in the Making*; and John Dewey, *A Common Faith.*
44:15	separation of church and state	This separation is insisted upon in some countries but largely ignored in others. For example, the queen of England is also the head of the Established Church of England. In the United States, separation of church and state is required by the Constitution: "Congress shall make no law respecting an establishment of religion."
44:18–19	religion and allegiance to the state	The U.S. Pledge of Allegiance mentions "One nation under God." The pledge, however, has no official standing, but is used almost everywhere by custom. For more on the problem of which allegiance takes precedence, that to the government or that to the church, see Aquinas, *Summa Theologica*; Hobbes, *Leviathan*, ch. 2; Spinoza, *Theologico-Political Treatise*, ch. 19; and Locke, *A Letter Concerning Toleration.*

44:27–28	Is something right because everyone does it?	One approach to this problem is that of Plato in the *Euthyphro*. John Stuart Mill deals with it in *On Liberty*, ch. 1, as "the tyranny of the majority." As a critical-thinking fallacy, it is sometimes called "the bandwagon fallacy." See W. W. Fearnside and W. B. Holther, *Fallacy: The Counterfeit of Argument*, pp. 92–93.
44:30–45:1	conflict of authority	Aquinas argues somewhere that if there is a conflict of authority between Christians and Jews or Christians and Muslims, it can be settled by an appeal to the Old Testament. And a conflict between Christians and nonbelievers can be settled by the use of reason.
45:6	interpretation	On interpretation, see Paul Ricoeur, *The Conflict of Interpretations: Essays in Hermeneutics*, ed. Don Ihde, and *Time and Narrative* (3 vols.). Also see Susan Sontag, *Against Interpretation*, and Paul Tillich, *Systematic Theology* (3 vols.).
45:8–11	fallibilism and infallibilism	The origin of fallibilism is to be found in Charles Peirce's article "The Fixation of Belief." Another strand of fallibilism comes out of Karl Popper and stresses the importance of falsification. See Popper, *Objective Knowledge*, and Henry Perkinson, *The Possibility of Error*, a Popperian approach to education.
45:10–14	Mr. Partridge's reasoning	Mr. Partridge, in line 6, has countered Dale's invocation of the Bible as an ultimate authority by asserting that we all have our interpretations and Dale's parents are entitled to theirs. Now he proceeds to suppose an interpretation that could be, for Dale, a matter of life or death. By introducing the notion of blood transfusions, Mr. Partridge attempts to show Dale that in such a crisis his parents would have to choose between following their interpretation of the Bible and risking Dale's death or giving up their interpretation and assuring his life. One way of understanding Mr. Partridge's reasoning here is to see it as an appeal to alarm. Traditionally, this and other appeals to emotion have been distrusted and called logical fallacies. The problem is that some decisions to act on such emotions as fear can turn out to be sound and justified conclusions. Just the same, appeals to emotion often mask weak arguments, as seems to be the case with Mr. Partridge's argument. See Douglas N. Walton, *Informal Logic*, particularly "Appeals to Emotion," ch. 4, pp. 82–107.
45:26	disagreement and disrespect	John Stuart Mill, in *On Liberty*, holds that diversity of opinions is healthy. (Dewey, influenced by Darwin, concludes similarly that the greater the variety in a species, the greater the possibilities of progress.) Mill goes so far as to claim that society needs the dissenter to point out

weaknesses that can be corrected but would otherwise be overlooked.

46:4	competing with ideas	Mill's notion that a democratic society ought to be as pluralistic as possible, with everyone competing with everyone else for excellence, is consistent with his defense of competitive laissez-faire capitalism. William James carried the same notion one step further when he argued that there are peaceable forms of competition that are the "moral equivalents of war." People should compete with one another in the fight against illness and injustice and poverty the same way that they had previously fought against each other for power or glory. At the close of the first chapter of *Human Nature and Conduct*, Dewey endorses James's argument. Expressions of James's point of view are to be found in his essay "Great Men and Their Environment" and in the collection *Essays in Radical Empiricism*.
46:6–10	Mr. Partridge's reasoning	Mr. Partridge first reassures Dale that he would not counsel him to disagree with his parents. He then immediately urges Dale to try to get his parents to see that it would be no dishonor if Dale came to his own conclusions. Since Dale has already indicated that he does think disagreeing with his parents would dishonor them, there seems to be an inconsistency in Mr. Partridge's argument. First he assures Dale that he wouldn't encourage him to disagree with his parents, and then he encourages him to do just that. A more precise classification might be to see Mr. Partridge's remarks about never counseling Dale to do something against his religious principles or to disagree with his parents as cases of what Kant calls "lying promises." See Kant, *Foundations of the Metaphysics of Morals*.

46:15–16	Mickey's reasoning	Mickey couches his argument as an analogy and couches the analogy as a hypothetical. The structure is
		    If (Dale's parents) are to be honored at (his disagreeing with them), then
		    (Mr. Partridge) should feel honored at (the students' disagreeing with him).

46:16–19	Mickey's defense of nonconformity	Mickey presents the possibility that someone may be justified in what he or she is doing, even though it is completely contrary to what everybody else is doing, if the action can satisfy two criteria: we must think that what we are doing is right; we must be able to say *why* we think it is right—we must be able to give a reason. If the individual can satisfy these two criteria, he or she is not being disrespectful. Mill, in *On Liberty*, holds that so long as we do not do harm to others, then we are within our rights to do whatever we please, no matter how odd

or eccentric our behavior appears. Others may try to
dissuade us from acting in such fashion, but they have no
right to stop us.

46:20–21   Maria's   Maria raises the criterion of harmful consequences. It is
           reasoning   generally agreed that Mill's invoking this single criterion
                            is at the risk of great oversimplification. It is one of the
                            reasons for the current rebellion against utilitarianism, as
                            well as the more long-standing rejection of Mill's laissez-
                            faire liberalism. The issue goes back to Mill's notion of
                            freedom being negatively defined: Freedom is freedom
                            from interference by others. Society should merely try to
                            restrict those who try to restrict others. It is easy to see
                            how Mill can use harm as a principal criterion for deter-
                            mining the meaning of restriction. In contrast, Dewey's
                            liberalism is positive, stressing freedom *to*. The free-
                            doms he espouses include freedom to grow, to lead a rich
                            life, and to have a share in making decisions that affect
                            everyone.

46:22–25   Mickey's   In *Utilitarianism*, Mill argues that we have to be able
           weighing of   to weigh the overall consequences of different courses
           harmful con-   of action, balancing their advantages and disadvantages.
           sequences   Thus, if people object to my freedom of speech because
                            they are hurt by having to listen to my views, I can reply
                            that the harm they do to me in depriving me of my right
                            of free speech is greater than the harm I do to them by
                            telling them what I think.

46:27   duty   Mr. Partridge argues that the schools have an obliga-
                            tion to let students know what society expects of them,
                            specifically using the word "duty." This reminds us that
                            a major philosophical theory of ethics, the deontologi-
                            cal theory, of which the outstanding champion is Kant,
                            has duty as the center. For a discussion of deontological
                            ethics, see W. D. Ross, *The Right and the Good*. The
                            ethics of duty has been much out of fashion in the twenti-
                            eth century and continues to attract much criticism. But
                            the focus of such criticism has now shifted to all theo-
                            retical or metaethical approaches to ethical education.
                            What is currently fashionable is the "virtues and vices"
                            approach, in which attention is paid to particular instances
                            or forms of moral behavior, such as friendship, charity,
                            altruism and the like. (See Alasdair MacIntyre, *After
                            Virtue*, and Bernard Williams, *Ethics and the Limits of
                            Philosophy*.) Philosophy for Children makes use of both
                            the theoretical and the "virtues and vices" approach.

46:28–29   schools and   See John Dewey, *School and Society* and *Democracy and
           good citizens   Education*, for a discussion of the relationship between
                            citizenry and education. Also see "Education for Civic
                            Values," in *Philosophy Goes to School* by Matthew Lipman.

This essay takes the position that the development of character in the individual is analogous to the development of due process in a democratic society.

47:1–3	questionable analogical reasoning	Mr. Partridge tells Mickey that if he accepts what Mr. Partridge has said, he'll be a better person in the same way that if he swallows some bad-tasting medicine, he'll be a healthier person. The analogy has a superficial plausibility. Mr. Partridge sees everyone, himself included, as being members of a community in which all must do their duty. The problem here is that this is not necessarily the conception of the community that the children have in mind, which seems to be a thinking and critical community. If Mr. Partridge is right, his analogy with the swallowing of the medicine makes sense. If the children are right, it doesn't.
47:4–6	Harry's reasoning	Harry is able to universalize what Mickey and Tony are requesting on the ground that what is permitted to one must be permitted to all. In a sense, this is a kind of categorical imperative. (Kant's version is considerably stronger: "Before performing an act, you should ask yourself whether you could will that it be everyone's duty to perform that act." See *Foundations of the Metaphysics of Morals*.)
47:7	Mr. Partridge's interpretation	Mr. Partridge caricatures what Harry is saying. He portrays it as a kind of anarchy in which anything goes.
47:8–9	thinking for yourself	Harry hasn't used the word "freedom" before, but now that Mr. Partridge mentions it Harry picks up the theme and argues in favor of freedom to think for oneself. This is a freedom that began to be recognized toward the end of the eighteenth century as something politically desirable for all people. It is mentioned specifically in Kant's *Logic*, published in 1800. But why does Harry raise the possibility that children may need this right even more than adults?
47:10–12	free and open discussion	Mr. Partridge claims that the discussion they had was "free and open." Harry acknowledges that they talked. But whether the discussion was free and open is highly questionable. See Ruth Saw, "On Conversation," *Thinking* 2, no. 1, who argues that a genuine conversation must be free of manipulation. (Also see Ronald F. Reed's essays in Part Five.)

CHAPTER TEN

Page, Line	*Theme*	*References and Sources*
48:6	clear and distinct	Clarity and distinctness are for Descartes the two criteria that are sufficient to enable a statement to be judged true. This is one reason that Descartes is considered an extreme rationalist. Tony does not take the rationalist position, but his manner of speaking (and perhaps of thinking) is similar to Descartes's.
48:7	opinion	This chapter is often thought of as the "critical thinking" chapter of the novel, and certainly distinguishing truth from "opinion" is one of the favorite exercises in critical-thinking courses. It would probably be a better policy, in such courses, to ask under what circumstances the distinction is valid or not. After all, as Plato pointed out, there are such things as true opinions.
48:13	referee	Harry's proposal that Mrs. Halsey act like a referee raises questions as to the proper role of the teacher in a community of inquiry. Is a referee a good model for such a teacher? Harry apparently conceives of the role of referee as that of an evaluator and adjudicator, in contrast to the facilitating function of the teacher who tries to get the community to engage in self-evaluation and self-correction. To give Harry his due, he is trying to persuade Mrs. Halsey to abdicate her usual instructional role and take part in a game instead. For another version of an instructor's role that is somewhat similar to the role of a teacher in a community of inquiry, see Alan Collins, John Seeley Brown, and Susan E. Newman, "Cognitive Apprenticeship," *Thinking* 8, no. 1: 2–10.
48:13–17	criticize	Harry introduces the notion of criticism because he recognizes that we have to go beyond our superficial likings and dislikings and begin to reflect on their justification. Thus Dewey, in the *Theory of Valuation* (pp. 5–6), distinguishes between valuing and evaluating, between prizing and appraising, and between esteeming and estimating. Following Dewey, Monroe Beardsley has assigned the task of aesthetic evaluation to the philosophy of criticism. See his *Aesthetics: Problems in the Philosophy of Criticism*. It is not an accident that Beardsley was a pioneer in the development of critical thinking. He had been an English teacher at one time, and his two earlier books, *Practical Logic* and *Straight Thinking*, have been enormously influential in applying the principles of criticism to the use of language, not only in critical-thinking

approaches generally but in the Philosophy for Children program in particular.

48:28–29	stating an opinion	Do we always have to give reasons for our opinions? Mrs. Halsey, apparently, is not claiming this, but she is maintaining that she can't do what Harry has asked her to do, evaluate the class's reasonings, unless the students provide reasons for their opinions.

49:2–3   reasons and feelings

Milly seems to be distinguishing between reasons and feelings. Is this justifiable? It raises the question of whether there are practical syllogisms that involve feelings as well as actions. For example:

> If you resent the war, blow your horn.
> (I resent the war.)
> (I blow my horn.)

Aristotle discusses practical syllogisms that involve actions rather than statements in book 6 of the *Nicomachean Ethics* and in *On the Movements of Animals*. If actions are permitted, why not feelings?

49:4–5   *Why* do you feel that way?

Mrs. Halsey evidently does not consider the possibility that a feeling can serve as a reason. Her rejoinder to Milly suggests that Milly's feeling needs to be explained if not justified. If Dewey is correct that all feelings have a cognitive germ, then its extraction would be the task of critical analysis. See *Experience and Nature*, pp. 252–61.

49:6–9   argument from alarm

Bill Beck's argument is based on the notion that there is a clear and present danger to the nation, so that in this emergency people cannot be free to do as they please. If this argument is unpersuasive, it is because there is no such emergency. Thus the appeal to alarm is a fallacy under certain circumstances (when there are not genuine grounds for alarm) and is not a fallacy under other circumstances. See W. W. Fearnside and W. B. Holther, *Fallacy: The Counterfeit of Argument*, and S. Morris Engel, *With Good Reason*. The appeal to alarm is one of many fallacies of relevance, where the argument trades on our emotions in order to persuade us.

49:10–17   Mrs. Halsey's argument

Mrs. Halsey accuses Bill of trying to scare us into agreeing with him. She rejects his argument with the claim that he hasn't proven that everything will explode if Dale doesn't stand up. Evidently, she understands his argument this way:

> If Dale does not stand up, everything will explode.
> Dale doesn't stand up.
> Everything will explode.

Mrs. Halsey is trying to show Bill that his argument is unacceptable because it rests on a major premise, the truth of which he is unable to demonstrate.

49:20–27	argument from ille-gitimate authority	Here we have an appeal to authority, and the question is whether it is a fallacious appeal. Some informal logicians see an illegitimate authority as someone who claims to be an authority but lacks the credentials that the community of inquiry would recognize. See Engel, *With Good Reason* (pp. 212–16), and Fearnside and Holther, *Fallacy* (pp. 84–88). See also Maurice Finocchiaro, "Fallacies and the Evaluation of Reasoning," *American Philosophical Quarterly*, January 1981; Gerald Massey, "The Fallacy Behind Fallacies," *Midwest Studies in Philosophy* 6:489–500; Trudy Govier, "Who Says There Are No Fallacies?" *Informal Logic Newsletter*, December 1982; and John Woods and Douglas Walton, *Argument: The Logic of the Fallacy*. Also see the work that is usually considered most authoritative, C. L. Hamblin, *Fallacies*.
49:28	judgment	Judgment has many meanings. In this context, it seems to be equivalent to verdict or ruling, very much what a judge hands down. It suggests finality, rather than ten-tativeness, fallibilism, discretion, and a sense of what is appropriate in a given context. For the latter meaning, see Aristotle, *Nicomachean Ethics*, bk. 6. For a celebra-tion of the role of judgment in education, see Michel de Montaigne's essay *On Education*. For a discussion of the role of judgment in inquiry, see Dewey, *Logic: The Theory of Inquiry*.
50:1–9	"rules are rules," or tautologies	Mrs. Halsey's claim that tautologies are sometimes meaningful is taken up by Beardsley in *Practical Logic*.
50:10	rules	See R. D. Gumb, *Rule-Governed Linguistic Behavior*. Also see Wittgenstein, *Remarks on the Foundations of Mathematics* and *Philosophical Investigations*.
50:11	exceptions to rules	Mickey proceeds from "every rule has an exception" to "rules are made to be broken." On the basis of this move, he claims that Dale doesn't have to stand up. However, Mickey's reasoning evidently involves a move from description to prescription and raises the question whether it is legitimate to move from "is" to "ought." The fact that rules *do* have exceptions is very different from saying that they *ought* to have exceptions. William Alston, "Comments on Kohlberg's 'From Is to Ought,'" in Theodore Mischel, *Cognitive Development and Episte-mology*. See also R. B. Brandt, *Ethical Theory*, and R. S. Peters, *Ethics in Education*.
50:13–16	Mrs. Halsey's reply	Mrs. Halsey says that since she allowed Suki to use an idiomatic expression as a reason, she should allow Mickey the same right. This seems commendable consistency until we see that the two cases are rather dissimilar. Suki uses an idiom as a reason, but Mickey uses it as one

premise in a very controversial argument. It is surprising that Mrs. Halsey does not take Mickey to task for his reasoning. And notice that no one in the class does, either.

50:20–25	Tony's argument	Tony appeals not to deduction but to induction. He is arguing that we very often make generalizations with full knowledge that there are exceptions. For example, we say that automobiles run on gasoline, even though we know that some are powered by alcohol or electricity. Tony's point could be the basis for a class discussion regarding the nature of inductive generalizations, because students will then begin to see that such generalizations are not usually true in the sense that definitional statements are true. As Cohen and Nagel remark, "Universal propositions which deal with matters of fact can never be more than probable" (*An Introduction to Logic and Scientific Method*, p. 279), because there is always the possibility of a counterinstance, as the fact that ebony sinks is the counterinstance to "all wood floats."
51:3–5	choice	Sandy seems to be saying that choice is the key to the problem. It is not our choice whether to go to school, nor do we have a choice with regard to religion. Bill Beck and Jane Starr chime in: neither do we have choice of our parents or whether to be born. But it is not clear why Sandy is making this claim. He doesn't explain why we don't have a choice in these matters, and it isn't even clear whether he thinks we should have. So what is he getting at? See Paul Goodman, *Compulsory Mis-Education*; Roni Aviram, "An Appeal for Total Intellectual Openness," *Thinking* 5, no. 2; and Ivan Illich, *Deschooling Society*. That we don't choose our parents or choose to be born is part of the nature of things and not a matter of social convention. See Heidegger, *Being and Time* (being thrown into the world), and Sartre, *Being and Nothingness* (facticity).
51:10–17	choosing to belong	Now Sandy says it's not just choice, but the prior choice: "choosing to belong." Once you do that, then everything else you do follows from that choice. Bill is saying that what takes priority is the choice people make in a state of nature when they form a social contract and establish a commonwealth. Everything follows from that choice. Thus, they cannot logically rebel against the commonwealth because this contradicts their having chosen it. Hobbes argues this way in *Leviathan*.
51:22–26	voluntary and involuntary associations	The notion that our obligations differ according to whether we belong voluntarily or involuntarily to a group is to be found in Alexander Meiklejohn, *Political Freedom*, pp. 18–28.

52:1	free will	On the topic of free will, see Saint Augustine, *The City of God* ("God's foreknowledge does not preclude man's free will"); John Calvin, *Institutes of the Christian Religion* ("What good there is in man is due to the grace of god"); G. W. Leibniz, "The Freedom of Man in a Predetermined Universe," in *Theodicy*; William James, "Some Metaphysical Problems Pragmatically Considered," in *Pragmatism*; Plotinus, "Free Will and the Will of the One," from the *Enneads*; Henri Bergson, *Time and Free Will*; and Nicholas Berdyaev, *Freedom and the Spirit of Man*.
52:5–6	trust	Cf. Erik Erikson, *Childhood and Society*, pp. 72–77; Simone Weil, *The Need for Roots*; and Martin Buber, *Between Man and Man* and *I and Thou*.
52:7	strangers	See Alfred Schutz, "The Stranger," *American Journal of Sociology* (1944): 499–507; and Margaret Mary Wood, *The Stranger: A Study in Social Relationship*, 1934. This latter work contains an excellent bibliography. See also Georg Simmel, "The Metropolis and Mental Life," in Donald Levine, ed., *Georg Simmel On Individuality and Social Forms*. Simmel's essay "The Stranger" is in *The Sociology of Georg Simmel*, ed. Kurt Wolff.
52:11	belonging	See Emile Durkheim, *Suicide*, and Martin Heidegger, *Being and Time*.
52:12–13	learning from one's students	See Sylvia Ashton-Warner, *Teacher*; Martin Heidegger, *Holzwege*; and *The Autobiography of Helen Keller*.

CHAPTER ELEVEN

Page, Line	*Theme*	*Sources and References*
53:6–10	feeling like a person	See Edmund Gosse, *Father and Son*, regarding the fallibility of grown-ups in the eyes of children. On teachers learning from children, see A. S. Palincsar and A. L. Brown, "Reciprocal Teaching of Comprehension-Fostering and Monitoring Activities," in *Cognition and Instruction* 1 (1984): 117–75.
53:11–13	putting yourself in another's place	Timmy's comment is an example of moral empathy. See Max Scheler, *The Nature of Sympathy*, and Maurice Mandelbaum, *The Phenomenology of Moral Experience*, pp. 210–12; Simone Weil, *Gravity and Grace*; and Carol Gilligan, *In a Different Voice*.
53:14–18	arithmetic vs. fact	Tony's statement is rather Cartesian (cf. Descartes's *Discourse on Method*, as well as *The Meditations*). Tony

seems to be contrasting not arithmetic and facts but induction and deduction. Inductive reasoning, as we know, can be at best only probable, while deductive reasoning can be certain. Deductive reasoning is also consistent, so it contains no contradictions. But our inductive experience of the world contains both instances and counterinstances.

Tony even suggests the criteria of simplicity, clarity, and truth, much as Descartes does. For a coherence theory of empirical knowledge, see Laurence Bon Jour, *The Structure of Empirical Knowledge*, pp. 87–190.

53:19–27	children's rights	See *Harvard Educational Review*, "The Rights of Children," 1974. A compilation of two issues of this journal, selections range from discussions of philosophical justification of children's rights to concrete examinations of policy proposals. See also Onora O'Neill and William Ruddick, eds., *Having Children*; John Holt, *Escape from Childhood*; and Leila Berg, *Children's Rights: Toward the Liberation of Children*.
53:19–27	patriotism	See Lord Hailsham, *The Conservative Case*.
53:23	the country as a parent	Plato, in the *Crito*, has Socrates say that the laws of Athens have been like a parent to him.
53:28–54:3	sharing creations	This is the sort of thing that is discussed in the work of Victor Lowenfeld. See his *Creative and Mental Growth*.
54:4–7	imagining as a criterion of truth	See Edward Casey's *Imagining*.
54:4–7	death	Cf. Simone de Beauvoir, *A Very Easy Death*; Leo Tolstoy, *The Death of Ivan Ilyitch*; and Rainer Maria Rilke, *The Notebooks of Malte Laurids Brigge*. On death and dying, see Freud, *Thoughts for the Times on War and Death*; Maurice Natanson, "Humanism and Death," in Paul Kurtz, ed., *Moral Problems in Contemporary Society*; Robert Fulton, ed., *Death and Identity*; and Thomas Nagel, "Death," and Mary Mothersill, "Death," both in *Moral Problems*, ed. James Rachels.
54:8–12	consciousness of identity	Locke holds that consciousness makes personal identity; Leibniz disagrees. See Locke, *Essay Concerning Human Understanding* (ch. 27) and Leibniz, *New Essays Concerning Human Understanding* (sec. 26, which deals with the principle of individuation). Note that when the word "black" appears in the paragraph with reference to physical characteristics, it is not capitalized, but when it has a cultural reference it is capitalized. This may be academic in that many members of this ethnic group now prefer to be known as African-Americans.

54:13   protesting   Nietzsche, in *The Genealogy of Morals* and *Beyond Good*
       too much   *and Evil*, prefigures Freud's "reaction formation." They
both suggest that civilization demands repression of basic
instincts but permits the expression of "civilized" versions of these instinctual needs. Sexual feeling becomes
dissolved in tenderness and sentimentality. People deny
the existence of their feelings. See Freud, *Civilization
and Its Discontents*.

54:14–16   Suki's poem   When Anne says that when she read Suki's poem "it was
       as a gesture   as if she had reached out her hand to me," she exempli-
fies G. H. Mead's contention that "in the case of the poet
and actor, the stimulus calls out in the artist that which it
calls out in the other" (*Mind, Self, and Society*, p. 148).
Mead is saying that in a communicative act the gesture
one makes toward the other person evokes in oneself the
same meaning and emotional response as the gesture
evokes in the person to whom it is addressed. Thus, all
community is based upon shared experience.
With regard to secrets, see Georg Simmel, "The Sociology of Secrecy and of Secret Societies," in Kurt Wolff,
ed., *The Sociology of Georg Simmel*.

54:16   friendship   Anne interprets Suki's gesture as one of friendship. See
Aristotle, *Nicomachean Ethics*, bk. 8, B (reciprocity of
friendship). See, in particular, ch. 8, where Aristotle
attempts to show that loving is more of the essence of
friendship than being loved. Compare Anne's remark with
Suki's (p. 54:1–2), where Suki finds Anne's reading the
poem an opportunity to rediscover it as all fresh and new.
Here the emphasis is on the poem, not on the friendship.

54:17–19   being un-   There is, in French philosophical literature (perhaps in
       wanted   Sartre's *Being and Nothingness*), some discussion of the
experience of being superfluous, or *de trop*. See also
Hannah Arendt, *The Origins of Totalitarianism*.

54:17–19   motivation   With regard to Jane's motivation for becoming a doctor,
she seems to analyze the factors in her life that serve
as incentives to her vocational goals. Dewey, in *Human
Nature and Conduct*, deals with the social character
of motivation, showing that it relates to social incentives rather than to "individual initiative" or some other
individual trait.

54:20–22   Mr. Spence   Martin Buber, in *Between Man and Man*, talks about the
       as a role   teacher as role model, as does Nietzsche in *Thus Spake
       model   Zarathustra*. Also, see José Ortega y Gasset, *The Revolt
of the Masses*, where he contrasts the "man of energy,"
whose motto is noblesse oblige and who thus demands
excellence of himself, with the "man of inertia" who does
what everybody else does.

54:22–24	Is religion a fairy tale?	See Karl Marx, *German Ideology*, and Nietzsche, *The Genealogy of Morals*. Also see Freud, *Moses and Monotheism* and *Thoughts for the Times on War and Death*. This latter essay can be found in Freud, *On Creativity and the Unconscious*, ed. Benjamin Nelson.
54:25–28	act and context	Maria notes a connection between Mark's behavior and its social context. See Solomon Asch's *Social Psychology*, an important Gestaltist approach.
54:28	trust	See Erik Erikson, *Childhood and Society*, in which he talks about the development of trust or mistrust as the first psychological stage that the child undergoes. Also see Martin Heidegger, *Being and Time*.
55:4	Aren't there reasons for everything we're told to do?	Political conservatives have generally taken the position that some human relationships are natural and not invented. For example, such family relationships as parental authority: One cannot construct a contract between parents and children. The same is true between rulers and ruled or teachers and students. Authority rests on faith and trust, not on reason. See Joseph de Maistre, *Essay on the Generative Principle of Political Constitutions*, and Michael Oakeshott, *Rationalism in Politics*. See, in particular, Oakeshott's essay "Political Education."
55:1–6	conflicting authorities	With regard to conflicting authorities, most thinkers believe that classic tragedy (e.g., *Antigone*) develops out of conflict between unyielding authorities so that there can be no rational or peaceable resolution. Fran perceives the conflict between Dale's parents and the school board as being one in which these are surrogates for the conflict between religion and state.
55:7–10	circular reasoning?	There are two kinds of possibly circular reasoning here. One is that the Blue Falcons are said to be the "greatest" only on their own authority—it is true only because they say so. Second, there may be a connection between Sandy's claim that "they are the greatest" and the Ontological Argument of St. Anselm: God is the greatest conceivable being. Whatever is in the mind and in reality is greater than <u>what is in the mind alone.</u> God exists. If God were just a figment of our imagination, God would be in the mind alone. But then there would be something greater, that which is in the mind *and* in reality. Therefore, since God is in reality, God exists.
55:14–15	the best of all possible worlds	Jill says, "I'm sure that the way things are is just about the best way they could be." This echoes the bland optimism of Dr. Pangloss in Voltaire's *Candide*, a satire written

in response to the Lisbon earthquake of 1755. Dr. Pangloss's views are intended to represent the contention by Leibniz that "this is the best of all possible worlds." However, Leibniz is often misunderstood on this point. He is not saying that the world is perfect, but that it *necessarily* contains a mixture of goods and evils. Any other worlds would also have a mixture, but this world contains the least amount of evil and the greatest amount of good.

| 55:16–20 | emulative behavior | One aspect of what Laura is saying here has to do with the ways in which children's play represents their efforts to emulate their parents' values. One can find various discussions on this topic in Johan Huizinga's *Homo Ludens* and in the writings of Erik Erikson and Lawrance K. Frank. The flaunting of cleanliness and propriety associated with middle-class morality is occasionally treated in Thorstein Veblen's *Theory of the Leisure Class*. |

| 55:21–28 | on looking like a dog | The incident on page 2 of *Lisa* can be traced back to this period when she was teased for looking like a Pekinese dog. (In *Lisa*, she says, "I'm a dog too.")

Lisa's simile "books and people are alike" is constructed, as she shows, on the understanding that both are full of thoughts; therefore, books are like people. Although not a logically valid syllogism, it does represent what Aristotle quite rightly prized very highly: the finding of an improbable middle term.

When Lisa says that "mirrors lie," she echoes Simone Weil. The quotation is very Platonic because it says that appearances are so deceiving. |

| 56:1–2 | the distinction between truth and reasoning | Perhaps what Harry has in mind is the explanation generally given to logic students—premises are either true or untrue, while reasoning is either valid or invalid. In argument analysis, the focus is on the reasoning, once the premises are *assumed* to be valid. On the other hand, for the argument to be sound, the premises must be true *and* the reasoning must be valid. (Some informal logicians, like John Hoagland, are now claiming that arguments can be sound even with untrue premises, but this is very controversial.) It may also be that Harry perceives Mrs. Halsey as a kind of Socratic figure who refuses to pretend to know the truth. |

| 56:5–6 | thinking well and thinking badly | Harry says that all you can do is try to tell the difference between thinking well and thinking badly. Harry here uses an analogy with an umpire, as earlier, on page 48, he used the analogy with the referee. What is more, on page 48 he twice characterizes what he would like Mrs. Halsey to do as "criticizing the way we reason," so as to "tell us whether we are thinking well or thinking badly." So Harry distinguishes between those who engage in a practice |

and perform skillfully and those who judge or criticize
such performances. Apparently, he sees Mrs. Halsey
and himself as, at best, merely judges or critics of thinking rather than as skillful thinkers. This may be why he
pessimistically concedes that he failed.

56:5–7   different   There is implied here the distinction between *thinking*
             types of   *how* and *thinking that* that is elaborated in Gilbert Ryle's
             thinking   *Concept of Mind*. That is, there is a difference between
thinking well and thinking badly, but there is also a differ-
ence between thinking well and thinking about thinking
well, or thinking how to go about thinking well. It is this
kind of metacognition that Harry seems to be particularly
interested in at this moment.

56:13–14   reasons of   For a superb analysis of children's constitutional rights,
             conscience   see James Herndon, "Ethics, Instruction, and the Consti-
             and chil-   tution," in *Thinking* 7, no. 1: 6–11. Herndon concludes
             dren's con-   that the kind of curriculum in ethics that is needed is an
             stitutional   open-ended, no-holds-barred one. This in turn would
             rights   result, he thinks, in the kind of ethical society most of us
would like to have.

CHAPTER TWELVE

Page, Line   *Theme*   *Sources and References*

57:8–9   Lisa's re-   Lisa first demands to know what reason people have
           quest for a   for not discussing Dale's leaving. She then supplies the
           reason   reason: We are ashamed of the way we think. She then
adds, "If people could realize the awful results of thinking
the way they do, they might not be so ready to do bad
things." Lisa seems to be making a case here for moral
reasoning—that if people could reason through what they
are considering doing, then they would act more virtu-
ously. This is a recurrent theme in Plato's Socrates, who
constantly argues that if people genuinely understood
what was involved in their choices, they would inevitably
choose the good. This raises countless questions about
human motivation, and about whether people are bound
to follow their interests and passions or whether they
are capable of an overriding rationality. See the discussion by Kurt Baier and G. J. Warnock on whether people
act on the basis of reasons in Peter French et al., *Mid-
west Studies in Philosophy*, vol. 18. See also J.-P. Sartre,
Existentialism, for a modern version of the argument
that "people always choose the good" (although one very
different from that of Socrates).

57:17–19   it was much   One of the maxims that guide scientific inquiry is that
             too big   when problems appear to be overwhelming they should
                                  be broken down into smaller, more manageable compo-
                                  nents and dealt with separately. See Cohen and Nagel,
                                  Introduction to Logic and Scientific Method. Whether this
                                  would have worked is another question, since the prob-
                                  lem here revolves around the conflict of authorities (the
                                  state vs. the parents). G. E. Moore (Monroe Beardsley
                                  points this out somewhere in his *Practical Logic*) used to
                                  say that there are two kinds of things we can't talk about:
                                  those so small we can't analyze them further, such as a
                                  point, and those so vast and so general that we have no
                                  larger frame of reference in which to place them. Perhaps
                                  the latter is what Harry feels he is confronted with now.

57:24   Lisa's praise   What action of Harry's does Lisa think is so praise-
                                  worthy? She says that he is "pushing us to think about
                                  the correct way to think." But this could be, as she put it
                                  a few lines earlier, getting people to realize the "awful re-
                                  sults of thinking the way they do." What she seems to be
                                  saying now is that if people could grasp the logical impli-
                                  cations of their ideas they would not be ready to do things
                                  that had adverse consequences. Harry is pushing the
                                  members of the class to become proficient in inference
                                  and to learn the implications of their thinking. By means
                                  of this kind of reflection, they can avoid impulsive actions
                                  that fail to take consequences into account. John Dewey
                                  takes this up when he deals with the way in which, before
                                  moral action, we can imaginatively rehearse what we
                                  might do and logically deduce the possible consequences
                                  of these hypothetical actions. See John Dewey, *How
                                  We Think*.

58:1–28   conversion   The conversion operation was discussed in the *Harry*
                                  manual with respect to A and E statements. Here we
                                  move to conversion of I and O statements. Unfortunately,
                                  Philosophical Inquiry, Chapter 12, provides no discussion
                                  of these additional operations. Virtually any logic text
                                  explains conversion of the four statements. An example
                                  would be David Kelly's *Art of Reasoning*. Kelly, like many
                                  traditional logicians, includes inference "by limitation."
                                  This does not appear in *Harry Stottlemeier's Discovery*,
                                  and most modern logicians have no use for this vestige of
                                  Aristotelian logic because it raises the problem of exis-
                                  tence. It means that from "All elephants are white" one
                                  can infer "Some elephants are white." Modern logicians
                                  do not consider the A statement as expressing existence,
                                  except in a hypothetical way, and therefore they reject
                                  the notion that particular statements can be inferred from
                                  universal statements. In the chart in the middle of page
                                  58, Harry has used dotted lines to indicate that the A and

O statements have no converses. Why the converse of an *A* statement is expressed by a dotted line has already been discussed in *Harry* (Chapters One and Two). Harry "explains" the reason for the invalidity of the *O* statement to Lisa by an example, but Kelly (p. 183) provides a somewhat fuller explanation. If, in the original statement, the subject term is a genus and the predicate term is a species, we can see at once that the converse does not follow. Thus, if the original statement is "Some animals are not dogs," we see immediately that we should not try to infer from that statement its converse, "Some dogs are not animals."

58:22	true sentences only follow from true sentences	Lisa says, "Don't you remember that we found out? . . ." Is there a point earlier in the book where Harry and Lisa explicitly found this out, or does she simply mean that as they worked with conversion they discovered that, using certain procedures, one could infer only true sentences from other sentences that were already true? In effect, Lisa is indicating that she and Harry earlier discovered the principle of validity, which is that kind of inference in which the truth of the premises is preserved in the conclusion.
58:28	contradiction	In Lisa's initial formulation of contradiction, it is presented as a characteristic of dialogue: when one person says something is true and another person says that it is false. Harry takes this into account and works with it, but it is not until the middle of page 59 that he formulates contradiction as something occurring between two statements, i.e., as a *logical*, not a dialogical, contradiction. Neither Harry nor Lisa reaches a definitive statement of what contradiction actually involves—a situation in which two statements are so related that when one is true the other is necessarily false. However, on page 59, Harry and Lisa identify the specific contradictories of each of the four types of statements.
60:5–10	naming the statements	The practice of nicknaming the statements *A, E, I,* and *O* comes from Aristotle, *Posterior Analytics*. By doing so, he was able to name each of the 256 different syllogisms. He applied the vowels to each premise and conclusion, and then constructed a proper name around the vowels. Thus, the syllogism of the form *A A A* became BARBARA.
60:18–30	gifts	In Bronislaw Malinowski's *Crime and Custom in Savage Society* (pp. 39–45), there is a discussion of reciprocal gifts. Other writers who have treated gifts philosophically or sociologically are Marcel Mauss and Georg Simmel.
60:27	souvenir	A souvenir is a remembrance. People give each other things in order to stimulate mental acts—so that the

things given become tokens of affection, charm, good
luck, or whatever it is that one wants the other to remember.

61:3

sharing an
experience

See John Dewey, *A Common Faith* and *Art as Experience*.
It was an unpleasant experience that led Lisa to realize
the preciousness of each of her classmates. The juxtaposition, in a way, is a kind of contradiction. In *Philosophy
in the Classroom*, it is pointed out that taking a child out
of the classroom should make a difference. If it doesn't,
there is something wrong with what is going on.
Although Dale's leaving hadn't been a pleasant experience, it was something the children shared. One of the
things one learns from Hannah Arendt's *Origins of Totalitarianism* is that, under certain circumstances, terror
creates solidarity.

61:8–62:17

an exempli-
fication of
contradiction

Gregory Bateson and Mary Katherine Bateson, in their
book *Angels Fear*, use the term *metalogue* to refer to a
dialogue in which what is happening in the subject matter is also happening in the conversation. In this sense,
this episode is a kind of metalogue because Luther and
Marty are discussing contradiction while analyzing it and
exhibiting it.

62:19–23

the boys
(with their
umbrel-
las) in the
treehouse

The image of Mark and Harry sitting in the treehouse
holding their umbrellas is somewhat Asian. This might
be an occasion for the class to ask itself what is being
represented here.

63:5–12

Harry's ac-
ceptance of
Bill

There is a rapid series of emotions, starting with the
happiness in the treehouse, then Bill scowling, then Bill
described as more miserable than angry, and finally Bill's
despairing comment, "nothing to go home for." In some
ways, Bill appears to be emotionally disturbed: He is
upset himself and he upsets others. There is a kind of
mirror image with the preceding episode. The children
give gifts to Dale, who is being forced out of the community; Bill, whose behavior has been antisocial, is being
invited into it.
    Note also Harry's apparent magnanimity. Bill, who
threw a stone at him, is now being invited to Harry's
home. (This is also in the context of Bill not answer-
ing Harry when he asks for an explanation about the
stone-throwing incident.)
    What makes Harry invite Bill home? He's already
suspected that Bill is more miserable than angry and that
he is not interested in fighting. It's when Bill says "nothing to go home for" that Harry reflects and issues the
invitation. It would seem that what has happened is not
that Harry is being forgiving or magnanimous. Instead,

Bill's behavior and statement enable Harry to *understand* to some extent. Also, Tony has probably told him about Bill's father (see p. 42). Once Harry understands the causes of Bill's behavior, his animosity disappears and there is no obstacle to bringing the previously antisocial Bill into the community. Spinoza, in part three of the *Ethics* ("The Origin and Nature of the Affects," proposition 59, *scholium*), writes of generosity as the desire by which from "the dictates of reason alone each person endeavors to help other people and to join them with him in friendship."

In part four of the *Ethics* ("Of Human Bondage," proposition 23), Spinoza writes: "A man cannot be absolutely said to act in conformity with virtue insofar as he is determined to any action because he has inadequate ideas (that is to say emotions), but only insofar as he is determined because he *understands*."

That deliberation comes from acting in accordance with one's understanding of the causes of things is a major thesis in the *Ethics*.

CHAPTER THIRTEEN

Page, Line	*Theme*	*Sources and References*
64:3–27	the boys' previous sleepover	This is a long paragraph with virtually no dialogue. It could very well be an account of a silent film, such a *The Little Rascals* shorts. (Timmy sitting unmoved amid the chaos is like the unflappable Alfalfa.) The pillow fight echoes the last scene of Jean Vigo's film *Zéro de conduite*. Mr. Stottlemeier's comment is almost like a subtitle in a silent film. And then, for the final comic note, the one thing that hasn't happened yet, happens.
65:1	amazement	Children often find adults as unpredictable as adults find children. But then children find many things astonishing and surprising: This is the link of wondering that children and philosophy share.
65:3	conversation	See Paul Grice, "Logic and Conversation," in his *Studies in the Way of Words*. See also Michael Walzer, "A Critique of Philosophical Conversation," in *Philosophical Forum*, Fall/Winter 1989–90. Also see Ruth Saw, "Conversation and Communication," in *Thinking* 2, no. 1: 55–64.
65:6	what Sandy showed Luther	In an early scene in the Vigo film already referred to, we see children on their way to school mysteriously exchanging secrets.

65:6	exaggeration	Children love exaggeration, and there are strong traditions of folk literature that are almost wholly composed of exaggerations, such as the stories of Paul Bunyan and Baron Munchausen. Also see Kenneth Koch's *Wishes, Lies, and Dreams,* where he argues that there are certain hilarious forms of lying (such as boasting and exaggerating) that make for the kind of metaphorical language that works very well in poetry.
65:8	sex education	The children in the novel approach the question of the origin of the universe after talking about where babies come from. One primitive explanation is that the world was reproduced sexually by the gods. Hume refers to this in his *Dialogues Concerning Natural Religion.*
65:11	Tony's dictum	"You can't get something out of nothing." This is of course a version of the medieval principle "out of nothing, nothing comes." Much of the layman's thinking about philosophical subjects is guided and regulated by just such dicta as this one, and the struggle, in ensuing discussions, is to find counterexamples to these principles. (Another illustration, which has been highly influential in the realism/idealism dispute, is that "there must be as much reality in the cause as in the effect.")
65:12	Mickey's counterexample	Mickey's counterexample is aimed at compelling Tony to say either that the world comes out of nothing (which he denies) or that it comes out of something else that was there previously. Tony chooses the latter, as we see on line 20 of this page. See Kant, *Critique of Pure Reason* ("Antinomies of Reason").
65:15	God	Luther here is referring to the Christian god. It wouldn't be the Greek gods, since they are not creators of the world. Luther is referring to Genesis. Students might do well to contrast the first paragraph of the Old Testament with the first paragraph of the Gospel according to John.
65:16	the scientific perspective	Mickey postulates that the earth was once part of the sun.
65:18–19	Harry's clarification	Harry distinguishes between the earth and the universe and claims that the question is how the *universe* began. Some philosophers might reply to Harry in the same way he replies to Mickey. They might distinguish between the *universe,* which for them is the largest context of scientific knowledge, and *nature,* of which the universe would be one manifestation. This is the position one finds in Aristotle and Spinoza; it is usefully examined in Milton Munitz's *Mystery of Existence.*
65:22	Luther's maxim	"Everything has to have a beginning." In part 1 of the *Summa Theologica,* Aquinas offers five proofs for the

existence of God. The first two take this principle to be axiomatic.

65:24–25	Could the universe be eternal?	Tony's reply to Luther is that the idea of nature as always existing is not self-contradictory. Like Aristotle in the *Physics*, Tony might say that the concept of nature as eternal is easier to grasp than the notion of a special Creation. From the point of view of William of Ockham, the hypothesis that the world has always existed requires no new explanatory entities such as God. And this, as Ockham would say (using Ockham's razor) is the simplest explanation.
66:1	imaginability as the criterion of existence	Many things are conceivable that are not imaginable. The origin of the universe may be as inconceivable as it is unimaginable. For more on this conceptual impossibility, see Munitz, *Mystery of Existence*. Also, there is very little literature, even in philosophy, on what we mean by "the world." One exception is Justus Buchler's *Metaphysics of Natural Complexes* (2d ed.), which contains a lengthy analysis of the concept of "the world."
66:3–6	Luther's remarks	These comments resemble St. Thomas Aquinas's second argument for the existence of God, except that Luther does not explicitly say that there must be a First Cause.
66:7–19	Tony invokes the fallacy of composition	Tony says that what is true of the parts need not be true of the whole. See Douglas N. Walton, *Informal Fallacies*, or John Woods and Douglas Walton, *Argument: The Logic of the Fallacies*. For criticism of Aquinas's Argument from Cause, see Kant, *Critique of Pure Reason*.
66:27	Bill's claim	Bill claims that the world had to be created by God and that this is the only possibility. It certainly is not the only *logical* possibility. Luther has just said, "Either the world was created by God or it was not." So what does Bill mean? Perhaps he is confusing possibility with truth. See Aristotle's *Metaphysics*, bk. 2.
67:1–12	four-part matrix	The origins of the four-part matrix probably go back to early Greek and Buddhist sources. See *The History of Logic* by William Kneale and Martha Kneale.
67:18–24	the four possibilities applied to the Creation	Tony makes use not only of the four possibilities but of the notion of contradiction. The consequent of the second possibility contradicts the consequent of the first; the consequent of the fourth contradicts the consequent of the third; and the antecedents of the third and fourth contradict the antecedents of the first and second. (Cf. the work of the early medieval philosopher John Scotus Erigena, as described in *The Encyclopedia of Philosophy*, vol. 3.) For Erigena, the unifying notion is Nature, which comprises both God and the world of crea-

tures. In his doctrine of Nature, there are four stages: Nature that creates and is not created, or God in his eternal reality; Nature that is both created and creative, or the archetypes of creatures in the Divine Mind; Nature that is created but does not create, or the world of creatures existing outside the Divine Mind; and Nature that neither creates nor is created, or God perfectly reunited with his creatures as the end and goal of the creative process.

67:23–24	Does the third possibility contradict itself?	Bill's objection is common. One response to it would be to invoke the notion of continual creation. See Plotinus, *Enneads*, and, among modern scientists, Fred Hoyle.
67:25–27	distinction between truth and possibility	See the *Posterior Analytics* of Aristotle for a discussion of this distinction.
68:1–2	Harry's remarks about looking for answers	If one looks at Gallie's article "Essentially Contested Concepts," one finds a conception of philosophy as inquiry into insoluble problems. Yet the inquiry is worthwhile because it turns up many interesting things along the way, even though it never answers the questions.
68:2	different ways of looking at things	This implies a kind of perspectivism. See George Herbert Mead, *Mind, Self, and Society* and *Movements of Thought in the Nineteenth Century*; E. B. McGilvary, *Toward a Perspective Realism*; and Justus Buchler, *Towards a General Theory of Human Judgment*. Nelson Goodman, in his essay "The Way the World Is" (in the first edition of *Discovering Philosophy*), argues that there is no "world" as such but only the various ways of experiencing the world.
68:2	modes of thinking	There are many treatments of this topic, ranging from Jerome Kagan's *Modes of Thinking in Young Children* and Howard Gardner's *Frames of Mind* to Whitehead's *Modes of Thought*. There is a stimulating anthropology of human thought in Heinz Werner's *Comparative Psychology of Mental Development*.
68:3	being taught and finding out for yourself	This distinction opens up a whole literature in education, involving arguments that education is not limited to school but that one can learn directly from experience. This position is to be found in Wordsworth, *The Prelude*, in *Leaves of Grass* by Whitman, in the essays of Emerson and Montaigne, in Thoreau's *Walden*, and in many other thinkers.

68:7	Is there a right way to think?	What Harry was talking about before—the many ways of thinking—is descriptive and empirical. The allegation that there is a right way to think is evaluative and normative. What grounds do Harry and Tony have to assume that there is a right way to think? According to a tradition that goes back to Plato, philosophy is excellent thinking. (He argues this way in the *Timaeus*.) It is also presupposed in Descartes's *Discourse on Method* and in Dewey's *How We Think*, where there is a problem-solving paradigm that Dewey suggests as the route to successful thinking. The problem here is not simply that Harry and Tony assume that there is a right way to think, but that they assume that there is only one right way to think. Harry's approach in line 5 is pluralistic and nonhierarchical. He wants to know all the different ways of thinking. Tony responds (and we are told that Harry would agree) that he wants to find out the "right way to think." One interpretation of what Tony is saying is that thinking, being a form of conduct, is an ethical matter to which the criteria of "right" and "wrong" apply. A proponent of such a view might be W. K. Clifford in his essay "The Ethics of Belief." See also his *Lectures and Essays* and his *Common Sense of the Exact Sciences*, ed. Karl Pearson. William James's essay "The Will to Believe" is a response to Clifford's position. See also the excellent article by Richard Brandt in the *Encyclopedia of Philosophy* (vol. 3), "Epistemology and Ethics, Parallel Between."
68:9–20	the dream	One can consider the dream and ask how it is to be interpreted. The name of the inn comes from the topic of the discussion earlier in the evening, as illustrated by the four-part square on the cobblestone courtyard. This, in turn, is associated with hopscotch, which unsurprisingly calls to mind Laura O'Mara. If what she is holding out to Tony is indeed an apple, it suggests Eve tempting Adam. The scene then changes to a baseball game. As Tony is trying to score, he finds a catcher blocking his path, who turns out to be his father. (See Sigmund Freud, *The Psychopathology of Everyday Life* and *The Interpretation of Dreams*.)

CHAPTER FOURTEEN

Page, Line	*Theme*	*Sources and References*
69:1	the museum	Insofar as the museum can be identified, it is the Frick Museum in New York City, which is small but, as art museums go, a jewel.

69:10   St. Francis   The painting of St. Francis by Giovanni Bellini is one of the most important in the Frick Collection.

69:12   Diana   The sculpture of Diana, also at the Frick, is by Houdon. About now, readers begin to suspect an analogical relationship between St. Francis and Suki, on the one hand, and Diana and Anne, on the other. That is, one can tease out a resemblance such that the sharp contrast between the saint and the huntress suggests the difference between Suki's gentleness and Anne's somewhat predatory disposition.

69:15–16   nudity   There is a contrast between nudity and nakedness. On line 15, Suki recognizes and applauds the beauty of the female nude. Anne's reply is more problematical. If, for example, she means that this particular sculpture would look awful if clothes were added to it (in the way that, during the Reformation, fig leaves and other garments were placed on nudes from antiquity), Anne is certainly right. Then she'd be making an aesthetic judgment. On the other hand, the modern aesthetic consciousness is considerably more complex. When Manet showed Olympia reclining on her chaise, wearing little more than a black choker, there was an immediate outcry from the outraged bourgeoisie, who recognized this as the portrait of a courtesan. In other words, the conventional attitude by the middle of the nineteenth century was that one had to be shown either completely dressed or completely undressed. A similar outcry greeted Manet's *Lunch on the Lawn*, which portrayed fully clothed men together with unclothed women.

         As for sources, look at Upjohn, *History of Modern Art*; Arnold Hauser, *The Social History of Art*; and John Rewald, *The History of Impressionism*.

69:17–18   Anne's last look at Diana   Why does Anne turn and look at Diana? Does she sense the connection suggested above?

69:19–24   the museum and the concert   The reference to architecture in this paragraph could be usefully explored with middle-school students, perhaps by showing slides of peristyles, pools, fountains, cherubs, and sculptured dolphins. The relationship of the peristyle to modern architecture can be noted (e.g., the Hyatt Regency hotels), and one can explore the history of the fountain, especially with a final illustration of the Trevi Fountain in Rome. This fountain has inspired many philosophers, from Plotinus, whose whole vision of the cosmos seems to be that of a series of pyramided fountains, to Santayana, who sometimes saw nature in the form of the Trevi Fountain. See Plotinus, *Enneads*, and Santayana, "Ultimate Religion," in *Obiter Scripta*. If one would like a playful connection between children, cher-

ubs, and fountains, look at the travel book *Rome and a
Villa*, by Eleanore Clark.

69:23–25	instruments	Students can certainly be queried as to the difference between a piano and a harpsichord and a viola and a cello. In a sense, it is a small exercise in finding appropriate criteria for classification. Using records and tapes would be helpful.
69:28	the human face	The classic analysis of the aesthetic significance of the human face is in an essay by Georg Simmel appearing in *Georg Simmel, 1858–1918*, ed. Kurt Wolff.
69:29	sketching	Sketching, like writing, is a form of expression and communication that philosophers have found particularly interesting. One can read, for example, John Dewey's discussions of children's drawings in *School and Society* or the book by the British philosopher Richard Wollheim, *How to Draw a Picture*. Students are particularly impressed by accounts of the creation of works of art; for example, many a young person has been entranced by Benvenuto Cellini's memoir of his casting of the *Perseus*.
70:1–3	gardening as therapy	See Holmes Rolston III, *Environmental Ethics: Duties to and Values in the Natural World*. There may very well be books on the philosophy of gardening, but we just don't know of them. British and Japanese sources, in particular, should be investigated.
70:7	death	Look at Florence Hetzler, *Death and Creativity*. See Erich Fromm, "Love of Death and Love of Life," in *The Heart of Man*, and Sigmund Freud's great essay "Thoughts for the Times on War and Death," in *Collected Works*, vol. 4. Also look at *Civilization and Its Discontents* by Freud. For a positive approach, see James Muyskins's *The Sufficiency of Hope*.
70:13	flowers	Poets often see flowers as emblematic of people and their situations. For example, in his poem "Gloire de Dijon" D. H. Lawrence compares the beauty of these yellow roses with the physical beauty of the female form. In one of the "Lucy" poems, William Wordsworth speaks about "gleeful daffodils," thereby comparing flowers and people in emotional terms; or, in another "Lucy" poem, he compares a modest and shy Lucy to "a violet by a mossy stone/Half hidden from the eye." On the other hand, Waller's poem "To a Rose" (or, "Song") addresses the rose as an intelligent being. Suki's poem below, dealing as it does with the way roses think, bears some resemblance in this respect to Waller's poem.
70:18	ordinary	On the distinction between the ordinary and the extraordinary, one might read Wittgenstein's *Lecture on Ethics*,

reprinted in *Discovering Philosophy*, or G. K. Chesterton, "The Ethics of Elfland," *Thinking* 1, no. 2. See also Ninian Smart, "In Defense of Religious Experience," in *Discovering Philosophy*.

70:20–22	Suki's poem	The original version of this poem comes from Fontenelle: "In the memory of the rose, no rose has ever seen a gardener die." There is an analysis of this poem in *Suki*, Chapter Four.
70:26	I don't like to watch things die	See Simone de Beauvoir, *A Very Easy Death*, in which she describes her mother's dying. There is a similar line, spoken by Katherine Ross, in *Butch Cassidy and the Sundance Kid*: "I'll go to Peru with you, but I won't stay till the end. I don't like to see things die."
70:28	night-blooming cereus	See Mircea Eliade, *The Sacred and the Profane*, and Roger Caillois, *L'homme et le sacre*. The theme of the flower periodically blooming after all the discussion on death may suggest to some readers the dichotomy of Lent and Easter or, for that matter, the sequence of winter and spring. The secular version of rebirth is the Renaissance, with its celebration of nature and life. An attempt to put all of this in half-Christian, half-pagan form would be Wagner's *Parsifal*.
71:5	happiness	See Aristotle on happiness in the *Nicomachean Ethics* (ch. 1), where he talks about it as the highest good. In this connection, Anne's happiness at seeing Suki happy is reminiscent of Harry Stack Sullivan's definition of love in *Conceptions of Modern Psychiatry*, where another person's happiness means as much as one's own.
71:9	collecting	Dewey talks about collecting as a "kind of spiritual capitalism" in *Art as Experience*. From the point of view of the rich collector, there is another case to be made, as in the recent book by Lord Duveen. John Fowles explores the perversity of the topic in his novel *The Collector* (also filmed, with Samantha Eggar). The question Why would anyone collect? is as philosophical an issue as Why would anyone paint?
71:12–13	Do animals feel pain?	Descartes claims that animals are simply machines. Cf. Peter Singer, *Animal Liberation* and *Practical Ethics*.
71:17	They'd find you so *interesting!*	In the "Observing, Looking on, Becoming Aware" in *Between Man and Man*, Martin Buber argues that the great artist is an onlooker who mistrusts traits, character, and expression and who remarks, "Forgetting is good . . . the interesting is not important."
71:18	like a butterfly	This line shows the power of analogy in literature. The good author hints at an analogy in such a way that readers themselves have to make the connection. Plato is full of

analogies, like lighting a candle with a candle, employed in the context of educational communication. There is a great deal of writing in the Thomistic tradition about analogy because this is the only kind of reasoning that seems capable of dealing with what would otherwise be ineffable, such as the love of God.

71:22   cruel   Hume says in "of the Standard of Taste" that moral terms have a built-in approbation or disapprobation, so whenever people use these words, in whatever language, they mean to express approval or disapproval. The words in any language that correspond to equity, justice, charity, and temperance are always used with approbation; those that correspond to treachery, inhumanity, cruelty, and revenge are always used to express disapproval. However, Hume adds, the acts that are classified in different societies as just or cruel are often utterly incompatible with civilized society. Hume, in effect, denies the position of Solomon Asch in *Social Psychology* (ch. 13), who maintains that the words standing for virtues and vices have the same meaning and incur the same respect or disapproval in all cultures. Many contemporary philosophers have become interested once again in virtues and vices. One can mention Philippa Foot, P. T. Geach, Sissela Bok, Thomas Nagel, James Rachel, and Edmund Pincoffs.

71:27   treating persons as things   In *Fundamental Principles of the Metaphysics of Morals*, Kant speaks of all rational beings as belonging to a kingdom of ends in which each such being must treat itself and all others as ends and never merely as means. Thus, to treat a person as a thing is a fundamental violation of Kantian morality.

From a Marxian point of view, capitalism violates Kantian ethics in that the workers are human beings who are used and employed as instruments for the benefit of the employers. Thus, as the Marxists say, it is no coincidence that Kant writes at the beginning of the Industrial Revolution. While there may be no opponent of Kant who would be willing to assert that any person can serve as a means, there are many ecologically oriented thinkers who would argue that there are countless ends in nature other than human beings. See Martin Buber, *I and Thou*, in which he discusses the I–it relationship.

For an analysis of the concept "person," see Peter Strawson, *Individuals*.

72:6–7   Titus   Titus may have been eight in the painting Anne refers to, but he didn't die until the age of twenty-eight, in the same year (1669) that Rembrandt died.

72:11   Are paintings persons?   Philosophers have been circling around the notion that works of art may be construed as persons, and they have been taking up one aspect of the problem after another. For example, Allan Tormey, in an article several years ago in the *Journal of Aesthetics and Art Criticism*, took the position that works of art, like human beings, have rights. And since the legal definition of a corporation holds that it should be treated as a person, there may be a sense in which the corporate human being includes all the characteristic products of that individual. In other words, according to this theory, the personality of the artist is embedded in the artwork.

| 72:16 | What is art? | Suki says on line 16 that she can only find aesthetic interest when art has something to do with life or people. It is not clear from this whether she is setting up as a criterion that art be representational or expressive or both. There are many such criteria with which aestheticians have attempted to pin down what is required for something to be a work of art. Expressiveness, representation, and decorativeness form one such group. Monroe Beardsley, in *Aesthetics: The Theory of Criticism*, offers the criteria of unity, complexity, and intensity.

For a source on the first trio and a discussion of expressiveness, see Susanne Langer, "Expressiveness," in her book *The Problems of Art*. See also Allan Tormey, *The Concept of Expression*, and Guy Sircello, *Mind and Art: An Essay on the Varieties of Expression*. For an analysis of representation, see Aristotle, *Poetics*. Also see an essay by Arthur Danto, "Artworks and Real Things," in *Theoria* 1973. |

| 72:21 | feelings | Santayana, in *The Sense of Beauty*, asserts that works of art give us feelings of pleasure and that beauty is simply this pleasure "objectified." Thus, the beauty is in us, not in the work of art. |

| 72:28 | having feelings and showing feelings | Some of the children discovered the four-part matrix in Chapter Thirteen. Apparently, Anne and Suki are here attempting to construct a similar matrix comprised of:

1. having feelings and showing feelings;
2. having feelings and not showing them;
3. not having feelings and showing them; and
4. not having feelings and not showing them. |

| 73:1 | the painter's thought | This brings up another theory, that art is a form of communication and that through art we disclose our thoughts to one another. One way of putting this is to be found in Collingwood, who, in *The Principles of Art* (pp. 225–99), treats art as a form of language. See also Jacques Maritain, *Creative Intuition in Art and Poetry*. |

| 73:2–5 | human face and body | This paragraph raises a number of questions: Do plants not show feelings? Do paintings always show feelings? Is |

the human body not man-made? Does the body necessarily show feelings?

For more on the philosophical relationship of the human face and body to the process of inquiry, see John A. Schumacher, *Human Posture: The Nature of Inquiry* (SUNY Press, 1989); also see M. Lipman, *What Happens in Art?* On the relationship between the human body, meaning, and reason, see Mark Johnson and George Lakoff, *Metaphors We Live By*, as well as, more recently, Mark Johnson, *The Body in the Mind* (University of Chicago Press).

73:7	yes, yes, yes	Molly Bloom's interior monologue at the end of James Joyce's *Ulysses* repeatedly uses these words and concludes with them. One can listen to the monologue as recorded by Siobhan McKenna. The short film *Joyce's Women* deals with several erotic episodes from *Ulysses* and other works and contains this passage of Molly's soliloquy.
73:10	movies	The preeminent figure in the philosophy of movies is Stanley Cavell; see, for example, his *Quest for the Ordinary*.
73:14	bride falling into the pool	Cf. Katharine Hepburn in the movie *The Philadelphia Story*.

74:1–4	Fran's reasoning	Fran's reasoning seems to work like this:
		    I want to do all I can for my people (who are black).
		    Those who can do the most for black people are lawyers.
		    Therefore, I want to be a lawyer.
		Technically, this reasoning is invalid; even if the premises are true, the conclusion doesn't necessarily follow. Fran might become a lawyer and still find that she is unable to do all she can for her people. On the other hand, it is good practical reasoning, since the problem would be the same no matter what group she would choose to belong to. So she's probably right, and her reasoning demonstrates good judgment.

74:10–17	the ethics of distribution	Fran's claim may apply to untouched tribal societies, but it is doubtful whether any still exist. The source of her position is Melville Herskovitz's *Economic Anthropology*. The claim is the Marxist one that distribution in precapitalist societies is based on need; see the Communist *Manifesto*.
74:24	privacy	Philosophically, privacy is related to subjectivity, individuality, the self, and human rights. Feminist philosophers have been particularly interested in this notion; their source has been Virginia Woolf's *Room of One's Own*. The relationship between private and public, or individual and social, is one of figure and ground, in the sense that

each is the reciprocal of the other. The sociologist Georg Simmel wrote many essays on subjectivity, social form and inner needs, subordination to the group and personal fulfillment, individuality and love, and the relationship between the mental life of the individual and the nature of the modern metropolis. See Donald Levine, ed., *Georg Simmel on Individuality and Social Forms*. As Simmel shows, the realm of privacy is very much connected with modern notions of freedom.

74:26–28   what Fran thinks Tony and Harry are doing   Evidently, Fran sees Tony and Harry as engaged in some kind of inquiry that is not quite the same as scientific inquiry. She thinks its chief characteristics are validity ("what follows from what"), asking for reasons, and explanation. The first two belong to philosophical inquiry, the third to scientific inquiry. See Michael Scriven's *Reasoning* (ch. 1).

75:4–11   Lisa's analogical explanation of the syllogism   Lisa understands Tony's syllogism as analogous to addition. One could ask whether the syllogism might not seem even more similar to subtraction (in view of the cancellation of the middle term).

75:15   the ethics of sexism   Lisa contends that Tony is probably sexist. For sources, see Simone de Beauvoir, *The Second Sex*; Shulamith Firestone, *The Dialectic of Sex*; Jean Grimshaw, *Feminist Philosophers*; Genevieve Lloyd, *The Man of Reason*; and Carol C. Gould, "The Woman Question: Philosophy of Liberation and the Liberation of Philosophy," in *Philosophy of Woman: An Anthology of Classic and Current Concepts*, ed. Mary Briody Mahowald. On the question of gender, see Nancy Julia Chodorow, "Gender, Relation, and Difference in Psychoanalytic Perspective," in *The Future of Difference*. Also see her "Rationality, Masculinity, and Modernity," in Terry Threadgold and Ann Cranny-Francis, eds., *Femininity, Masculinity, and Representation*.

75:16–17   Fran on people trying to prove things   Fran's statement has the ring of paradox. She may mean that if one doesn't believe something, one is always trying to prove it. This sounds implausible. More likely, Fran means that, like a person who protests too much, Tony's efforts at proving things conceal or are a symptom of his own insecurity about what to believe.

75:17–18   Fran's comparison of Tony and Harry   Fran suggests that Tony is so insecure that he fails to take the kind of risks that Harry takes. She may be suggesting that Tony tends to be analytic and Harry experimental. There is a literature on intellectual risk taking; see *Unstable Ideas: Temperament, Cognition, and Self* by Jerome Kagan.

75:20–77:18	speed reasoning through pattern recognition	Lisa and Fran are looking for a speedy way of determining the validity of a syllogism through pattern recognition. That is, they identify two types of patterns that are associated with invalid reasoning. But as Lisa says on page 77, they can't be sure that these patterns are guarantors of false conclusions. The patterns are therefore unreliable. In certain cases, the premises may be true, the syllogisms may be formally invalid, and still the conclusion is true. For example:

> All beagles are canine.
> All dogs are canine.
> All beagles are dogs.

Obviously, this case relies on the two subjects having a genus–species relationship. But once one understands this possibility, it is easier to use the pattern-recognition approach than to use the traditional method that relies upon distribution. It is likely that fallacies of illicit major and illicit minor are among those most frequently committed in reasoning. The speed-reasoning, or "pattern-recognition," analysis is much more efficient than the traditional method, which is difficult, time consuming, and intuitively unappealing. But this particular kind of analysis works only with certain types of syllogisms, such as $A\ A\ A$ (BARBARA).

CHAPTER FIFTEEN

Page, Line	*Theme*	*Sources and References*
79:12	Mr. Stottlemeier's reason for smoking	Is Mr. Stottlemeier's reason a good one? And is it sufficiently good to justify his smoking? Kurt Baier, in "Good Reasons," *Philosophical Studies* 4 (1953): 1–15, discusses reasons for smoking and notes that "smoking in order to satisfy a craving can be considered action in accordance with a good reason, *other things being equal.*" Smoking because one likes to is a consideration or prima facie reason, Baier says, that has to be weighed against other prima facie reasons. After deliberating, one may come to a final or sufficient reason for doing something in the circumstances in question. One can also look at Robert E. Goodin, *No Smoking*, a book on the ethics of smoking.
79:13–14	When does one smoke too much?	Mr. Stottlemeier's answer would seem to lead to circularity in that, if Harry should ask, "When does one smoke too much?" the answer would be "When it causes cancer." Circular arguments are often considered examples of the fallacy of "begging the question." See Humphrey Palmer,

		"Do Circular Arguments Beg the Question?" *Philosophy*, July 1981.
79:17	habit	See Dewey on the psychology of habit in *Human Nature and Conduct*.
79:20	not liking something at first	Many addictive substances are not initially attractive, especially to children. The aversion has to be overcome by peer pressure, advertising, etc.
79:25–80:14	analogy between smoking and fighting	At the bottom of p. 79 and the top of p. 80, Harry seems to be trying to establish an analogy between the way smoking starts and the way that fighting starts. He seems to be pointing out to his father that smoking is thought to be the consequence of liking to smoke, as wars are said to be the consequence of people's hating one another. Harry questions the underlying assumptions of both accounts. He says (p. 80, lines 10 and 11) that in his father's case the fighting preceded the hating, rather than the other way around. He wants an explanation. He particularly wonders if the same thing could be true regarding smoking: Could the smoking precede the liking to smoke (p. 80, line 22)? For an account of the commonly held presumption that human habits, customs, and institutions are natural reflections of underlying passions and appetites, see Dewey's *Human Nature and Conduct*, pp. 95–124. Attacking the notion that there are specific instincts, such as aggressiveness, that inevitably lead to war, Dewey tries to show instead that human motives are themselves the effects of social conditioning.
80:25–81:6	Mr. Bradley's dismissal of animism	Mr. Bradley is trying to show that scientific thinking represents a triumph over animistic thinking. Animistic thinking endows the physical world with mental qualities. This is quite common in primitive thought (see Heinz Werner, *Comparative Psychology of Mental Development*). But it is also to be found in poetic thought. (For a description of water as a psychotic person, see Francis Ponge, *Le Parti pris des choses*.) Sartre and Derrida have commented on this book in lengthy essays.
81:7–8	Tony's counter-example	Tony does not show that Mr. Bradley is incorrect but contends that his formulation readily lends itself to misunderstanding.
81:12–14	prescription and description	Mr. Bradley distinguishes between prescriptive and descriptive laws. Prescientific knowing takes the modes of production found among humans (such as cooking by recipe) and imposes them on nature, with the result that nature is understood to be obeying laws. Scientific understanding attempts to show that the laws merely are summary descriptions of how nature does in fact behave. This positivistic formulation continues to be

questioned. See Marx Wartofsky in *Conceptual Foundations of Scientific Thought* (ch. 3, "Prescientific Ways of Knowing").

81:25	description, explanation, and definition	Mickey asks Mr. Bradley how he can see through the mica. Mr. Bradley explains that one can see through mica because it is transparent. This leads Harry to ask, "Can you see through it because it is transparent or is it transparent because you can see through it?" Harry is raising the question of whether science uses operational or non-operational, conditional definitions. As Robert Ennis puts it in *Logic and Teaching*, (pp. 236–37), "a conditional definition with an If . . . clause specifies a condition under which the rest of the definition is to hold. . . . When a conditional definition's initial condition is an operation, the definition is *an operational definition.*" Thus, "if mica can be seen through [operation], then it is transparent." The alternative, "if mica is transparent, then you can see through it," is not operational because the concept of transparency could conceivably involve many operations other than "seeing through." In the operational definition, being able to see through something is a *sufficient condition* for its being transparent.
82:11–12	the connection between naming and describing	There is a helpful discussion of the relationship between naming, describing, and explaining by Martin Tamny, "Can Children Do Science Philosophically?" in *Growing Up with Philosophy*, ed. Lipman and Sharp. Tamny discusses the conceptual interchange between description and explanation, the way names are continually reassigned to keep up with revisions in our understanding of events.
82:13–17	the "hurricane"	Tamny might say that the name "hurricane" is not merely a name, despite what Tony says: It stands for a complex understanding of an event, and that understanding contains both descriptive and explanatory elements.
82:21–22	the "racist"	This would be an opportunity to illustrate Ennis's approach to operational definitions. One might legitimately say, "If you hate the members of ethnic groups X without a reason, then you are a racist." But one would not want to say, "If you are a racist, then you hate members of ethnic group X without a reason." You might love them but hate some other ethnic group. The next three examples (elasticity, solubility, and combativeness) are taken from Dewey, *Human Nature and Conduct*, pp. 95–124.
83:15–16	causes and effects turning into one another	A symptom of nervousness may increase nervousness, as in stuttering. This represents a closed retroactive causal relation. Similarly, a traffic jam is a positive feedback system in which the appearance of the gridlock makes

the gridlock worse. For discussion, see Marx Wartofsky, *Conceptual Foundations of Scientific Thought*, pp. 306–8.

83:17–24   causes and reasons

Harry objects to his father's evasive replies because he feels that his father is merely *explaining* why he smokes, rather than trying to *justify* it. We can restrict the word "reason" to justification and the word "cause" to explanation. (This eliminates the mischievous category of "explanatory" reasons, which many people, scientists included, enjoy invoking.) For further discussion of the distinction between "causes" and "reasons," see Kurt Baier, *The Moral Point of View*; John Hospers, *Human Conduct*; and the opposed readings of R. S. Peters and Donald Davidson in *The Nature of Human Action*, ed. Myles Brand. Another useful article is "Why Questions?" by Sylvain Bromberger, in *Mind and Cosmos*, ed. R. Colodny.

CHAPTER SIXTEEN

Page, Line	*Theme*	*Sources and References*

84–89:25   hypothetical, or conditional, syllogisms

There is almost nothing about this kind of syllogism in Aristotle, but a theory of conditional reasoning was well worked out by his contemporary Chryssipus. (See *A History of Logic* by William Kneale and Martha Kneale.) The presentation here can be corroborated in virtually any standard logic text.

90:2   harm

Harm is a major criterion in ethics for Mill's utilitarianism. There are discussions of harm and blameworthiness in Richard Brandt, *Ethical Theory*, and in A. I. Melden, ed, *Essays in Moral Philosophy*. Among classic sources, in addition to Mill, one should mention Jeremy Bentham, *An Introduction to the Principles of Morals and Legislation*.

90:9–10   being right for the wrong reason

Plato discusses this in *The Republic* when he distinguishes between merely having the right opinion and having the right opinion together with an adequate reason. Tony explains his phrase "wrong reason" with the elaboration that it is a guess, the product of luck. It cannot be proven. To say that it is a guess is hardly distinguishable from saying that it is an intuitive judgment. It is becoming quite fashionable among philosophers of science to make a case for intuitive judgments. For example, Patrick Suppes, in a recent book, has pleaded for a recognition that scientists constantly judge intuitively. Introducing the notion of luck does not seem to carry much weight, if we accept Aristotle's understanding of luck as simply the particular way in which the universal laws of nature happen to be carried out. Thus, if an airplane runs out of fuel, it is determined that it should fall; it is your bad luck that it falls on your house, but this is in no way contrary to natural law. However, Tony's charge that Lisa cannot prove her allegation—meaning, presumably, that she has no evidence to substantiate it— is a more serious criticism.

90:11–14	Could a hunch be a reason?	Lisa says she had a feeling, which she defines as a kind of hunch. She offers that as a reason. One can imagine Tony rejecting this on the grounds that it is not a reason but an explanation. In Chapter Ten, we considered the possibility that under certain circumstances feelings might very well serve as reasons. However, were such circumstances present in this case? Tony could argue that the kind of situation that might permit a feeling to serve as a reason (e.g., marrying a woman because you love her) does not operate here.
90:13	hunch	Peirce argues somewhere that there is a greater likelihood that hunches are right than wrong. His explanation is that over the course of human evolution people who had wrong hunches were more likely to be eliminated by natural selection than those who had right hunches.
90:13–20	Is being right what's important?	Lisa says that the important thing is to be right. But Mr. Spence replies that he doesn't like reckless accusations. What are we to make of this confrontation? One way we can view it is as a conflict between an emphasis on method and an emphasis on successful results. Mr. Spence apparently feels that inquiry cannot deviate from a scrupulous adherence to appropriate procedures. Lisa argues, as do many who take the problem-solving approach, that the heuristic method is to solve the problem without too much concern for just how it is done. Both of these approaches have their place in science. It is probable that the danger begins to appear when the reliance on method excludes all creativity, or when the reliance on results excludes all rigor.

A version of this conflict is to be found in the disagreement W. K. Clifford had with William James. Clifford advocated undeviating commitment to scientific methodology. James, however, in his essay "The Will to Believe," attempts to make a case for a situation in which abandoning such rigorous procedures is justifiable. He argues that if there is a class of truths that cannot be reached by scientific method, with the result that the truth we possess is incomplete and seriously deficient, we are justified in abandoning the method and permitting ourselves to use whatever alternative would give us access to those truths.

CHAPTER SEVENTEEN

Page, Line	Theme	Sources and References
91:8–11	relationship of philosophy to other disciplines	The Aristotelian view that philosophy is queen of the sciences lasted through the Middle Ages and into the Renaissance. It was only then, with the rise of natural science, that philosophy's role was reduced to that of a handmaiden to the sciences. The question of philosophy's actual relationship to the other disciplines is now being reexamined. An example of an astute reappraisal is to be found in Jacob Lowenberg's essays on Hegel, which argue persuasively that no discipline can turn to reflect upon itself without becoming the philosophy of itself.
91:20	what is worthwhile and what is a waste of time	Some of the things that Plato considers essential to education in *The Republic*—for example, music—are no longer seen as basic, nor would many educators today agree with medieval schoolmen about the importance of the trivium and quadrivium. The point is that we cannot decide what is not worthwhile unless we have a goal or objective that the course in question would help achieve. Among the philosophers who, in recent years, have attempted to analyze not simply the goals of education (as Whitehead does in *The Aims of Education*) but the goal of an educated person have been Jane Roland Martin in *The Educated Woman* and R. F. Dearden in *The Concept of Education*, which he edited with R. S. Peters.
91:21–26	recollection	Lisa seems to be suggesting that whatever she learns in the philosophical community of inquiry is something she already knew. She does not seem to be generalizing that all learning is recollection. If we then restrict her claim to the shared philosophical experience, it would seem to be a restatement of Plato's *Meno* (a good commentary on which is to be found in Jerome Eckstein's book *The Platonic Method*). If the recollection theory is taken seriously, it embraces Freud, Bergson, Proust, Jung, and many other advocates of a universal but forgotten knowledge that each of us is capable of bringing back or of a personal knowledge, long repressed, that is always capable of emerging into consciousness. Another interpretation of what Lisa is saying is that understanding begins with the acquisition of language, and, to the extent that she was using language well before the philosophical experience, she hasn't learned anything new. Lisa may be saying that the experience provided her with no new knowledge. But did it equip her with many additional skills—and a certain self-consciousness—that she did not have at the beginning?

92:6–7	what was important and what wasn't	Harry's phrase "what was important and what wasn't important" suggests that one of the things he cherished most about the class discussions was the inquiry into values, which is what he presumably means by "matters of importance." The question of importance is taken up by Whitehead in his stimulating little book *Modes of Thought*, in which he argues that nature contains hierarchies of intrinsic importance. Justus Buchler disputes this strenuously, arguing instead for a principle of "ontological parity" in which all values stand on the same footing. Buchler's position seems to be close to that of Spinoza, except that Buchler would argue for the objective equality of values in nature, while Spinoza holds that any difference of greater or lesser importance would be due to subjectivistic differences of interpretation.
92:10–11	understanding in different ways	Here Harry seems to be saying that there are not only different styles of thinking but different forms of intelligence. The most articulate contemporary statement of this pluralistic position is by Howard Gardner in *Frames of Mind*.
92:15–17	counting on one another	The source of Harry's feeling is to be found in Sartre's essay "The Republic of Silence." Sartre maintains that a member of the Resistance captured by the Nazis suffered extreme internal anguish. One would be expected to withstand torture and not reveal the whereabouts of one's companions. Yet the captive knew that those companions would make no effort to save one of their number who had been captured. *They counted on him, but he couldn't count on them.*
92:19	contradiction	Mickey is right that contradiction, as logicians understand it, is seldom taught in courses in English, which stress instead notions of opposition or contrast. Opposition, insofar as it refers to what is at opposite ends of a spectrum (hot vs. cold or tall vs. short), represents differences of degree, while contradiction is a difference of kind. For more on this point, see Robert Fogelin, *Figuratively Speaking*. Fogelin's discussion is, in turn, based on a treatment of the topic in Nelson Goodman's *Languages of Art*.
92:21–24	nonconvertibility of the *A* statement	Laura could have stopped by simply citing the rule of conversion, but she doesn't—she offers an example of the rule.
92:29	learning styles	Much has been written on learning styles of children, particularly by Jerome Kagan. His work with Michael Wallach, linking learning styles to creativity, is especially worthwhile. One should be wary, however, of drawing the inference that one should adapt one's teaching style to each child's learning style. Identifying a child's learning

style is a complex procedure, and just when someone
may be so typed is a very open question.

93:1   jumping to conclusions

As S. Morris Engel points out in *With Good Reason*, we
are dealing with an informal fallacy that may take either of
two forms: sweeping generalization or hasty generalization. These are mirror images. Sweeping generalization
is committed when a warranted general rule is applied
to a specific case, even though the rule is not applicable
because of special features of that case. In hasty generalization, on the other hand, an exceptional case is taken to
be a rule for a generalization that is unwarranted.

93:4   tautology

The logical aspect of Tony's remark, which Lisa noticed,
is the principle of tautology. A tautology is a proposition
whose contradiction involves a self-contradiction. Thus
the contradiction of *All A is A* is *Some A is not A*. And the
latter is self-contradictory.

93:4   what's true is true

We have seen earlier (in Chapter Ten) that some statements may be tautologies but are not empty—e.g.,
"business is business" or "boys will be boys." It may be
that Tony considers his remark to be of this kind when
he says, "what's true is true." Perhaps he feels it is not
empty. But then, what does it mean? For Tony, it might
mean that once something is true, it is always true. It is
not just true in some contexts and not true in others. Lisa
makes fun of Tony's claim, saying that it is equal to "cows
are cows." Here again, Lisa may be jumping to conclusions. If Tony wanted to rely on a remark by Peirce, he
might say that two plus two will always be a tautology in
that it will always equal four, but we have no guarantee
that two fish plus two fish will always equal four fish. The
world does not have to conform to our number system.

93:10–15   two methods of thinking

Harry contrasts two methods of thinking. One is Tony's
method, which is rule governed, step-by-step, and
therefore analytical. The other is instantaneous and immediately produces an answer—so that it can be called
intuitive. For a discussion of these two complementary
modes of thinking (sometimes described as rule governed
vs. intuitive, analytical vs. contextual, or phenomenological or critical vs. creative), see Matthew Lipman,
Thinking in Education, Chapter Four. One should remember that the community of inquiry as a pedagogical
model involves complementarity, not only of critical and
creative thinking, but of one form of cognitive complementary with another form of cognitive, and one form of
affective complementary with another form of affective.

In *Harry* the entire community models this complementarity in several ways. One might ask a question, and
that may liberate others to ask other questions. That is

solidarity through replication. On the other hand, one may ask a question, another give an answer, and still another draw an inference from the answer. This is solidarity through division of labor. Both types of solidarity can be manifested in the same community of inquiry. For more on the distinction between mechanic and organic solidarity, see Emile Durkheim, *The Division of Labor in Society.*

93:23   the same room for all of us

This is not Locke's room—"dark room"—which is his figurative model of the mind and another way of expressing the idea that our minds are empty before experience. The room that Fran is talking about is the world we all find ourselves in. The sources here are three essays by Leibniz: *Discourse on Metaphysics*, *Monadology*, and *Principles of Nature and of Grace*. For Leibniz there is only one world, or nature, but it is represented differently in every monad.

93:26–28   different points of view in nature

Fran notes that each of us observes this common world from a different point of view and, consequently, each observes a different aspect of the same world. In Leibniz, particularly in the *Monadology*, each monad, or individual being, represents within itself the entire world as it might be perceived from its unique point of view. Therefore, each monad is a microcosm that reproduces the same macrocosm, yet each microcosm is different. For more on perspectivism, see G. H. Mead, *Movements of Thought in the Nineteenth Century*, E. B. McGilvary, *Toward a Perspective Realism*, and the chapter on perspective in Justus Buchler's *Towards a General Theory of Human Judgment.*

94:4–9   Anne's pluralism

Anne does not think there is one world. She thinks there are many worlds. This is similar to Fran's view, insofar as it says there is an infinite number of worlds, one for each person. It fails to mention the other aspect of Fran's argument, however, which is that all these countless worlds are at the same time representations of one single world, or nature. It would not be fair to Anne to say that her position is subjectivistic, although this is a possible interpretation. But it does follow from her view that we can't share perspectives. In many ways, Anne's view is closer to relativism. There is some similarity between her aesthetic position and the qualitative pluralism in Dewey (see his *Logic*, pp. 66–70), as well as Peirce's "Firstness" in his essay "Phenomenology" or Bosanquet's "Tertiary Qualities" in *Three Lectures on Aesthetics*. One should also look at Santayana's "essences," which are discussed in his *Realms of Being*. Santayana's position is rather ironical in that he is a materialist who finds a material universe uninteresting. He is only interested in

meanings—qualities and essences—all of which are for
him not part of physical nature.

94:10–14 Harry's correction

Harry attempts to correct Anne. He criticizes her *interpretation* of Fran's remark. ("Interpretation" is a major category in recent philosophical writing, particularly among Continental philosophers like Paul Ricoeur and Jacques Derrida. For more on interpretation and its complementary concept, translation, see George Steiner, *After Babel*.) Harry attempts to rectify Anne's remark by arguing that perspectives can be shared. We have only to assume other people's points of view in order to appreciate and grasp the way they see things. This is certainly a cardinal point of scientific method, in that experimental results are publicized with the express intention of getting other investigators to replicate the experiment and see if they get the same results. Where observations among particular investigators differ, we can presume that this can be accounted for by the differing situations of the observers. Thus, if the sky I see is different from the sky you see, this could be accounted for by the fact that I am standing in the northern hemisphere and you are in the southern hemisphere. If I were to visit your hemisphere, I would see the same sky you do. See Claude Bernard, *An Introduction to the Study of Experimental Medicine*, and Mill's *Logic*, bks. 3 and 6. Also, see Dewey in *Essays in Experimental Logic* (pp. 231–41) on agreement.

94:15–17 Lisa's interpretation of Harry

Lisa's interpretation of Harry's remark is that we can come to agreement with other people by replicating their perspectives and sharing their points of view. It is questionable whether this is an adequate formulation of his position. Harry is not simply suggesting that everybody in the community can try to assume the other person's point of view. He holds, rather, that we can allow for other points of view without attempting to simulate other people's experience, and that, insofar as there is objective knowledge, it is the result of assuming that there are countless different points of view other than our own, so that objectivity is a composite result of all these perspectives. Once I realize that there is a multiplicity of points of view and that the differences in what we observe can be accounted for in the differences in our points of view, there is no longer a need for me to replicate everybody else's experience. Our experiences are all complementary as well as different, and, if they are not complementary, that is a problem for further inquiry. See Aristotle, *Metaphysics* (bk. 1) and *Physics* (bk. 1).

94:17–20 Lisa's objection

Anne has said that "everyone lives in his own world," and she sees no problem with such pluralism. She simply accepts the fact of ontological diversity. Harry says, yes, there is diversity, but there is also a unity of human knowledge to be approached by sharing perspectives. All these diverse observations add up to a confirmation of Fran's point that there is only one world. Lisa asks, "Why doesn't anyone try to understand *my* point of view?" What does she want when she demands understanding of her point of view? (Aristotle, in the *Nicomachean Ethics*, bk. 7, conceives of understanding as the product of deliberation and the ground of judgment.) Lisa does not merely wish to be tolerated. She would like it understood that her point of view is legitimate, authentic, and represents, possibly, a correction of the understanding shared by the other members of the community. The case Lisa is making is one that has been made before by such individuals as Socrates and Thoreau, Luther and Galileo, Kierkegaard and Nietzsche. All of these see unorthodoxy as possibly creative, deviance as possibly constructive, and dissent as possibly corrective. What is classified as an error in one generation may come to be classified as a profound insight subsequently. This is not because understanding is relative from one generation to the next, but because successive generations understand matters more and more comprehensively.

94:23–24	point of view	Points of view are not identical with perspectives. From the point of view of a mountaintop, one may look at the landscape stretching out below in a certain perspective. From the point of view of a certain individual—her history, attitudes, values, etc.—one can understand her perspective on the world. A point of view is a standpoint; a perspective is an angle of vision. See Buchler's chapter on perspective in *Towards a General Theory of Human Judgment*.
94:27	What started you thinking this way?	Mr. Spence has gotten nowhere asking Lisa for an explanation. He now resorts to asking her to give an account of what "led her to think" in this fashion. He wonders if someone said something in class that triggered her view. Questions such as these are psychological rather than philosophical, and this is the first time Mr. Spence has resorted to this kind of query. Such questions are discussed in Terry Meyers, Keith Brown, and Brendan McGonigle, eds., *Reasoning and Discourse Processes* (Academic Press, 1986). See, in particular, chs. 2–3, 10, and 11.
95:4–5	the mind	She and her classmates, Lisa thinks, are trying to discover how the mind works. At least this is what she reports to her father. We may question whether this formulation is not overly psychological.

95:7–9   the first poem

The first poem Lisa's father shows her is "The Mind Is an Enchanted Thing" by Marianne Moore. It is not as tightly constructed or as profound as the Wilbur poem, "Mind," but it has its sparkling moments, such as the remark that the mind is "like Gieseking playing Scarlatti."

95:9   the cave

First, there is the analogy "thoughts are in our minds as bats are in a cave." The analogy is then amplified. Ideas fly blindly within the walls of the mind, as bats fly about without crashing into the walls of the cave.

95:11   graceful error corrects the cave

The analogy referred to above is a graceful one, but it needs to be corrected. Wilbur does this by pointing out something that happens in the mind that does not happen among the bats. If a bat makes a mistake it will smash itself against the wall of the cave. If we think deviantly, however, we may, now and then, discover that our thinking has changed the shape of the whole of our knowledge. What Lisa perceives in the Wilbur poem is a defense of intellectual autonomy and a recognition of its social utility. The wonderful phrase "graceful error" is perilously close to being a self-contradiction. Nevertheless, it precisely captures Wilbur's meaning. One can see why Lisa is so attracted to it. It may even remind her, in its own way, of that episode early on in the book when Fran's conduct, seemingly so improper, involved a graceful leaping from desk to desk.

A useful source with regard to the role of error in education is Henry Perkinson's *Possibility of Error*, an essentially Popperian account. See also Simone Weil's *Lectures on Philosophy*.

95:15–19   the Columbus illustration

It would seem that the Columbus example is a good illustration of the general principle that Lisa is trying to establish. While exemplification has not attracted nearly so much attention in philosophical circles as has generalization, there is some interest in the topic. For example, a paper to be given in a forthcoming *APA* conference will be devoted to the nature of examples by Betsy Newell Decyk.

95:18–19   changing paradigms of knowledge

This portion of the book may seem to echo Thomas Kuhn, but it was not written with any knowledge of his work and, as a matter of fact, has a different emphasis. (Cf. *The Structure of Scientific Revolutions* and *The Essential Temper*.) To some extent, Kuhn views science as a shifting cultural phenomenon whose history, like that of art, shows great pendulum swings but not necessarily any forward progress. Whether the accusations of relativism leveled against Kuhn are accurate is not the issue here. The Columbus example suggests progress by the very notion of correction. If the concept of progress then becomes a difficulty, one can invoke Collingwood's dictum that there is progress in science when a new theory answers all the questions that an older theory answers, plus other questions that the older theory fails to answer. The progressive interpretation of science that underlies Chapter Seventeen is closer in inspiration to Ernest Nagel's *Structure of Science* and to *An Introduction to Logic and Scientific Method*, which he coauthored with Morris R. Cohen.

95:20	Tony's remark	Tony's remark can be interpreted as being sarcastic, but it reveals the gulf between him and Lisa. She seems to be interested in ideas and in the clash of ideas. He seems to think that the enterprise the class has been engaged in is, instead, the development of proficiency in "straight thinking," or "critical thinking." Tony's interest seems to be in the reasoning: He can take the philosophy or leave it, whereas Lisa seems to be interested in the philosophy and can take the logic or leave it.
95:22	open-mindedness	One of the goals of the Philosophy for Children project, in addition to the cultivation of judgment and proficiency in reasoning and inquiry, is the cultivation of open-mindedness. William Hare has written two excellent books on this subject, *Open-Mindedness and Education* and *In Defense of Open-Mindedness*, both published by McGill–Queen's University Press. See also Matthew Lipman's review of *In Defense of Open-Mindedness* in *Teachers College Record* (Winter 1986).
95:24	It was fun.	Johan Huizinga remarks in *Homo Ludens*, that the word "fun" appears only in the English language. Whether this is true or not, there is a difference between fun and play. Play is behavioral; fun is presumably affective. What is important here is that Lisa recognizes the category of intellectual play and that philosophy, for her, fits into it. In Jerome Bruner's afterword to *Thinking and Learning Skills*, edited by Segal, Chipman, and Glaser, he pays a great deal of attention, as he does in subsequent works, to the notion of play. But he seems to identify it very infrequently with *intellectual* play and never with philosophy. Lisa obviously thinks that "fun" is an important criterion to take into account when considering whether one should keep studying a certain discipline. She also points out that "it does seem to work." Lisa appears to be contradicting here the dichotomy commonly made between work and play. The course worked, it was fun, and perhaps it was fun precisely because it worked. To what extent Lisa's word "fun" and Aristotle's word "happiness" approximate each other deserves study.

95:25   It works with   First, what does "it" refer to? The "it" apparently refers
          the way we   to the logic they have been studying. One point that Lisa
          talk but not   is making is that the logic may not apply to the world, as
          with the way   the Scholastics thought, but it does apply to language.
          we imag-   Her other point is that logic does not work with the way
          ine, feel,   we imagine, feel, or dream. One can certainly differ with
          or dream.   her in this regard. For example, see G. K. Chesterton,
                               "The Ethics of Elfland," in *Thinking* 1, no. 2. On the
                               other hand, it remains an open question whether logic
                               is applicable to dreams. Here one might cite such works
                               as *Alice in Wonderland*, or Freud's essay "Negation"
                               in the *Collected Works*. Freud argues that some con-
                               cepts are inherently ambiguous, so that the principle of
                               noncontradiction does not apply.

About the Authors

MATTHEW LIPMAN   is the director of the Institute for the Advancement of Philosophy for Children, Montclair State College, Upper Montclair, New Jersey, and the creator of the Philosophy for Children curriculum that is now being taught to young people in many nations.

MICHAEL S. PRITCHARD   teaches philosophy at Western Michigan University at Kalamazoo and works with Michigan schoolteachers in Philosophy for Children.

RONALD F. REED   teaches philosophy and education at Texas Wesleyan University in Fort Worth and is the director of the Analytic Teaching Center. Editor of *Analytic Teaching*, he has been a teacher–educator in Philosophy for Children since 1979. President of the International Council of Philosophical Inquiry with Children, he is coeditor of the council's *Bulletin* and author of *Talking with Children* and *Rebecca*.

ANN MARGARET SHARP   is the associate director of the Institute for the Advancement of Philosophy for Children. She has worked with Matthew Lipman since 1973 in the creation of the Philosophy for Children program and has been primarily responsible for its dissemination abroad. As director of the graduate program in Philosophy for Children at Montclair State College, she has been involved in the preparation of future teacher–educators in Philosophy for Children.

MARTIN BENJAMIN   teaches philosophy at Michigan State University in East Lansing.

EUGENIO ECHEVERRIA   is a graduate of the master's degree program in Philosophy for Children and is a doctoral candidate at Michigan State University. He now teaches education and Philosophy for Children at ITESO University in Guadalajara, Mexico. As director of the Mexican Center for Philosophy for Children in Guadalajara, he is actively involved in teacher education and the preparation of future teacher–educators in Philosophy for Children.

PHILIP C. GUIN   is a teacher–educator in Philosophy for Children. He is based at the Institute for the Advancement of Philosophy for Children at Montclair State College, and, as director of field services, is responsible for the dissemination of the curriculum throughout the United States.

JOHN C. THOMAS   teaches philosophy at Lindfield College in Portland, Oregon, and is actively involved in teacher education in Philosophy for Children.

LAURANCE J. SPLITTER   is a director of the Australian Center of Philosophy for Children in Melbourne.

CLIVE LINDOP   teaches philosophy of education and teacher education at the Warrnambool Institute of Advanced Education, Victoria, Australia. A graduate of the master's program in Philosophy for Children, he is actively involved in teacher education in Philosophy for Children.

FREDERICK S. OSCANYAN   was the director of the Berea Center of Philosophy for Children, Berea College, Berea, Kentucky. Coauthor of *Philosophy in the Classroom* and the manual that accompanies *Harry Stottlemeier's Discovery, Philosophical Inquiry,* he had been actively involved in all aspects of the Philosophy for Children movement since 1975.